ON ALTERING ARCHITECTURE

ON ALTERING ARCHITECTURE explores the alternative to the sequence of demolition and new building that makes up the usual practices of architecture. Bringing together ideas of what might constitute a theory of interior, or interventional, design, Fred Scott fills a wide gap in the literature covering the evolution of interior space.

This new text examines the craft of altering buildings, reconsidering established ideas and practices. The masterworks of interventional design found in architectural history are compared and contrasted in a compelling way, in order to show how theory might be derived from previous practice. Extending the ideas of Viollet-le-Duc in particular, via Structuralism, this book aims to outline the criteria for an art of intervention and change.

Beginning with a rehearsal of the arguments for works of architecture remaining unaltered and sacrosanct versus the case for alteration, the philosophy of conservation, preservation and restoration is also introduced. Exploring the many social and political issues involved, the scale of change is analysed, suggesting that processes applied to the individual building can be echoed at the neighbourhood and city scale.

Of interest to those in the professions of architecture and interiors, town planners, and students in architecture and art schools, *On Altering Architecture* forms a body of thought that can be aligned and compared with architectural theory.

FRED SCOTT is Visiting Professor of Interior Architecture at Rhode Island School of Design and was previously course leader for Interior Design at Kingston University, London.

Fred Scott

ON ALTERING ARCHITECTURE

Routledge
Taylor & Francis Group

LONDON AND NEW YORK

First published 2008
by Routledge
2 Park Square, Milton Park, Abingdon, Oxon OX14 4RN

Simultaneously published in the USA and Canada
by Routledge
270 Madison Avenue, New York, NY 10016

Routledge is an imprint of the Taylor & Francis Group, an informa business

Typeset in Meta and Interstate by
Keystroke, 28 High Street, Tettenhall, Wolverhampton

Printed and bound in Great Britain by
The Cromwell Press, Trowbridge, Wiltshire

British Library Cataloguing in Publication Data
A catalogue record for this book is available from the British Library

Library of Congress Cataloging in Publication Data
Scott, Fred, 1939–
     On altering architecture / Fred Scott.
          p. cm.
     Includes bibliographical references and index.
     ISBN 978–0–415–31751–1 (hbk : alk. paper)—ISBN 978–0–415–31752–8
     (pbk : alk. paper) 1. Interior architecture. 2. Buildings—Repair and
     reconstruction. 3. Architecture—Conservation and restoration.
     4. Architecture—Philosophy. I. Title.
     NA2850.S38 2007
     729–dc22   2006039499

ISBN10: 0–415–31751–7 (hbk)
ISBN10: 0–415–31752–5 (pbk)
ISBN10: 0–203–59059–7 (ebk)

ISBN13: 978–0–415–31751–1 (hbk)
ISBN13: 978–0–415–31752–8 (pbk)
ISBN13: 978–0–203–59059–1 (ebk)

CONTENTS

LIST OF FIGURES

ACKNOWLEDGEMENTS

TO BEGIN, JULIAN POWELL-TUCK, to whom this book is dedicated, first set me off thinking that alteration might be a discrete preoccupation, and not an impoverished relation of architecture, or perhaps we set out together. I have taken his advice at numerous points in the writing. We share the same view of the subject; he invariably has had a sharper focus and a quicker grasp of key issues than myself, and in addition, I have always been able to rely on his unvarnished opinion; he has no other kind, as far as I know.

At RISD, my sponsor, Professor Brian Kernaghan, and my friend Professor Dietrich Neumann at Brown University have been important sounding boards for numerous ideas in the book. In London, the glittering array of part-time staff that taught with me on the Interior Design course at Kingston was of crucial assistance over many years, as were many students. In addition let me record my gratitude to Martin Dyke-Coomes, out of whose office windows I have stared empty headed and undisturbed for countless hours.

My thanks also go to Professor Robert Harbison at London Metropolitan University for reading the early drafts and for his encouragement to my publishers to publish this book. I must thank the commissioning editor at Routledge, Caroline Mallinder, for her unhurried tolerance.

Most of the final draft was completed in Providence, Rhode Island, while I was teaching at the Rhode Island School of Design. Here I was helped immensely by the resource of three marvellous libraries in the town, a couple across the road from one another and the third a little way up the hill, one beautiful, one very beautiful and one vast: the RISD Library, the Providence Athenaeum, both on Benefit Street, and the Rockefeller Library at Brown University. Without them, and the unremitting patience and helpfulness of the staff in all three, the task would have been impossible. I must include in this the equally supportive role of the staff in the Library of the Design Faculty at Kingston University while I taught there, in particular the help given me by Susan St Clair. Over the years, the Kingston University Design research panel awarded me fifteen days' leave to work on the manuscript.

My friend in Sydney, Australia, Diana Tilley Winyard sent a flock of e-mails, to get permissions for the illustrations. I couldn't have done it without her sustained assistance.

At the time of writing, both Katherine Shonfield and Cedric Price, whose work is mentioned in Chapter 1, have died within weeks of one another. This is not the proper place for a full appreciation of these two exceptional people, but not to record the loss that is felt by the architectural community in London and further afield would be a violation. One thinks of them both as vital elements of the collective mind of London, and their loss will take much bearing in the time to come, both intellectually and emotionally. Both had important things to say, which still lack proper responses from the wider community. They were both great company.

I want also to thank my wife, Liz Davis, family and friends, whose collective patience I must have sorely tried, waiting for this book to be finished. To all I would like to record here my deep thanks for your unflagging confidence in the work. And finally my thanks to Elena Massucco who told me the trick by which I could bring myself at last to let go of the text.

Fred Scott
London, July 2006

PREFACE

THE GENERAL INSTINCT IS PROBABLY that the built environment, if it is of any architectural merit at all, should not be altered. The money spent on refurbishment now, however, is greater than that spent on new buildings, and this balance continues to change in favour of alteration. Although this may be thought of as the consequence of mere expediency, one can be reminded that theory follows in the wake of the expedient.

This book began from a partisan argument for the contribution of art school designers to be recognized as being as valid in the alteration of the built environment as the more celebrated work of architects in making new buildings. It was in the beginning an argument against a widely assumed hegemony. All environmental work may be termed architecture, and be the better for it the argument ran, but this is not to assume that it is all exclusively within the remit of the chartered architect; others are involved, and other considerations. In truth many people apart from architects are responsible for shaping the built environment.

I may appear at some points to be like a drunk looking for a fight, where no real contention exists between the practices of architecture and alteration and intervention, but throughout the book I have tried to identify characteristics and attitudes relevant to the work of intervention in existing buildings, and to compare and contrast those with what I have generally called 'pure architecture', which means no more than the making of a new building on a cleared site. In contrast to this, the designers work with that of others who have preceded them, when working to alter a building, and also in precedence of those who will come after them. The work of intervention and alteration is thus collective, across generations, whereas the work of architecture may often be considered to be individual. I have tried to say here and there how there may be contrasting sensibilities, contrary imaginations suited to changing the existing, compared with the making of a new building.

Beneath this discussion there probably is what would resolve itself into an argument regarding profession, that is a continuation of the incipient turf war that is always imminent between an established profession and the under-appreciated contribution of others. Because of this, there still remains with me a desire to call attention to the less well publicized work of designers, and in so doing to celebrate the tradition and achievement of the art schools that trained them. The art schools commonly contain a set of affinities that may find in intervention a basis for common work, the interior designer, the installation artist, the colourist involved in a collective undertaking. Along with this is an opposite sense of admonition, of a desire to raise up and establish their collective production on a level comparable with pure architecture, an aspiration to raise the level of dialogue and intention with regard to works of intervention and alteration. As it is generally, cross-discipline work is too little encouraged in the art schools themselves.

I think there is a case to be made that there are different tendencies in the production of art-school-trained designers, compared with the work of architects. In their use of colour in particular, eclectic use of materials, and variety of finishes, the designer often has the edge over the architect. Of course in the more solemn aspects of building, this position may well be reversed.

There are in the United Kingdom alone any number of magazines and a newspaper dedicated to the work of the architectural profession, compared with the paucity of publications covering other aspects of environmental or spatial design. One can find evidence of editorial imbalance in many ways; whereas in recent years the contribution of engineers to architectural projects has been more fully recognized, it is still quite common for a review of a new museum to be published and reviewed with only the architect of the building mentioned, and no reference made to the teams of designers of the interior, of the design of the exhibit, which for most lay people will be the reason for and the most lasting memory of their visit.

But to claim any exclusivity of background for those who undertake the work of alteration would be as blind as any other obliqueness. Of course both architects and designers can practise alteration, and to draw attention to any differences is to deal only in niceties. The work is the thing, and this book sets out to show the rich potential of such undertakings. Alteration is more like a duet than a solo. It is about an art of response as much as it is an art of individual genius; it sets out to make a concord between the new and the existing, or even a discord. Either way, it is a proposal concerning how the designer may form a response in their new work to the host building. These writings are intended to confer on the processes of alteration a certain consciousness, for the purposes of supporting a radical intelligence with regard to the work. The proposal herein is that interventional design can be usefully examined as a discrete activity, and looked at in order to see if one might be able to suggest proper practices, if only in order to begin to discourage some of its excesses. The more positive thought is that by raising the consideration of alteration, we may at the same time begin also to raise the practice.

This undertaking is not intended to reach hard and fast conclusions regarding building, for I lack both the depth of knowledge and the breadth of experience to do that, but it is intended to lay out a geography of a discrete topic within the general realm of the disciplines of the built environment. As I write this preface, as usual as one of the final tasks, I am struck by the questions that remain unresolved, which may of course be only because of the author's lassitude or ineptitude. There is not a considered discussion of the social aspects of alteration, for instance, even though change of use always carries with it class implications, as any unworthy visitor to a National Trust grand house may testify. Many similar issues may not have been exhaustively explored, sometimes for the reason that they verge on the unfathomable. Such a topic is the similar question of inappropriate use, whether in regard to a spatial fit or the less certain territory of appropriate use. The first is a question of practicalities but the second may invoke questions of propriety. Such judgements are beyond the scope of this book, except to mention that the twelfth-century St Bartholomew's church in Smithfield in London was used as a blacksmith's and stables at some time after the Dissolution of the Monasteries in England under Henry VIII, and may be again for all we know. Buildings, unlike ships, are unlikely ever to die of shame. In an everyday sense, propriety is a question for the client and the designer, whether the proffered relationship is accepted or refused; the history of the twentieth century is as good as any for examples of the problematic nature of such relationships.

Another point requiring further thought, for instance, is the issue of the later designer, the interventionist being more talented and informed than the originators of a building, able to see in a sense more clearly than the original builders what they were aiming for, although whose judgement it is which decides such matters is another matter entirely. Conversely at other times the opposite may be true. In the event of honesty and authenticity being shown to be unachievable in the realm of restoration, it would seem that the present designer should be at least of the same ability and vision as the initial architect. In the case of whole-hearted restoration of works of genius, this question looms impossibly large. The comprehensive recent work on Hawksmoor's Christchurch Spitalfield in London sets questions regarding the architectural abilities of the alterers. In passing, one may note the lack of comment or critical response to this work within the architectural community.

However, it seems to me that it is sensible to identify issues with regard to working on the existing, but premature to attempt a comprehensive resolution of them, were there ever to be such a thing. Generally my ambition for the book is that if it fails to provide answers to every aspect of altering architecture, at least it unearths questions. All questions derive from the one question that the designer faces, as suggested in the beginning by Julian Powell-Tuck, which is, 'How much can I change the building that I'm working on?' The work of alteration is paradoxically a function of the general impulse to conserve, perhaps to try to keep hold of something within an assumed universe of increasing entropy, a response to the general anxiety that not all will be lost by the passage of time, and the purpose is to work the existent and the ideal together through the processes of intervention, to keep the existing occupied and significant. In doing so, one lives to a certain extent with the inadequacies and aspirations of an earlier time.

UNCHANGING ARCHITECTURE AND THE CASE FOR ALTERATION

Nietzsche said, 'The purpose of our Palaces and public gardens is to maintain the idea of order.'

(quoted by John Pawson)

ALL BUILDINGS, ONCE HANDED OVER by the builders to the client, have three possible fates, namely to remain unchanged, to be altered or to be demolished. The price for remaining unchanged is eventual loss of occupation, the threat of alteration is the entropic skid, the promise of demolition is of a new building. For the architect, the last course would seem the most fruitful.

In a perfectly functioning state, according to the precepts of functionalism, buildings would either fulfil their purpose or be demolished, except perhaps for a few exceptions. Alteration would be unknown. Through forethought and prescience, buildings would remain unchanged from the moment of their inception to their eventual demise. In such a world, devoid as it would be of any taint of sentiment, what might be the qualities that would save a building from destruction?

The functionalists were the early saints of Modernism, even though sometimes their beliefs seem to float between the moral and the aesthetic, deserting one for the other in the face of argument. Their intention was to keep the purposes of Modernism free from doubt. John Summerson has said that the one singular characteristic of Modernist theory was the commitment to a social programme, that is architecture in the service of progressive tendencies in society. He further stated that without this, architectural theory would be indistinguishable from architectural thought since the eighteenth century, although this was said before the onset of postmodern writings. In some less than obvious way, functionalism is the agent of this commitment: function is generally supposed to envelop without contradiction progressive social purposes. The Machine Aesthetic presumes a clarity of purpose, as that which the machine itself has. The Machine is the vehicle that will carry society towards Utopia.

In contrast to the machine, the difficulties in defining the elusive exact correspondence between function and built form is that which hinders the realization of such a perfect state, but does not entirely disprove its propositions. It may be that the elusiveness is a result of compounding the animate with the inanimate.

Le Corbusier's own attitude would seem to have been made explicit by his claiming that the house is to be 'a machine to live in'. But as Philippe Boudon has pointed out, this is not without ambiguity. He quotes from Le Corbusier's notes:

> The dictionary tells us that *machine* is a word of Latin and Greek origin meaning art or artifice: 'a contrivance for producing specific effects' . . . which forms the necessary and sufficient framework for a life that we are able to illumine by raising it above the level of the ground through the medium of artistic designs, an undertaking dedicated in its entirety to the happiness of man.[1]

Thus we read the clear qualities of necessity and sufficiency amalgamated with 'the medium of artistic designs', with no contradiction recognized by the author therein.

In several instances in later architectural theory, function is equated with Vitruvian commodity. Robert Venturi, for instance, at the Art Net conference in London in the 1970s[2] said that Classic architecture consisted of Commodity, Firmness and Delight, as propounded by Vitruvius, and that Modern architecture consisted of Firmness plus Commodity equals Delight. In making this proposal, it is evident that he was relying on the commonly held assumption that the commodity of Vitruvius is the equivalent of function in Modernist theory. Dr Robin Evans once observed that in referring to commodity, Vitruvius gives the example of the rich merchant leaving his house and of how the design of the portal can help to give an appropriate setting as he emerges into the city. Thus in this exposition there are traces of the client's vanity and status that are at odds with the concept of efficient, economic and selfless function in the service of social progress.

Function assumes qualities of precision and absence of ambiguity. Perhaps it is because these qualities are manifest in the architectonics of Modernist built form that they are used through allusion to make reference to the assumed conduct of life within the buildings. To put it more succinctly, following Le Corbusier's pronouncement that the house is a machine for living in, it would seem that the precision of servicing, construction and structure of Modernist buildings has been commonly taken as a metaphor for the life intended to be led in such buildings. The actual conduct of life, of course, is always more elusive than the architect's will.

One can suggest that this metaphoric link was the means by which Modernist tendencies identified with the forces for social progress, that there was an assumed parallel between architectonic reform and the contemporaneous attempt to reform the populace's thought and behaviour, to bring into being an intelligent and cohesive proletariat. By this assumption Modernist buildings could be thought of as active agents in the crusade for social progress, and thus a means of connected commitment between theory and practice.

In addition a further attraction might be that it offered a way by which the architect might allay the loneliness of genius through such a social commitment. Such an alliance might be said to underlie the various progressive crusades in architecture in the twentieth century.

Latter-day proponents of functionalism such as Cedric Price and Peter Blundell Jones have sought to re-establish its potency with arguments for a greater clarity with regard to the workings and purposes of buildings. However, this has a key difficulty: precision is a difficult quality to apply to thought and behaviour, which are crucial components of inhabitation. Intent in particular has no immediate spatial requirement.

Peter Blundell Jones talks very persuasively of the attributes of functionalism, using as primary evidence the cowshed and other farm buildings at Garkau near Lubeck by Hugo Haring[3] (Figure 1.1). It is a further difficulty of functionalism indicated by this choice of paradigm, that proving the case for one building by definition disqualifies it for exact translation to others, because of the dependence on the particulars of specification. Philippe Boudon, of

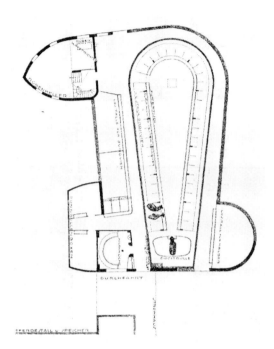

whom the reader will hear more later, expressed a similar observation thus: 'The desire for authenticity and truth of the function . . ., the rejection of connotation (since the form must come strictly from the function) leads to incommunicability . . . All this puts modern architecture in a very precarious position: incapable of being taught because of its incommunicability'.[4]

Cedric Price long argued for the demolition of obsolete buildings, buildings that have outlived their usefulness; at the time of his untimely death, he had been trying to prevent Camden Council proposing one of his own buildings for listing to save it from demolition. A lesser but more ennobled mind has recently called for the demolition of a certain building on the grounds that it was a 'waste of space', and coincidentally in the way of one of his own proposals. Of course the intellectual integrity of the first puts the second to shame, and perhaps all doctrines have a raw edge, but the idea of obsolescence in architecture is quite a strange one. It is peculiarly distinct and separate from the intrinsic qualities, whether spatial or physical, of the building that is in question, the qualities for which a building is liable to be considered for preservation.

It is difficult not to associate it with censorship, or at least with a licence to censor. Thus in a functionalist model, all works of architecture stand in danger of being considered at some time or other, by some agency or other, as a waste of space. Because of the uncertainties in being able to fit function tightly to the built form, the idea of obsolescence is amenable to other interpretations, such as, for instance, what might be considered aesthetic obsolescence.

In this model of the world and architecture's place within it, however, the buildings remain unaltered; their obsolescence therefore is a result of something extrinsic, as it is with military aircraft. They both can be considered as obsolete through changes in the patterns of use which can no longer be accommodated. Whereas with the weapon, such changes can be decided with considerable exactitude, the dismissal of a building on similar grounds is more difficult to achieve. This is perhaps further evidence of the entwining of function and behaviour in Modernist thinking.

The residual idea of functionalism is probably that which envisages buildings as purposeful in achieving social progress, and consequently becoming obsolete once the stated purpose has been achieved: that is, prisons would be demolished once all criminals have been corrected through their use and mental hospitals closed once their inmates were returned to sanity.[5]

The function of buildings in human affairs is more correctly described through patterns or rituals of occupation. Buildings will otherwise resist description in terms of more precise functions; as James Gowan has sometimes commented to me, 'I can eat a sandwich in any size of room'. The intended fit between function and space can be elusive, unfocused, but the image is vivid, which is a reason why the idea of obsolescence is so uncertain with regard to buildings.

The Modernist pursuit of the minimal dwelling was perhaps at root as much an attempt to avoid this difficulty in functionalist theory as it was a concern for cost. It is the alteration in the rituals of occupation that will cause a building to be considered obsolete.

The mutability of function may be more easily described by considering a specific typology, for instance a railway terminal such as King's Cross Station[6] in London, today and at its inception. The change from steam to diesel electric has been accommodated but not exploited, as for instance in not occupying the huge air volume previously required for the dispersal of coal smoke and steam. Unlike with military hardware, technological advances are perhaps less threatening to the existing built form than changes in the conduct of everyday life, because it is these that render the functional description of the building today at odds with its original form. A primary function of railway termini now, as with other transport interchanges such as airports, is the correct siting of retail units, which is the result or the cause of changes in our collective behaviour.

Peter Reyner Banham's obituary for the Machine Aesthetic[7] made similar comparisons in attacking it as an outmoded and misleading symbol of clarity and purpose. He most clearly recognized the delusion that the phrase *form follows function* could apply equally to machine and human behaviour, and that pure built forms would promote a desired way of life. However, I don't believe that he entirely lost an allegiance to the notion; part of him remained an unreconstructed Modernist.[8]

Architecture operates in the world in similar ways to ideology, that is by being clearly conceived in the beginning by the authors, and more diffusely received by the populace.

The purest architecture appears always from seismic shifts in the human psyche. Buildings are too expensive for it ever to be otherwise. The purest buildings are set up to propagate a deep collective conviction. Architects are tempted to believe that the very quality of the architecture is proof or otherwise of the strength of those convictions. Nothing happens without self-interest. The priests at the Council of Trent must have been at least a little concerned about their future stipends when prescribing the architecture of the Counter-Reformation, but underlying all great epochs of building are deeply imbibed systems of belief. It is just this that gives architecture its tragic stature. Architecture sets out time and again to construct Utopia, and in so doing the accompanying act of widespread demolition may be legitimized as ridding the world of a heresy.

The architect has his own agenda, deeply intuitive in impulse and some-how in that strange human way detached at the point of insight from the very convictions to which he is required to give expression.

Katherine Shonfield[9] has talked brilliantly of the basket domes of the Baroque churches in and around Turin as a response by Guarini and others to the admonitions of the Counter-Reformation to represent in built form a 'faith beyond reason'. One might add that Vignola's Jesuit church in Rome is the first great response to the new Catholic doctrine, and go on to trace the correspondence between architecture and eruptions of belief, to include of course the projects of Ledoux and Boullee for the Revolutionary society in France at the end of the eighteenth century. In particular, Ledoux's project for the Saltworks near Besançon that was intended as a matrix for the ideal community (Figure 1.2). In the last century, of course, Le Corbusier in writing *Vers une Architecture* (1923) and *La Ville Radieuse* (1935), created his own scriptural texts which were as much a call to a new way of life as they were a recipe for how buildings were to be made. From the work of such architects we derive our understanding of a building as a work of art.

The idea of a work of art is one that attempts to exclude alteration. In practice, this is generally undertaken through strict environmental control. Just as it seems strange sometimes that the universe is not just an infinite fizz of basic particles and their anti-matter shadows, that things appear discrete and separate-natured, there is nevertheless a chemistry between the animate and the inanimate which alters all things. Although one might observe that this does not seem to lead to an increase in entropy, established material order

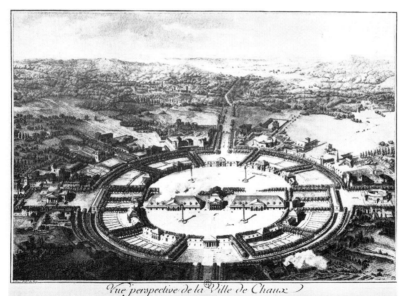

Vue perspective de la Ville de Chaux

1.2   Project for saltworks at Chaux near Besançon by Ledoux, 1773–79

is constantly corroded, everything physical changes. Corrosion results from the work of art harbouring alien life forms. In a painting this can be confined to the molecular level; in a building the most potent chemistry is the interaction between the built form and its inhabitants.

This can best be explained by the description of an exception. Let us consider the building which is most like a painting, the interior of which is experientially most like being absorbed into a painting, the house built in Utrecht for the widow Truus Schröder-Schräder, herself an interior designer, by her close friend Gerrit Rietveld (Figure 1.3). Here is a house where the occupant, once the boys were grown up and off her hands, lived as the curator conserving a monument at once personal and cosmic. In so doing she assiduously repressed the interplay between the house and the everyday that threatened to usurp the initial order.

1.3   The Schröder House, Utrecht by Gerrit Rietveld, 1924

Mondrian said: 'The tragedy of life and art can only be reduced by the depiction of the elements and the balance of the proportions between them.'[10] Trapped on a visit home by the Netherlands' neutrality at the outbreak of the First World War, marooned from his chosen home in Paris, and from *la vie Boheme*, thrown back on his own resources, he adapted to his new circumstances. In so doing, he exhibited the historic resourcefulness of the Dutch people, famed for landscape paintings while lacking any landscape of note, and for creating a realm where water runs uphill. Mondrian set out with others on the path to the universal language of de Stijl. He set out in search of the source of the deep pleasure that paintings share with the mind.

Anyone who has visited the Schröder House at the end of Prins Hendricklaan may have the memory of being shown the house by two women, one slight and one strong, one to supply a commentary and one to move the partitions. To some the utopian intention will have been made most evident in the relatively primitive construction techniques employed in the house. The insistent detailing of such houses as the Maison de Verre is entirely absent, and so the abstract shines through. In the bedroom is a small shelf, a block of cut stock timber, to take Mme Schröder's treasured watch while she slept. Its placement holds anyone who enters the space like a well-placed punctuation mark.

Rietveld claimed that he never met Mondrian, and Mme Schröder said after being persuaded to attend a lecture by van Doesburg, the chief theorist of De Stijl, that the philosophy he propounded wasn't for her. Nevertheless, the house is rightly described as the most convincing use of De Stijl's principles of form. Each Sunday, while he lived, the cabinet maker-architect would come for lunch. In her eighties, the by-then sole occupant had to be dissuaded by her sons from her habit of placing the purpose-made ladder on the top rail of the balustrade at the top of the stairwell, so as to climb into the lantern on the roof to sit and read and to look over the flat land. The purpose of the unchanging rituals was at once the affirmation and preservation of the architecture.

In the eighteenth century, it was the habit of some English landowners with newly landscaped grounds, often made available by the Acts of Enclosure of common land, to employ a hermit to live in a grotto on the estate as a living metaphor for certain virtues. There exist lists of instructions for anyone taking up one of these posts regarding the correct conduct as a hermit;

indulging in banter or soliciting money from guests of the landowner and smoking were strictly forbidden, for example. After Mme Schröder, anyone occupying her house would need a list of instructions to maintain the rituals. This would promote the farce of repeated history, behaviour without conviction, and the best reason why the house, although much visited, is now uninhabited.

At some time someone allowed a motorway to be built across the front of the house, as if to confound its magic. One day the architects of the world should organize and block the motorway with their bodies until the European Union agrees to the resiting of the road.

There is usually over time an interaction between the built form and its occupants that is like chemistry. It is this phenomenon that has to be excluded if a building is to be saved from functionalist oblivion. Adaptation, which is the outcome of the interaction, would need to be forbidden in the services of a perfectly functioning built environment. Only Cedric Price's theory has intellectual integrity within true Modernist thought. His recent death robs architecture of one of its most brilliant critics. Perhaps within the theory there is a case for exemplary buildings such as the Schröder House to be pardoned and granted eternal life on instructive as well as aesthetic grounds; or as Cedric would have said, for our delight.

The price of survival would properly be vacant occupation, emptiness. If the practice of architecture was always high art, if the production of architects was unrelentingly exemplary, then each epoch would make in time an empty preserved quarter of the city. The vacated core would be progressively encircled by a living ring, where the inhabitation would have a finite lease.

The greatest works of art are exemplars. All have their progeny or potential progeny; no such work of art exists without this; the single and the many. But the paradigm contains the essence and its contradiction, to paraphrase Hegel, and it is these that the act of preservation hopes to secure. The case for the conservation of a building rests as much upon commemorating lost social and political aspirations as upon the material preservation of architectonic form.

In the preface to *Scope of Total Architecture* Walter Gropius, founder of the Bauhaus, wrote, 'In the course of my life I became more and more convinced that the usual practice of architects to relieve the dominating disjointed pattern, here and there by a beautiful building is most inadequate and that we must find, instead, a new set of values, based on such constituent factors as would generate an integrated expression of the thought and the feeling of our time.'[11]

All crusades founder on the corruption of their axiomatic origins. An inertia of belief in Modernist thought, supplanted by formalism, leaves us today with an arch conservatism regarding use, in partnership with a rabid policy of demolition: the present building boom in the City of London is a vivid example of this. It is a parody of the Modernist crusade, bereft of association with any idea of social progress.

In this respect, buildings chosen for preservation are memorials to failed collective architectural endeavour; the reason for preserving such paradigms is to retain examples of how architects attempted to devise a built form fitting to the emergent convictions of particular times and places, which is the purpose of pure architecture.

The atmosphere of all preserved buildings is unavoidably instilled with the qualities of *fetish*. The idea of alteration is to offer an alternative to preservation or demolition, a more general strategy to keep buildings extant beyond their time, that is to be inhabited, occupied. One may suppose that such undertakings will be simply expedient, and of course many such changes will be prompted by extraneous needs, but if one considers the survival of the original building, the host so to speak of the new works, then the activity assumes a wider scope. It becomes like an act of transition or translation, from the past into the present, with logically also a consideration for the future of the host building. Without such promise, the undertaking of alteration would seem liable to be doubly destructive: on the one hand causing the destruction of the host building within a facsimile exterior, and on the other losing the hope of a new building, following total demolition of the existing.

One might then deduce that if there is to be a structure of ideas relating to alteration, a theory or an approach to a theory, then this might begin with a consideration of the designer's attitudes towards the host building, and the ordering of such attitudes. Alteration changes the previous condition, to state the obvious. Consequently processes of change to facilitate re-colonization will tend to usurp a building's initial integrity and create mongrel buildings. Because of this, the proposition that alteration needs to be approached on theoretical grounds is obstructed by some widespread problems of perception.

In his *Architecture in Britain 1530–1830*,[12] Sir John Summerson refers extensively to Hampton Court Palace at two separate points in the book; firstly the palace appears as the joint Tudor creation of Cardinal Wolsey and King Henry VIII, and secondly two hundred pages later as the creation of Sir Christopher Wren. The consideration of architectural style requires this ersatz purity of vision, a perceptual requirement to see buildings as discrete entities and complete unto themselves, even when, as is the case with Hampton Court, the whole is a composite affair.

Many other famous buildings have been first published with doctored photographs to pretend a singularity which is fictional: the Maison de Verre was published regularly with the top floor of the nineteenth-century house above it, which the old lady resident had refused to vacate, vanished.

It may be that Hampton Court is a collection of different parts, or it may be that our terms of description are inadequate. It would seem clear from the casual manner of the junction between the Baroque and the Tudor that Wren was not over-concerned with integration (Figure 1.4). But the experience of visiting the palace is not one of distinct entities, where you step from one to another across emphatic boundaries, where one thing ends and another begins. In fact the very mechanisms of separation seem rather to be the means of transition from one space to the next, heightening the unity of sensation. Many people would consider that one of the best architectural promenades in Great Britain is the journey from front to back of the palace, bridging across the small mock moat, going through the passage from the Tudor Clock Court, from where another goes off to the left, finding the huge windowed swing doors, and going through these into the high, gloomy, voluptuous stairwell of the Queen's Stair, with its William Kent murals, then from there emerging into Wren's Fountain Court, with its fake bull's-eye windows, and around the arcade and into the columned loggia, perfectly scaled for a figure mounted on a horse, which connects the palace to garden, which also is by another hand. There is nothing discordant in the experience of the sequence to suggest any discontinuity. The experience can be thus described in cinematic terms, and yet escapes explanation in architectural terms, and one must believe that Summerson is possibly unequalled in his ability to write about architecture. Perhaps this suggests that the terms of such descriptions are inapplicable to describing buildings that are other than singular and complete.

1.4   Junction of Tudor and Baroque buildings at Hampton Court

This would suggest that buildings that have been altered, that are assemblages in some way, can only be devalued by classic architectural criticism. How then can the alteration that is inevitable if a building is to remain in use be executed and be recognized as the equivalent of that which is altered? How might the original and the alteration become intrinsic?

The sense of existential exhaustion after the extremes and experiments of the last century is palpable, and would seem to make more doubtful any ideological revival in the near future, although the writing of this feels like tempting fate. The great Modernist project is stalled, pulled over, and no one will believe yet awhile in the abilities of unhindered progressive thought to offer solutions. Architects now are needed in the service of the Spectacle. Despite the difficulties surrounding the subject of housing, the one-time flagship project of Modern architecture, for instance, no one will suggest an architectural solution to the difficulties. 'Modernist' form is presently reserved for entrenched programmes, the private house, the office block, the museum, the concert hall, the art gallery: the trough may be deep but functionalism now is uncoupled from social progress.

I am not sure whether the habit of compounding rational and aspirational thinking is more prevalent in architecture than in other fields, but it is endemic in the writings of the early Modern Movement. How else, one may ask, can the often utopian intentions of the various movements be articulated within a movement that has such a reverence for mechanization references?

One may answer that architects should stay out of the territory of society and politics, and draw on the history of architecture alone for direction or inspiration. The early decades of the twentieth century proved the impossibility of such an admonition; buildings over time will alter their status with regard to society and always have done; their cost alone at their inception will always bring them within the scrutiny of the wider society. The history of architecture is just such a story.

How may one account for changes of style in architecture? It was proposed by a certain theorist in the nineteenth century that all true styles of architecture were rational within their context, but to attempt to remove status for instance from the production of buildings, related either to client or architect, seems at least myopic. Styles may be post-rational or retro-rational, that is capable of rationalization in retrospect, but in the entanglement of architecture and everyday life, not even such a modified explanation will work. Architectural form is delineated, everyday life is not, it is 'base' in Hegelian terms, and hence in a continuous state of mutation at the edges.[13] Look at the demographic statistics if you doubt it.[11] The idea of 'fit' that is at the centre of the idea of functionalism cannot claim exactitude in respect to the relationship between the living and the built. However, the idea is not rendered impossible because of this; the potentiality for realization is still contained within it. It is within the region of the conceivable, its repeated failure is to be expected as is its repeated resurrection. In a sense all styles of architecture are failed social, religious or utopian experiments, that is how the history is made up: the Baroque failed to push back the tide of Reformation following the Council of Trent and failed to return Europe to the Holy Roman Church, just as public housing in Europe failed to create a contented and progressive proletariat in the twentieth century, but neither failure was complete.

After driving the Moors from Spain, the triumphant forces of Christendom built a cathedral which appears to crash straight through the roof of the Mosque at Cordoba (Figure 1.5).[14] The mosque is a masterwork of Islamic architecture and is usually published ignoring the later savage Christian intrusion. For all their brutality, the cathedral's builders dealt with the world as it exists, and in so doing provoked a commemoration that may have been the opposite of their intentions.

The single high purpose of architecture is to create new order, to sweep away the present in the service of Utopia or paradise on earth. Le Corbusier's Plan Voison[15] for Paris is the clearest statement of this. But such high purpose is of variable availability at different times (Figure 1.6).

Alteration seems to work against this high purpose; it has a different agenda. If only for this reason the practices and theory of alteration may be seen as different from those of pure architecture; this is not meant to imply that architects are in any way disqualified from its practices.

1.5   Fifteenth-century cathedral built through the eighth-century mosque, Cordoba, Spain

1.6   Le Corbusier's Plan Voison for Paris, 1925 model

1.7   Change of use as a consequence of wider socio-economic changes: the Michigan Theater, Detroit

Alteration is the mediation between preservation or demolition. In this less than perfect world the cause of obsolescence is more generally derived from social and economic changes in the wider society (Figure 1.7). In the city, uses and occupations migrate from quarter to quarter in quantum shifts; the one-time brothel becomes software offices, the soap factory becomes artists' studios. Change of use causes a massive change in the rituals of occupation. Buildings change as the city changes.

NOTES

1   Philippe Boudon, *Lived in Architecture* (Cambridge, Mass.: MIT Press, 1972), p. 32.
2   Venturi was quoting from his own *Learning from Las Vegas* (Cambridge, Mass.: MIT Press, 1972, p. 134). Art Net was the gallery run by Peter Cook at the time he was Fifth Year Master at the Architectural Association.
3   Cowshed, hayloft and barn at Garkau. Peter Blundell-Jones, 'Hugo Haring and the Search for a Responsive Architecture', *AA Files* 13 (1983), pp. 30–43. Some might think that the paradigm of functionalist architecture is the oil refinery, or others the chemical works, where each space is specific for a clear purpose; the manner in which such industrial assemblies influenced the Archigram group in the 1960s might bear witness to this. In actuality, the anonymity regarding function is a characteristic of many Modernist prime examples, such as the Van Nelle factory in Rotterdam and its many derivatives. Functionalism has had its critics for some time. This is Martin Pawley (from the Time House, a student project from when he was at the AA, published in *Meaning in Architecture*, ed. Charles Jencks and George Baird, New York: George Braziller, 1970, p. 121): 'it is impossible to functionally define the act of dwelling, which is a continuously evolving drama, not a pattern established once and retained forever', And earlier, Martin Heidegger (*Poetry, Language and Thought*, trans. Albert Hofstadter, New York: Harper & Row, 1971, pp. 145–46): 'residential buildings do indeed provide shelter; today's houses may even be well planned, easy to keep clean, attractively cheap, open to air, light and sun, but – do the houses themselves hold any guarantee that dwelling occurs in them?' Spatial excess, which transparency requires, confounds functionality, whose metaphors are the oil refinery, the internal combustion engined, the mechanical watch, where surplus space has been squeezed out. The need to marry the Machine Aesthetic, the functionalist intention that implies a closedness, to the nature of transparency can reasonably be said to qualify as the outstanding paradox in Modern architecture, theory and practice. Other aspects of transparency are discussed in later chapters.
4   Philippe Boudon, 'Project in the Manner of . . . Notes on a Pedagogic Concept', *Daidalos* 8 (1983), pp. 63–74.
5   Aneurin Bevan, Minister of Health at the initiation of the National Health Service in the United Kingdom, believed that the service would become less and less needed with the advance of socially progressive measures.
6   This station is currently being restored as part of the development of the whole quarter, masterplanned by Foster Associates. The contrasting fates of the two main stations in New York City also show the transience of function. The beautiful cast-iron Penn Station was destroyed in order to incorporate it into an encompassing commercial development, and Grand Central, some twenty years later, was restored, treated as if it were a cathedral. Consequently one can see that other issues, those that might be considered by the true functionalist as sentimental, can now affect the alteration of a building. Issues of patrimony are clearly set to clash with the purposes of efficient operation in all cities.
7   Reyner Banham was to write the obituary of the Machine Aesthetic in typical fashion, berating architects from his engineering background, in a short piece in *Architectural Review* 118 (April 1955), pp. 355–61:

If we make these [regular geometrical forms] the last term in the Ozenfant–Corbusier model of the design process, we get a proposition of this order: objects of maximum utility and lowest price have simple geometric shapes. To most architects this proposition would appear watertight, but to most production engineers it would appear too abstract to be useful, and demonstrably false in its outcome. To them, Utility, in the Rationalist sense which the authors clearly intended, is a marginal factor – only one among a number of factors bearing upon sales . . .

But after the Second World War, in which a whole generation had been forced to familiarize themselves with machinery on its own terms, the disparity between the observable facts and the architect's Machine Aesthetic had become too obtrusive to be ignored. In the Jet Age these ideas of the 'twenties began to wear a very quaint and half timbered look.

This, of course, made it easier for some feeble intellects to 'adopt a modern style' and we are all familiar with the dandified figures in their draughty and obsolescent sports-cars who practise modern architecture as if it were a finished period style, with all the answers in the books. Such men are academics, since their authority is the past, and their skin deep modernism is soon seen through . . .

The Machine Age is dead and we salute its grave because of the magnificent architecture it produced, but we cannot be sentimental over its passing.

The combative tone of the piece may now seem surprising; it represents the tensions within the English architectural community as a new aesthetic or ethic, Brutalism, for which Banham was the spokesman, was emerging to challenge the ageing first generation of British Modernists. One inclination to be noted is the sympathetic attitude towards marketing, treated as if it might adequately replace the machine entirely as the new generator of form. This is a change in political positions, from left to right, which was to become a characteristic of much of the work in the 1950s of the Independent Group and the Institute of Contemporary Art, with which Banham was associated.

8   Thus the Machine Aesthetic is used as metaphor at some times (as in *la machine à habiter*, for instance) and as historical necessity at others. There may be something else beneath all this; when one considers the charm of early Modernist chair prototypes, and the loss of this charm in serial production, it might suggest values beyond the virtues of mass production. Reasonably one might think from the stated intentions of the designers that the processes of mass production should increase the beauty of the prototype. In developing the bent tube furniture at the Bauhaus in the 1920s, Marcel Brueur set out to use bicycle manufacturing machinery for their production. When he found that the machinery was incapable of making the formed radii that he needed, he resorted to hand manufacture of the prototypes. This is to suggest a kind of reversal, where the aesthetic specifies the machine, which was then of necessity evolved to mass-produce the chairs.

9   Katherine Shonfield, Lecture at University of North London, c. 1993.

10   Mondrian cited on the back cover of Carsten-Peter Warncke, *De Stijl 1917–1931* (Köln: Benedickt *Taschen, 1994*).

11   Walter Gropius, *Scope of Total Architecture* (London: Macmillan paperback, 1980).

12   John Summerson, *Architecture in Britain 1530–1830* (London: Pelican History of Art, Penguin Books, 1953; seventh revised and enlarged edition, 1983).

13   Statistics indicate that now in the USA there are more single occupancy habitations than family homes (*New York Times*, 23 November 2003).

14   In *The Arabs: A Short History* (Princeton: Princeton University Press, 1943) Philip K. Hitti explains in the chapter 'Cordova: Jewel of the World' the mosque's origins thus: 'With his realm consolidated and temporarily pacified, Abd-al-Rahman turned to the arts of peace, in which he showed himself as great as in the art of war. He beautified the cities of his domain . . . Two years before his death in 788 Abd-al-Rahman founded the great Mosque of Cordova as a rival to the two sanctuaries of Islam in Jerusalem and Mecca.'

15   I am aware of the recent article in *AA Files* (No. 38) entitled 'Restoration in the Machine Age: Themes of Conservation in Le Corbusier's Plan Voisin', by Thordis Arrhenius which is extremely well researched and rather beautifully written. But just because the great man was gracious enough to run a strip of parkland between the Seine and his layout of spaces and superblocks, and to preserve a few chosen buildings (the usual suspects, Notre Dame, la Madeleine, the Palais Royal

the Louvre, etc.) like the remaining teeth in an ancient's mouth, this hardly constitutes an approach to conservation. Everything within the main layout was to be banished from the face of the earth once and for all. I must acknowledge my debt to the writer, however, for the extensive research that went into his piece, of which I have made use, here and elsewhere. I am reminded by Rodrigo Perez de Arce that there were several projects in the 1960s and 1970s which took the ability to alter as a characteristic of the original design. I remember them quite well; they were often associated with the idea of mass-produced houses, intended to make such productions more responsive to the needs of the inhabitants. Mainly the proposed flexibility was concerned with being able to move internal walls. One might view it as a strategy to limit change, and thus to ensure that the architect retained indefinitely some overall control. This seems to me to want to weaken the principle and pleasures of cross-reference between any present engagement of a building with previous and future engagements.

CHAPTER 2
THE LITERATE AND THE VERNACULAR

'I think Corb would have liked it. When we visited the Villa Savoye, it was full of students squatting everywhere drawing the building, with workmen in blue overalls stepping over them painting the walls white in relays.'

Alex de Rijke recalling a recent field trip to Poissy

LE CORBUSIER USED TO PRETEND to casual enquirers that the Villa Savoye at Poissy had been demolished during the time when it was photographed by Rene Burri in a neglected and ruinous condition.[1] Bernard Tschumi remembers visiting the villa as a student when it was in this state, and remembers the smell of defecation (Figure 2.1). The building was of course adopted as a Monument Nationale by the French Government in 1965,[2] and after extensive restorative works was opened to the public. It is today one of the most visited modern buildings in Europe. Shortly before the order to preserve the villa, the municipality had applied for permission to demolish it in order to extend the school that had already been built to encroach on the edge of the site[3] (Figure 2.2).

No-one saw the potential of the Modern age more clearly than Le Corbusier. In the early 1920s in defining the necessity of a house as a '*machine à habiter*' he proclaimed:

Modern life demands and is waiting for a new kind of plan, both for the house and for the city.

2.1   The Villa Savoye as a ruin in the late 1950s

2.2   The Villa Savoye at Poissy, restored

A great epoch has begun.

There exists a new spirit.

Industry . . . has furnished us with new tools adapted to this new epoch, animated by the new spirit . . .

The problem of the house is the problem of the epoch.

Industry on the grand a scale must occupy itself with building and establish the elements of the house on a mass-production basis.

We must create:

- the mass-production spirit
- the spirit of constructing mass-production houses
- the spirit of living in mass-production houses
- the spirit of conceiving mass-production houses.[4]

He was a man inspired by the advance of technology, and in particular in 1920 the advances that derived from warfare. His vision was expansive, and entirely free of sentiment; for him at this time Progress excused all things. In his book *Aircraft; 'L'avion accuse . . .'* (1935), which is itself a rapturous expansion of the chapter on aircraft from the 'Eyes Which Do Not See' section in *Vers une Architecture*, he wrote the following:

The Great War came. Man had acquired 'the bird's eye view'. What an unexpected gift to survey the armies in front from above! But the bird can be dove or hawk. It became a hawk. What an unexpected gift to be able to set off at night under cover of darkness, and away to sow death with bombs upon sleeping towns. But the hawk swoops on its prey and seizes it in its beak and claws. What an unexpected gift to be able to come from above with a machine gun at the beak's tip spitting death fanwise on men crouched in holes.

The war was a tremendous lever for aviation. In a feverishly accelerated rhythm, at the command of the State, the order of authority, all doors were opened to discovery, Success was achieved, the aim reached, astounding progress made . . . War was the hellish laboratory in which aviation became adult, and was shaped to flawless perfection.[5]

The villa at Poissy, the Villa Savoye or *les Heures Claires* is the culmination of the campaign by Le Cobusier, together with Ozenfant and his cousin Pierre Jeanneret, to define through writing and action the nature of Purist architecture. In defining Purism at the beginning of the 1920s (in their magazine *L'Esprit Nouveau*), this definition is put forward:

The highest delectation of the human spirit is the perception of order and the greatest human satisfaction is the feeling of collaborating or participating in that order . . . The perception of order is mathematical in kind . . . The Purist element, derived from the purification of standard forms, is not a copy in all its generality and invariability. Purist elements are therefore comparable to well-defined words; the Purist syntax is the application of constructive and modulor means; it is the application of the laws which govern pictorial space.[6]

The progress of Le Corbusier's architecture in the 1920s may be seen as part of a European-wide pursuit of an *elementalist* architecture as espoused elsewhere by Theo van Doesburg and Cornelis van Esteren in Holland, and Waschmann, Mies van der Rohe and Malevich. There were of course certain key differences. The house at Poissy marks the furthest point the architect reaches in developing the language of Purism, before beginning in the 1930s a much broader development of his genius.[7]

So this villa, standing in its diminished setting in the Seine valley to the west of Paris, marks as clearly as the Schröder House at the end of Prinzhendrikslaan in Utrecht the high water mark of the most magical phase of Modern architecture, when thought and instinct saturated one another in the creation of these two houses. This is the case for their enshrinement as monuments, protected as far as is possible from alteration. Savoye embodies the clearest realization of the Purist phase of the twentieth century's greatest architect. It was he who added to the singular edict of functionalism, that form follows function, with the definition of the house as 'a house-implement', and 'a machine to live in'. As noted in the previous chapter, this was not without its ambiguities. These were perhaps compounded by Le Corbusier's tendency to slip from the rational into the poetic in further endorsing these exhortations. As noted in Chapter 1, the architect had a tendency to ambiguity when speaking of the machine, treating it at once as both functional and poetic, to suit his purpose.

So here was an edict which could be made to inform not only how the house was made, its spatiality, the life to be led within it, but also by extension the future of our species. The machine for Le Corbusier was both a functional and a poetic metaphor, a cult object from which the qualities of exactitude and precision could be derived, and perhaps with more difficulty, ideas of purpose, without which the machine itself would never have come into existence. There is then inevitably an air of determinism hovering around the supposed purposes of the house; it is difficult to suppress the delinquent feeling that Poissy in particular needs to be inhabited in order to prove or test the more diffuse point concerning conduct of life and the production of happiness. The house would seem to be a test case for the fusion of architecture and accommodation, an elegantly composed set of spatial apparatus.

The building of the post-war secondary school on the boundary of the site has damaged its once seemingly solitary situation. The school's running track, that beloved component of much of Le Corbusier's later planning, has stolen six hectacres of land, and cramped that side of the site. The exquisite Virgilian solitude of the original untrammelled orchard site,[8] with its once seemingly infinite prospect, has been lost. In visiting the restored building now, one is only too aware that the setting, the spatial context of the villa, is irredeemably changed. It no longer commands the view from the roof of an apparently uninhabited landscape, which it once did, as from the terrace at nearby Versaille, at the edge of an urban condition before the vastness of the natural world. Today the sweet building gives a sense of being both stranded and over-manicured, encroached upon by the school built in the 1950s and perpetually freshly painted and gleaming. It was built as a demonstration of *le machine inhabiter*, precision in the service of an erotic and hedonistic way of life. Now the villa at Poissy has in force the rituals of an uninhabited building; visitors are allowed no inappropriate postures, there should be no touching, and consequently only furtive intimacies are possible.

Everything changes, everything changes. At Pessac, on the edge of Bordeaux, Le Corbusier designed a suburb of villas for a local admiring developer, M. Fruges, of which fifty houses were built and completed in 1926. The development is called Les Quartiers Modernes Fruges (Figures 2.3a and 2.3b). They represent Le Corbusier's first extensive exercise in standardization of building components and the industrialization of building methods. The general spirit regarding housing in France at the time was akin to the 'homes fit for heroes' movement in the United Kingdom, the rush of sentiment following the terrible slaughter of the war:

> During the war all house-building projects were brought to a halt whilst at the same time people's expectations grew considerably under the impact of

2.3   Newly completed houses in Les Quartiers Modernes Fruges, Pessac, near Bordeaux, 1926

the stupendous events which had thrown normal life into a turmoil from 1914 to 1918.

From 1918 onwards workmen, who would once have been perfectly happy to find accommodation for themselves and their – in some cases – large families in a two-roomed flat, began to look forward to the day when they would be able to order their lives more agreeably in a small maisonette with 4 or 5 rooms. Although perfectly natural, this desire was none the less one of the salient features of social life in the post-war period.

(a contemporary issue of *Petite Gironde*)

The emphasis became therefore to discover rapid methods for building housing.

On reading Le Corbusier's writings specifically regarding mass production, Henry Fruges contacted the architect and discussed first a development of six houses in Bordeaux, and following the completion of those the building of the larger project at Pessac. One of the attributes of the industrialized methods the architect intended to employ with which he pressed his case with the developer was the ability to dig trenches rapidly, using machinery developed during the First World War. Fruges was a remarkable man of enormous energy and a willing client. Le Corbusier called him 'a natural phenomenon', and the people of Pessac, whose affection he retained throughout his long life, called him 'a true artist'.[9]

The houses at Pessac were Le Corbusier's first chance to try out the implication of mass-producing elements of the house, 'derived from the purification of standard forms'. At the inauguration of Les Quartiers Modernes Fruges the architect expounded, 'The basic component in Pessac which was determined by the standardized design was a cell measuring 5×5 metres, which could be broken down into smaller units of 5×2.50 metres. The whole estate was built on this basis. Each house accommodates 6, 8, 9 or 10 cells, depending on its size.'[10] In fact the walls were made *in situ* but they were designed as a prototype for factory production, or rather a simulation or play.

Ironically, the municipality virtually refused to allow water pipes to be laid for several years after the completion of the houses, despite the trench digger. This is Doctor M, a municipal councillor at the time, and later the mayor of Pessac: 'I had no confidence . . . it was strange, it broke with tradition . . . it was rumoured that these houses belonged to Abd-El-Krim . . . in their simplicity people imagined they were harems! . . . public disaffection stemmed more from objections to lack of amenities than from aesthetic disapproval.'[11]

The reading of the development as 'Arab' was far from universal. The other strong proponent for the project was the French Fascist group Faisceau, to which Le Corbusier is rumoured to have belonged for a time (one needs to remember that *La Ville Radieuse* was dedicated to 'Those in authority'). The proclamation in support of the Pessac development by the French Fascist writer Dr P. Winter, published in *L'Intrasigeant* (25 June 1926) must have been largely dictated by Le Corbusier. It required the repeated intervention of two ministers of state to see the project completed.

After completion, and after a period of three years of planning wrangles, the houses were occupied by low-income families, and were subsequently largely forgotten by the outside world. The client, Henry Fruges, troubled with depression, perhaps exacerbated by the resistance to the development by the municipality and others, had withdrawn in the late 1920s to live in Algiers. He returned in the 1960s; his interest in Pessac meanwhile had remained undiminished.

At about the same time Philippe Boudon made a study using sociological methods of the extensive changes the occupants had wrought on their houses, and from which he published a book containing his interviews with the occupants and others, as well as his wonderfully sober photographs of the altered dwellings. The book was called *Lived-in Architecture* in English. It documented the addition of the metal and glass canopies beloved of the French, the partial blocking of strip windows, a profusion of various planters, the enclosure of exterior spaces, and the addition on some pitched roofs. By splicing separate photographs together, he showed jolly rows of dwellings, bedecked, begoniaed and Renault Dauphined (Figure 2.4). When questioned by Boudon about their alterations, the residents often said the original features were out of date, but one might notice that the most widespread alteration is the conversion of the strip windows into the more time-honoured rectangular opening, that type which the architect had sought to dismiss through scientific reasoning in expounding the Five Points of the New Architecture. It is reasonable to observe that the changes to the houses were more extensive than is usually observed in small housing developments elsewhere. Many of the residents stated that the original designs were well suited to conversion.

The book caused outrage among all right-thinking people within the architectural community. The conflict was between the pure and the colloquial. However, when the architect was asked his opinion after perusing the book, he was more sanguine. Le Corbusier responded when asked his opinion of the changes to his work: '*Connaissez-vous, c'est toujours la vie qui a raison, l'architecte qui a tort.*' (You know, it is always life which is right, it is the architect who is wrong).

2.4   Altered dwellings in Pessac as recorded by Philippe Boudon in the 1960s

The changes wrought by the occupants often obscured the best qualities of the project, as with the common enclosure of the roof terraces recorded by Boudon which destroyed the 'see through' quality from one house to another along the row, and with it the loss of a sense of a collective life of the community, lived out as predicted by the architect on the roof gardens on warm summer evenings, *les jardins du toit* as prescribed by the Five Points.

Martin Pawley, in reviewing the book in *Architectural Design* (September 1969), said it indicated

> a method which is not fundamentally *anti-architectural* . . . The Corbusier who emerges from the analysis of Pessac is not reduced to the status of a fool, nor merely made to seem out of date. The fantastic pitched roof mutations which were once 'machines a habiter' are now composite structures in time, carrying within their structure the memory of their previous form. They can, without irony, be compared to the cathedrals of medieval times for that reason.

For Pessac to have remained unaltered, or to have appeared so, would have required that the populace behave as had Mme Schröder in her similarly sized and similarly aged house in Utrecht. One can imagine that such discipline would be beyond almost any group of people, outside of the armed services or a religious order. However, this is the degree of rigour regarding the conduct of daily life that such day-to-day maintenance would require, year in, year out, regardless of the change of inhabitants due to ageing, marriage, death and birth, or in relocation, or moving away from Pessac. This in itself would contradict the liberation of daily life that the architect intended to promote through the design of these houses.

In looking at the photographs in Boudon's book over a long period of time, the original design increasingly reasserts itself. The regulating lines and careful massing begin to show through so that the ensemble begins to disclose a double nature in which the vernacular is wedded with the magnificence of the original. Although or maybe because the alterations are neither respectful nor erudite, the houses exist as a strange proof of the architect's genius. Perhaps the old boy could see this before anyone else, and as a result could exhibit a relaxed response to these alterations of his work.

The Conclusion to Boudon's book contains the following assertion:

> Certain aspects of the Pessac development have now been clarified. In the first place we have seen that the Q.M.F. were not an 'architectural failure'; the modifications carried out by the occupants constitute a positive and not a negative consequence of le Corbusier's original conception. Pessac could only be regarded as a failure if it had failed to satisfy the needs of the occupants. In point of fact, however, it not only allowed the occupants sufficient latitude to satisfy their needs, by doing so it also helped them to realize what those needs were. Because of the individuality of certain houses in the district – and it was in these that the most extensive conversions were carried out – the district itself acquired a highly individual character. It is, in fact, a small world in itself, closed and open at one and the same time and imbued with an individuality that I was privileged to study. On the other hand, there were certain zones in the settlement where the houses were far more impersonal with the result that they were converted to a much lesser extent; this merely goes to show that, in certain circumstances, a settlement is more likely to inhibit individuality than encourage it.[12]

The uncertainty of the tone must be evident to all. The sidestep early on from 'to satisfy their needs' to 'allowed . . . sufficient latitude to satisfy their needs' cannot pass unnoticed. Later, Boudon quotes Steen Eiler Rasmussen, recalling his visit to Pessac when it was newly completed:

Sitting in a garden on the roof of one of the houses, in the shade of a leafy maple tree, I could see how the sun dappled the Havana-brown wall with blobs of light. The only purpose of the wall was to frame the view. The building opposite could be perceived as houses only with great difficulty. The one to the left was simply a light-green plane without cornice or gutter. An oblong hole was cut out of the plane exactly like the one I was looking through. Behind and to the right of the green house were row houses with coffee-brown facades and cream-coloured sides and behind them rose the tops of the blue 'skyscrapers'.

Boudon comments: 'With his sculptural attitude to the urban scene this critic is clearly poles apart from the occupants and no doubt even further removed from le Corbusier.'[13] This latter comment is wrong.

Lived-in Architecture has been quoted at length so as to explore the difficulties that architectural theory has in coping with change and alteration to the built form following completion, even with a well-plotted method such as the one devised by Philippe Boudon for this book and despite the many delightful critical excursions around the Quartiers, classifying changes as he goes. The phenomenon of alteration manages to avoid explanation despite the author's efforts, which otherwise might have allowed the subject to take its place among the other varied discourses on architecture.

In 1973, admirers of Le Corbusier began the first restoration of one of the Pessac houses, in the Rue des Arcades. Following this the Quartiers' significance were recognized nationally by their incorporation as a Zone de Protection du Patrimoine Architectural, Urbain et Paysager. The local authority at Pessac purchased one of the 'skyscraper' houses in Rue Le Corbusier, in order to transform it, as the latter-day guide explains, into '"a model dwelling" of the neighbourhood, acting as a sort of museum of the site. It is open to the public and fulfills a pedagogical role through its function as a "showcase" of the architectural solutions and techniques developed for restoring the Quartiers Modernes Fruges.'[14] The guide contains only photographs of the houses in the course of construction and before they were occupied, or photographs of the few restored houses. It goes on, quoting from Vers une Architecture:

indeed did not the architects themselves declare at the time: '. . . we will always opt for the banal, the commonplace, the steadfast rule, rather than individualism, the fruit of impetuosity. The common, the rule, the common rule, seem to us to be the strategic bases in the quest for progress and beauty. We see general beauty as attractive and dismiss heroic beauty as pure drama.'

One wonders what is served by reprinting this quotation in the context of the guide. It comes from a time of high optimism concerning the promise of Modernity and an unquestioning of its precepts by its devotees, and it is presented here as if still pertinent today. Within the guide only one mention is made of a single altered house, citing Boudon for its notoriety, so what is the attitude to the residents implicit in this wilful ignorance of their work on the houses over several generations? The residents from the outset did not intend to opt for the banal or the commonplace, nor to be rendered invisible by the later official guide. It is difficult to read the quotation in light of the exclusions from the guide without understanding it as a censure on the efforts of the occupants.

When one visits the scheme today, the altered buildings still constitute a considerable majority, and the Quartiers communicate a strange tension now in the contrast between the used and the restored.

It is intended that the Quartiers will undergo a slow process of attempted purification, but in so doing certain ethics of the original undertaking will be destroyed, in particular the sense that these were a gift of genius to the people, to do as they would wish with them. In Pessac this is more true than in other places; when the properties were finally occupied in 1929, no deposit was required from the new owners.

There are now in Pessac several agencies committed to persuading residents and newcomers to restore the houses to a facsimile of their original condition. What happened singularly at Poissy is intended to be produced collectively at Pessac, except here the buildings are intended to be inhabited. It is intended to expunge the colloquial by these means, one suspects from both the built form and the society. The processes of the new intended colonization may frustrate this[15] (Figure 2.5).

The enigma of Pessac is contained within the contrast between high and low art, the perceived conflict between the quixotic temperament of the occupants and the broodings of genius. What does an act of restoration imply? The removal of the history of the building since its inception? What is the status of the alterations? One is impressed by the confident nature of some of them.

2.5   Restored and unrestored houses in Pessac, 2005

In the rather large detached house and its alterations, documented in Boudon's book in photos 49–54, the owner's changes are assured and comprehensive; their removal since these pictures were taken and the return of the building to its present overall white feel a little like a loss (Figure 2.6). As one first arrives at the Quartiers, in Avenue Henry Fruges, there today are the strange globular planters beneath the bedroom window on the façade of the Type 1 house, as recorded by Boudon, as well as the 'gabled' roofline above. These have the feeling now of historical fact, true additions, rather than imposters, which is how one feels the other changes are viewed by the restorers. Is no synthesis possible between high and low art?

From the evidence of the early photographs of the project, it is difficult to believe that the intended colour scheme, evident in the original model (which has survived and is on display in the 'museum') was ever universally applied (Figure 2.7). There is a photograph of the main block in the Avenue Fruges painted deep ochre as the model, but little other evidence of the overall implementation of the scheme. If it was implemented, it would appear to have been short-lived; the pejorative nicknames that the area attracted, 'the

2.6   Altered house, Pessac, 1960s

Moroccan quarter' and the like, would seem to suggest that the houses were mainly white at the time of occupation. Apart from Rasmussen's attractive commentary on his visit to the newly completed houses, there seems to be little evidence for the original polychromatic scheme existing for any length of time; the three-year period when the houses stood empty between completion and occupation, one suspects, was a time when the original intentions were frustrated. This begs the question, in the planned restoration, to what previous condition is the restoration intended? Restored to the scheme as it was when it was handed over by the contractors or when it was first occupied, or to an assumed purity of completion that may or may not have ever been achieved?

2.7   Original model of Les Quartiers Modernes Fruges, Pessac

One might ask the question: which is the more authentic, the houses restored by the agencies or the others, those altered by the residents, which still have as their basis within them the original structure? Restoration and authenticity are not necessarily exactly coincidental.

One may wonder also why so little is written on alteration in the canon of architecture; let me suggest that it is in fact antipathetic to the crucial architectural impulse. At its root, architecture seeks to sweep away the present and build a better, or certainly different world, and this is why alliances so naturally form between architects and the reigning powers. The idea that such high intentions would ever need altering is a heresy. Alteration, it must be believed, aims to frustrate and subvert the most noble undertakings of architecture. However, one may also concede that the beauty of old cities is the result as much of the glacial changes that sequential occupations have wrought as of their planning and their architecture. Left to time and casual occupation, buildings will alter, and with them the city.

Within the limited existing literature of alteration, Rodrigo Perez de Arce's long article 'Urban Transformation and the Architecture of Additions'[16] is a landmark text that will remain so because of the quality of thought and the extent of his pioneering research. The article is a chronicle of an archaeology of continuous imposition. In it, Perez de Arce charts the changes through time of various European and other buildings and cities. He documents the processes of successive colonizations of the city and the concomitant changes. The article is illustrated throughout with his own careful, intelligent drawings, which expose a marvellous historical imagination.

Early on, he draws in a series of town plans the absorption over the centuries into the general urban fabric of the Roman amphitheatres at Arles, Nimes, Florence and Lucca, and the Diocletian Palace at Spalato or Split in former Yugoslavia (Figure 2.8). This last example may have undergone other changes since this article was published. This is Perez de Arce description of its inception and subsequent history:

> The Roman Palace of Diocletian in Spalato (Split) on the Dalmatian coast was built in an unusually short period, for the Emperor had abdicated and wanted to spend the last years of his life in this quiet and beautiful locality.
>
> The enormous rectangular building (180 × 215m) was divided, in the usual Roman manner, by two roads which crossed each other at right angles.

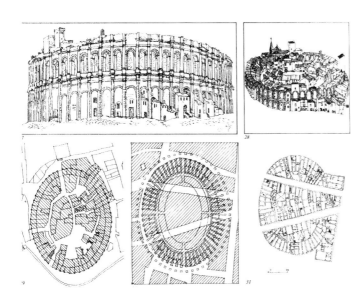

2.8   Amphitheatres and urban absorption

2.9   The Roman Palace of Diocletian in Split (Spalato)

The area next to the seaside was designated for the Emperor's quarters, for the palace proper. These buildings were built over enormous basements which extended all along the front of the palace. Direct connection was provided from the peristyle court through the basements to a small door which led to a pier and the vastness of the Adriatic Sea. The other quarters were inhabited by soldiers and servants [Figure 2.9].

The Emperor died in 316 AD. And the palace complex fell into a long period of decay. Peasants and villagers of the neighbouring areas created legends around this imposing building, half palace and half fortress. But an unexpected event was to have perdurable consequences in the history of the palace, when the nearby city of Salona was invaded and sacked by the Slavs around the year 614 AD. The inhabitants who escaped the massacres first fled to the safe refuge of the islands in the Adriatic Sea, but once they could return in safety they did so, not to their destroyed town but to the remains of the palace.

A conversion operation of enormous scale took place from that moment onwards: the ruins of the palace were gradually transformed into a town and the social stratification of the inhabitants was reflected in the way the grounds and available spaces were used. Thus the wealthy took possession of the areas inside the palace precincts where they could build their mansions, the less powerful citizens inhabited the rooms and spaces which had remained from the original fabric, and the plebeians were left with the crypts, basements and cellars. New buildings and a new street layout were superimposed on the Roman ones. Existing buildings were converted: the mausoleum of the Emperor was transformed into a church and a campanile was built next to it; the Palatine temple was transformed into a baptistry.[17]

In addition, Perez de Arce compares the palace in Spalato with the Spanish/Inca city of Cuzco in Peru and with Rome to this end:

> Cuzco, Spalato, and Rome testify to the validity and permanence of an urban plan well beyond its original and foreseeable development. But in the three cases (which are taken as archetypical ones) there has been one rule which has commanded the process: a correct relationship between urban morphology and building types has been maintained.[18]

The piquancy of the urban transformations chronicled by Perez de Arce is the imagining of the repeated colonization of the ruined city, and each colonization matched with a desertion. This may have happened as a result of war, pestilence or famine, or may have come about because of a change in fashion. Thus to welcome the insidious, creeping, undermining workings of time which reveal a different truth is a critique of the established order, of that part which has historically provided the most sponsors for architecture.

This is not intended to detract from the high opinion this long article deserves. On reading Perez de Arce's brilliant writings, one might conclude, as with looking at Rene Burri's beautiful photographs of the ruined Villa Savoye, that time itself is the architect. But if that is so, where is the space for conscious action in the process? The question implicit in Perez de Arce's writing is: can the designer gain their identity through works of intervention in the existing city, but also be part of the anonymous continuity of alteration of the built fabric, of which he, Perez de Arce, is the narrator?

The writing is an expression of praise of the innate genius of the populace. This stance requires in its turn an uncritical attitude to colloquial alterations. The interaction over time between the urban fabric and citizens that slowly transmutes the city must be treated implicitly as a type of inevitability. All reverence for the vernacular comes up against a similar observation and an objection: true vernacular cannot be appropriated; it can be parodied but the risks are high.

The stance is uncritical and indiscriminate; this is spontaneous folk art, and all changes must be treated as of equal value. The new additions are necessarily read in a way that is free of censure, since the vernacular is beyond the reach of the critical. Colloquial changes eschew the discriminate, no blame is to be purported to any act of 'pop' alteration. Such common-place changes depend on an innocence which is unavailable to the designer.

Two objections to this view also might be made, the first regarding spatiality; this type of alteration is almost always a process of encrustation, of diminished spaces, and of a usual loss of spatial clarity. It is like the over-layering of the underlying form, similar to the processes in nature that absorb organisms into the surroundings, while somehow retaining a trace of the original form, as, for instance, with how ammonites form (Figure 2.10). It is an increase in entropy, and as such should be contested by the creative will. The second is the implication that in the past, mistakes were never made (Figure 2.11). The traces that result from such processes, however, must be thought of as authentic, in some way unsullied.

Rodolfo Machado, writing in *Progressive Architecture*,[19] makes another metaphorical connection between remodelling and writing. In an article called

2.10   Processes of encrustation: the ammonite

2.11   Gothic window inserted into a Romanesque apse

'Old Buildings as Palimpsest', written while he was teaching at RISD, Providence, Rhode Island, he sees the processes of serial alteration through the ages as being like the writing on a palimpsest, a piece of stretched suede or vellum used by the Romans as a substitute for paper. It was inscribed with the point of a metal stylus, and once the message was conveyed, the surface could be scraped back and a new message written. As the palimpsest wore, traces of previous messages would remain. Using as an illustration the walls of a Romanesque palace in Lucca, he makes the comparison with how a building might also be like this, that is written over, partially erased and written over again so that traces of the previous writings remain discernible (Figure 2.12).

As with Perez de Arce, this would seem to give equal relevance to all work done during a building's lifetime, and its original condition. Everything existing is taken as authentic. The article is an elegant piece but a little lacking in development. It is, however, a new contribution to the debate between the

2.12   A Romanesque palace 'over-written' through time

contrasting attitudes to restoration which derive from either Viollet-le-Duc or John Ruskin.

Perez de Arce and, to a certain extent, Machado are writing of unconscious processes in history, the workings of a latent genius in the populous to affect the built environment, generation after generation to a fruitful end. The writings assume that the vernacular can never make a mistake. Perhaps nothing more needs to be said. Perhaps the creeping persistent metamorphosis by diminutive change is best left to the laity and collective genius; how else might one prevent it? As at Pessac, it seems low art needs to be left to work its transformations unhindered by any external scrutiny, like experiments in quantum mechanics, following Heisenberg's Principle of Uncertainty. This proposed state of innocence, however, as with all similar states, once transgressed cannot be retrieved. The designer is a being beyond innocence, and the task of their consciousness is to raise low art to a higher level. Opposition to such an elevation might come from professional and political sources; on the one hand the architect might suspect that their assumed monopoly of philosophies of the building is eroded by this development; and on the other, romantically inclined historians of the masses might object also that this once collective activity should not be removed to the rarefied atmosphere of the artist.

At the end of his essay Perez de Arce uses two contrasting quotations, the first from Benito Mussolini:

> I should like to divide the problem of Rome, the Rome of the 20th Century, into two categories: the problems of necessity and the problems of grandeur. One cannot confront the latter unless the first has been resolved . . . The problems of grandeur are of another kind: we must liberate all of Ancient Rome from the mediocre construction that disfigures it . . . but side by side with the Rome of Antiquity and Christianity we must also create the monumental Rome of the 20th Century.[20]

The second is from Aldo Rossi:

> To understand monuments as pieces of cities, sedimentations of materials that can be transformed, adapted and arranged for a fresh life, does not mean a cultural adventure, but a great project for the principal nations of Europe. This to some extent happened – and often catastrophically – during the Napoleonic era and after the Unification of Italy, but despite the way it was carried out, it constituted a progressive fact.[21]

NOTES

1 Rene Burri/Magnum Photos, *Le Corbusier, Moments in the Life of a Great Architect*, ed. Arthur Ruegg (Basel, Boston, Berlin: Birkhauser, 1999).

2 Andre Malraux, whom General de Gaulle had appointed as his Minister of Culture, was responsible for the decision to save the villa for posterity.

3 The fact that the original site has lost six hectacres for the school's running track, an element that Le Corbusier himself introduced into the language of the architectural plan shows that irony and history can be indistinguishable.

4   Le Corbusier, *Towards a New Architecture*, trans. Frederick Etchells (London: The Architectuals Press, 1927) n.p.
5   Published London: Trefoil, 1987, n.p.
6   Le Corbusier and Amédée Ozenfant, *L'Esprit Nouveau* I (1920), n.p. The architect's intentions are formalized by the publication of the Five Points of the New Architecture (Le Corbusier and Pierre Jeanneret, *Berlin: Die Form*, vol. II, 1927, pp. 272–74). The Five Points consist of Roof Gardens, the Grid of Supporting Columns (or *pilotis*), the Free Plan (made possible by the structure having been assigned to the grid of columns), the Long (or Strip) window, and the Free Façade. The explanation ends: 'The five basic points laid out above involve a fundamentally new aesthetic. Just as we can get very little from the literary and historical instruction meted out at school, so nothing remains for us any more of the architecture of earlier epochs.' The several inconsistencies and contradictions in the Five Points are quite easy to identify: The raised ground floor on *pilotis* is wilful, and is not for instance a property of the original paradigm, the Domino House of 1914–15.
    Plans in a building are never entirely free from one another, they are connected by circulation and plumbing. Neither can the grid of columns be entirely ignored. It has been noted elsewhere that this idea of the plan allowed Le Corbusier to compose plans as if they were drawings for paintings, so producing strikingly beautiful plans through his skill as a graphic artist.
    The long window is less independent of the internal divisions than the 'awkward' vertical windows. The problem of running the strip window past the end of internal walls is unavoidable and very difficult to solve. The explanations of the window's virtues assume that the designer will welcome a high light intensity in all situations. In other places the window is recommended for its evenness of light, which might be seen as an agent of the lack of emphasis that the aesthetic of transparency requires. Of course at other times, and with Le Corbusier too in his later works (at Ronchamp, for instance), evenness of light is not a priority.
    The free façade is not free, it must be made with strip windows and must conform to the Regulating Lines, as expounded in *Vers une Architecture*.
    Only the least reasonable of the Five Points, the roof garden, manages to escape unscathed.
    Nevertheless, from this formula he made wonderful houses and villas during the 1920s. So much still can be said of Le Corbusier, but for the moment we may recognize him as Superman and move on. His shadow passes over us like that of an aircraft flying over the desert.
7   By 1929, Le Corbusier was able to claim in a letter to a client: 'now I am famous'. The retreat into the role of Unique Genius was short-lived, however. The architect's conviction of the universal relevance of his theories, and of their architectural, cultural and social significance, prompted Le Corbusier's greatest book, *La Ville Radieuse* (*The Radiant City*, published in 1933; in English translation in 1967). This was a magnificent amplification of his architectural thinking, and has remained the fullest account he ever gave of his great mind with respect to the built environment.
8   Colin Rowe in his essay 'The Mathematics of the Ideal Villa' says of Savoye that it has a Virgilian nostalgia and the qualities of a contemporary pastoral; *Mathematics of the Ideal Villa and Other Essays* (Cambridge, Mass.: MIT Press, 1976).
9   There is an interesting commentary on the origins of Pessac by Brian Brace Taylor (*Le Corbusier at Pessac*, Cambridge, Mass.: Carpenter Center for the Visual Arts, Harvard University, 1972).

    Two decisions taken at the outset by the architect and client were certainly inextricably linked. One related to the technical system which le Corbusier proposed, namely the cement-gun technique of the Ingersoll-Rand company; the cost of purchasing this equipment was not justified by the scale of M. Fruges' initial proposal. Thus the other decision taken at the time that the gunite system was adopted enlarged the scope of the building program. It was enlarged to include several residential quarters in the Southwest of France . . . The grandeur of their joint endeavor had a special, rather ancient, precedent in the area which both men were well aware of. This was the rich tradition of thirteenth-century villes neuves in southwestern France. Le Corbusier was familiar with these medieval towns from an article which had appeared in January 1925, which had been translated from English for his use. The English and the French conquerors alike had settled large tracts of land by founding such planned new towns as Creon, Sauveterre, Monpazier, and Libourne. Streets set out in a carefully rectilinear grid, with a main plaza at the centre, characterizes the urban pattern of many of these colonial settlements; a noteworthy architectural element, namely, a covered arcade around the four sides of these plazas and termed cornieres, was a feature which M. Fruges specifically requested the architects to include in the Quartier Moderne Fruges at Pessac. M. Fruges' stature as industrialist, community leader, and artist suggests that he wished to see himself as a grand seigneur of the 20th century, developing the region by means of model communities.

10 Philippe Boudon, *Lived-in Architecture* (Cambridge, Mass.: MIT Press; London: Lund Humphries, 1972) (*Pessac de Le Corbusier: 1927–1967 Etude socio-architecturale* in French), p. 11.

11 Ibid., p. 14.

12 Ibid., p. 161.

13 Ibid., p. 162.

14 Marylene Ferrand, Jean-Pierre Feugas, Bernard Le Roy and Jean-Luc Veyret, *Le Corbusier: Les Quartiers Modernes Fruges* (Paris: Fondation Le Corbusier / Basel, Boston, Berlin: Birkhauser, 1998).

15 To comment briefly on the general restorative strategy adopted by the district, all householders are required when considering repainting either to apply the architect's original colours or to paint their house white. One wonders if other suggestions would not be more apt. The most obvious phenomenon that presently obscures the sense of 'laboratory' that both architect and client were aiming for is the proliferation and maturity of the planting. It is this that makes certain corners of the scheme look like any other suburban development. Some encouragement to the inhabitants to inhibit and cut back plant growth would allow the original intentions to be more apparent. Standing on the roof of the restored 'skyscraper' house that serves as the museum, one is struck by widespread later covering of the roof terraces with sloping roofs, many of the most basic corrugated construction. The reason for this was that the original flat roofs leaked. One clear proposition for conduct of life in the Five Points is the use of roof terraces; Rassmussen nicely implies in his description quoted earlier the wedding of community and aesthetic that would have resulted had the roofs been more widely used as intended. Philippe Boudon discusses the ambiguous attitudes to the 'roof terraces', which were viewed as being sometimes simply the lack of a real roof, and sometimes an invitation to inappropriate behaviour. If, however, now the residents could be persuaded up onto these terraces, on any warm evening, what we owe to the architect's foresight would be apparent. Perhaps sometimes a radical proposal must wait before it is taken up. To encourage the residents to restore these terraces, and for the authorities to make available new technologies to waterproof the terraces reliably, would achieve a more powerful indication of the original spirit than the rather timid suggestions concerning repainting.

16 Rodrigo Perez de Arce, 'Urban Transformations and the Architecture of Additions', *Architectural Design*, 4 April 1978.

17 Ibid., p. 244.

18 Ibid., p. 248.

19 Rodolfo Machado, 'Old Buildings as Palimpsest', *Progressive Architecture*, November 1976.

20 Mussolini's speech on the development of Rome, 1924, quoted from S. Kostoff, *The Third Rome*; seminar at the University of Art Museum, Berkeley, 1973.

21 Aldo Rossi, quoted from a panel discussion recorded in *Lotus* 13 (December 1976), n.p.

CHAPTER 3
RESTORATION, PRESERVATION AND ALTERATION

RESTORATION IS OF COURSE A type of alteration; considering issues of restoration and conservation removes the act of alteration from the realm of low art by way of the intrinsic intellectual requirement of such an undertaking. All such issues would require the comprehension of that which is to be studied, an understanding of the host building, its spatial context and temporal context. Any work of alteration that begins with a restorative component is thus raised into a more general discourse from the local incoherence of the colloquial. Perhaps it is proof of the dialectical nature of the practices of alteration that one must first think about attitudes to restoration and conservation.

Since the nineteenth century, the practice of restoration has been torn between two opposing orthodoxies. The editor of *Domus* in 1990 stated the situation thus:

> There are two paths restoration can take. One starts from the building and meditating on the material and the period in which the building was erected finds materials which can't be reproduced and time that doesn't return, so pursues the conservation of the materials' consistency, *hic et nunc*, as a guarantee of the attained texts' authenticity. The other arrives at the monument only after delving in the fields of Aesthetics, Idealism, and Art History, to win the devastated physique of the manufactured article, by transformimg it, so different now from the reassuring image of its 'original state'. An old story, the definition of modern restoration . . . the paths remain two, that are incompatible: on one hand restoration and its adjectives and on the other preservation.[1]

3.1   Viollet-le-Duc, study of Sainte Chapelle, Paris (*Dictionnaire raisonné*)

Viollet-le-Duc wrote, '*Restaurer un edifice, ce n'est pas l'entretenir, le reparer ou le refaire, c'est retablir dans un etat complet qui peut n'avoir jamais existe, a un moment donne*'[2] (Figure 3.1).

In *The Seven Lamps of Architecture*, John Ruskin wrote:

> Neither by the public nor by those who have care of public monuments, is the true meaning of the word restoration understood. It means the most total destruction which a building can suffer: a destruction out of which no remnants can be gathered: a destruction accompanied with false description of the thing destroyed. Do not let us deceive ourselves in this important matter; it is impossible, as impossible as to raise the dead, to restore anything that has ever been great or beautiful in architecture.[3] (Figure 3.2)

3.2   John Ruskin, part of Cathedral of St Lo, Normandy (*The Seven Lamps of Architecture*)

Of these two great theorists, both of them enthusiasts of the Gothic, it would seem that from these two differing points of view, Viollet-le-Duc was the despoiler, and Ruskin the protector of old buildings.

I remember reading a Stephen Bayley essay on these two, where he tells the story of their both, at different times, drawing the same range of the Alps, near the Jungfrau perhaps, and separately conducting an analysis of the mountain forms. Viollet-le-Duc found an underlying cubic organization, and Ruskin found the serpentine line that Hogarth had proposed as the essence of beauty.[4]

Both, however, were united in a disapproval of any stone cladding of metal structures (as too was Le Corbusier, when praising the George Washington Bridge a century later[5]). Ruskin was able to draw and write like an angel: Viollet-le-Duc loved cats.

A legacy of the nineteenth century is this contest of views regarding restoration. The first appears to be an argument for licence to alter, and the other is an opposite admonition against meddling. Each in their way reflects social and political conditions in the authors' respective home countries, and the engagement of one against the nonconformity of the other; a positive social and political radicalism contrasted with a querulous resistance to the trends of the day.

In subsequent commentaries, there is an occasional suggestion that restoration is permissible in France, but not in England. For instance, in writing about the disapprobation of the various restorative works of Sir George Gilbert Scott and others, reported in the essay 'Scrape and Anti-scrape', Nikolaus Pevsner notes William Morris's remarks that Viollet-le-Duc 'invented for Clermont-Ferrand Cathedral . . . a piece of scholarly conjecture, not of wild fancy as Lord Grimthorpe's . . . west front of St Albans'.[6]

Apart from his writings, Viollet-le-Duc is probably best known for the extensive work on Notre Dame in Paris, in particular the design for the lantern over the crossing, the reconstruction of the walled citadel of Carcassonne and the rebuilding of the chateau at Pierrefronds (Figure 3.3). Carcassonne is among the greatest tourist attractions of France. Among its competitors is Disneyland, Paris. Disney himself said that along with the castles of Ludwig of Bavaria, Carcassonne was one of his primary influences.

Works of scholarly restoration are akin in some ways to the making of a new building. Both have the same purist tendencies, and the drive towards

3.3 Pierrefronds, before and after restoration

completeness. The clear difference is that in not working in a contemporaneous style, certain sinews are severed, certain narratives rejected that would connect the building with the ever-present in which we are all ensnared. They are therefore removed from human affairs, and, except for the recluse, uninhabitable as a result.

For Ruskin, the closer was the copy, the greater was the deception. His empathy was with the dead craftsman, as when he goes on to say, concerning restoration:

> That which I have above insisted upon as the life of the whole, that spirit which is given only by the hand and eye of the workman, can never be recalled. Another spirit may be given, and it is then a new building; but the spirit of the dead workman cannot be summoned up, and commanded to direct other hands, and other thoughts. And as for direct and simple copying, it is palpably impossible. What copying can there be of surfaces that have been worn half an inch down? The whole finish of the work was in the half inch that is gone; if you attempt to restore that finish, you do it conjecturally; if you copy what is left, granting fidelity to be possible, . . . how is the new work better than the old? There was yet some life, some mysterious suggestion of what it had been, and of what it had lost; some sweetness in the gentle lines which rain and sun had wrought. There can be none in the brute hardness of the new carving . . . Do not let us talk then of restoration. The thing is a Lie from beginning to end. You may make a model of a building as you may of a corpse.[7]

Ruskin's true attitude to restoration was closer to terror than simple hatred, a deep fear as if from childhood, a fairy-tale terror of Red Riding Hood and the Wolf, the fear of the doppelgänger.

In 1874 Ruskin refused the Royal Institute of Architects' gold medal because of 'the destruction under the name of restoration brought about by architects'. His devoted disciple William Morris was converted to his master's views on restoration at an early age.[8] Ruskin was celibate, essentially removed from the world, while Morris was the phenomenal man of action. The younger man must have soon seen the impracticality of Ruskin's vow of chastity regarding building. His response was to establish what became the Society for the Protection of Ancient Buildings, and to lay down guidelines for working on ancient buildings. He was prompted to do it, as he explained in a letter to the *Athenaeum* in March 1877:

> Sir, my eye just now caught the word 'restoration' in the morning paper and on looking closer, I saw that this time it is nothing less than the minster of Tewkesbury that is to be destroyed by Sir Gilbert Scott. Is it altogether too late to do something to save it? . . . Would it not be some use once for all,

and with the least delay possible to set on foot an association for the purpose of watching over and protecting these relics . . . What I wish for, therefore, is that an association should be set on foot to keep watch on old monuments, to protect against all 'restoration' that means more than keeping out wind and weather, and by all means, literary and other, to awaken a feeling that our ancient buildings are not ecclesiastical toys, but sacred monuments of the nation's growth and hope.

The letter had immediate effect, and the Anti-scrape Club was founded with Morris as Honorary Secretary.[9] His involvement was assiduous and lifelong.

He even overcame his ingrained hatred of English Baroque: Thomas Carlyle's support was solicited, and the latter wrote a passionate plea for the saving of Wren's churches, the one style Morris himself would have happily seen banished from the face of the earth. Perhaps persuaded by Carlyle's letter, and recognizing his own insupportable prejudices, Morris was later to attack the City of London's widespread destruction of the churches in a letter to *The Times* in April, 1878. After Gilbert Scott's death that year, Morris later called him 'That happily dead dog'.[10]

The manifesto Morris wrote for the Society for the Protection of Ancient Buildings is used unaltered to this day.[11] The third paragraph begins:

For Architecture, long decaying, died out as a popular art, just as knowledge of mediaeval art was born. So that the civilized world of the nineteenth century has no style of its own amidst its wide knowledge of the styles of other centuries. From this lack and this gain arose in men's minds the strange idea of the Restoration of ancient buildings; and a strange and most fatal idea, which by its very name implies that it is possible to strip from a building this, that or the other part of its history – of its life that is – and then to stay the hand at some arbitrary point, and leave it still historical, living, and even as it was once.

In early times this forgery was impossible, because the knowledge failed the builders or perhaps because instinct held them back. If repairs were needed, if ambition or piety held them back, that change was of necessity wrought in the unmistakable fashion of the time; a church of the eleventh century might be added to or altered in the twelfth, thirteenth, fourteenth, fifteenth, sixteenth, or even seventeenth or eighteenth; but every change, whatever history it destroyed, left history in the gap, and was alive with the deeds done midst its fashioning. The result of all this was often a building in which the many changes, though harsh and visible enough, were, by their very contrast, interesting and instructive and could by no possibility mislead. But those who make the changes wrought in our day under the name of restoration . . . have no guide but each his own individual whim.

Morris later made a concession: if new work was to be done in an old building, then it should be in a contemporary style. But to qualify this, he stated that all insertions were to be reversible, that is, could be removed without leaving a trace.

Here is a double difficulty. Firstly, what, to someone like Morris, was a contemporary style, soaked as he was in a devotion to the Gothic? The second problem was clearly seen by Pevsner in his essay 'Scrape and Anti-scrape':

> The Victorian restorers removed 'original' features, Perpendicular and later, and especially Georgian, and we tell them they were vandals. What they put in their stead a hundred years ago, should not that now be as sacrosanct as the Georgian pieces a hundred years old when they were removed? . . . Scott's and Skidmore's screens, for example . . . ought to be protected against the zeal of today's Ecclesiologists, the men of the Liturgical Movement who just like their predecessors plead for destruction in the name of worship . . . [T]he aim of closer participation in the service can be achieved without sweeping away what is of architectural value.[12]

Old churches are and will continue to be required to absorb changes; what is important is that these changes are both well conceived and well carried out, and not regrettable.

The penultimate paragraph of the manifesto sets out the proposed attitude to old buildings. The paragraph before it begins:

> For what is left we plead before our architects themselves, before the official guardians of buildings, and before the public generally, and we pray them to remember how much is gone of the religion, thought and manners of time past, never by almost universal consent, to be Restored: and to consider whether it be possible to Restore those buildings, the living spirit of which, it cannot be too often repeated, was an inseparable part of that religion and thought, and those past manners . . .

It is for all these buildings, therefore, of all times and styles, that we plead and call upon those who have to deal with them, to put Protection in the place of Restoration, to stave off decay by daily care, to prop a perilous wall or mend a leaky roof by such means as are obviously meant for support or covering and show no pretence of other art, and otherwise to resist all tampering with either the fabric or ornament of the building as it stands; if it has become inconvenient for its present use, to raise another building rather than alter or enlarge the old one; in fine to treat our ancient buildings as monuments of a bygone art, created by bygone manners, that modern art cannot meddle with without destroying.

Thus, and only thus, shall we escape the reproach of our learning being turned into a snare to us; thus, and only thus, can we protect our ancient buildings, and hand them down instructive and venerable to those that come after us.

This is a close paraphrase of Ruskin's exhortations in *The Seven Lamps of Architecture*.[13] Both are attempting to remove from alteration buildings whose very charm they both had admitted had come from alteration, whether by the weather or by now dead craftsmen. Because of their abhorrence of the present, they deny those working on old buildings just that engagement and association that Morris in particular was dedicated to allowing his own studio workers. So in attempting to be true to Ruskin's absolute prohibition, Morris denies the workmen of his own age, those who were otherwise the focus of his life's effort, any hope of pleasurable involvement with their labour, of obtaining that unalienated condition that Ruskin worships elsewhere in *The Seven Lamps of Architecture*, when writing on the quality of Savagery in architecture.

Having recognized the validity of past alterations in the manifesto, Morris disallows the possibility of any future permanent change.

William Morris was man of action, of extraordinary energy, increasingly devoted in later life to socialist politics, and increasingly revolutionary socialist politics at that. Perhaps having realized the impotence of his attempts to replace the thundering means of production of his time with craft-based guilds, he gave himself increasingly to left-wing causes; his integrity remained undiminished all his life, and as with many great men, this was the root of his tragedy.

Ruskin suffered a mental collapse in old age, increasingly unable to cope with 'the restless and discontented present'. 'I have fallen down the stair of my senses,' he wrote in a letter. His sad infatuation with a young girl is another melancholic feature of his later years. In his prime he wrote beautifully and persuasively on a wide range of social issues of his time, as well as on architecture, the natural world and painting. His prose was so admired that he was offered the post of Poet Laureate (the quotation above is from the letter refusing that honour). His mind when strong was for many like a beacon, in a country denied the liberation of revolution. Ruskin's sympathy for the working classes of his own day is evident in everything he did, and the reverence for the dead builders of ancient buildings repeatedly surfaces in his writings. It informed as much as anything else his views on restoration. The culmination of his arguments in Chapter XX of 'The Lamp of Memory', from *The Seven Books of Architecture*, reads:

> I must not leave the truth unstated, that it is again no question of expediency or feeling whether we shall preserve the buildings of past times or not. We have no right whatever to touch them. They are not ours. They belong partly to those who built them, and partly to all the generations of mankind who are to follow us. The dead have still their right in them: that which they laboured for, the praise of achievement or the expression of religious feeling, or what so ever else it might be which in those buildings they intended to be permanent, we have no right to obliterate.[14]

Of course in time 'the generations who are to follow' will become the living, and in their turn also will be forbidden from touching ancient buildings. Ruskin's definition therefore reveres only the dead, without, as later theories would have it, the chance of dialogue across generations.

Ruskin's love of the picturesque is revealing:

> in architecture, the superinduced and accidental beauty is the most commonly inconsistent with the preservation of the original character, and the picturesque is therefore sought in ruin, and supposed to consist in decay. Whereas, even when so sought, it consists of the mere sublimity of the rents, or fractures, or stains, or vegetation, which assimilate the architecture with the work of Nature, and bestow upon it those circumstances of colour and form which are universally beloved by the eye of man . . . But so far as it can be rendered consistent with the inherent character, the picturesque or extraneous sublimity of architecture has just this of nobler function in it than that of any other object whatsoever, that it is an exponent of age, of that in

which, as has been said, the greatest glory of the building consists; and, therefore, the external signs of this glory, having power and purpose greater than any belonging to their mere sensible beauty, may be considered as taking rank among pure and essential characters; so essential to my mind, that I think a building cannot be considered as in its prime until four or five centuries have passed over it; and that the entire choice and arrangement of its details should have reference to their appearance after that period, so that none should be admitted which would suffer material injury either by the weather-staining, or the mechanical degradation which a lapse of such a period would necessitate.[15]

One is tempted to say that Ruskin's attitude to old buildings is prescribed entirely by his love of surface, lost or otherwise. One thinks of both Ruskin and Viollet-le-Duc, together with Pugin, as the great proponents of the virtues of Gothic architecture. Viollet-le-Duc's approach[16] was the most structured and far-reaching, and he had no such partisan restraints as affected the other two. His *Dictionnaire* is a disinterested and extensive enquiry into how buildings of all ages came about, despite a certain emphasis on the Gothic, from which the author concludes that all different styles of architecture are rational, apart perhaps from their different inceptions. As such, the work can claim to have relevance not merely historically, but also in the present and into the future. For him 'taste' properly understood was simply unconscious reasoning at work.

John Summerson called Viollet-le-Duc and Alberti 'the two supremely eminent theorists in the history of European Architecture',[17] and the universality of Viollett-le-Duc's writings is confirmation of this.

Ruskin would seem to want to quarantine a building for centuries before even comment on it were allowed. Contradictions abound in his thinking, not least the counter-claims that a building 'cannot be considered as in its prime until four or five centuries have passed over it', and the insistence that a building only becomes architecture through its ornamentation, considered by him as the messenger of the joyful 'savageness' of the original mason; how could that survive so clear for so long?

The impracticalities in Ruskin's thinking were addressed to a certain extent by Morris, but both men seem to want to withdraw buildings from everyday use, in the service of preservation. Whereas these ideas may apply to buildings more than five hundred years old, if only because of such buildings' comparative rarity, as a matter of defence, their helpfulness in the task of alteration of buildings less than fifty years old, for instance, would seem questionable.

The issues concerning how to treat old buildings are more alive in Continental Europe than in Great Britain; somewhere or other the assumption here is that Anglo-Saxon pragmatism and 'common sense', that ever-popular substitute for thought, will cope in confronting the issues case by case.[18] But, even in the most accepted of cases, there are many complications.

Only one flutter of doubt creeps into Ruskin's exposition of the evils of restoration. Regarding imitation, he writes:

> the second [step to restoration] is usually to put up the cheapest and the basest imitation which can escape detection, but in all cases, however careful, and however laboured, an imitation still, a cold model of such parts as can be modelled, with conjectural supplements; and my experience has as yet furnished me with only one instance, that of the Palais de Justice at Rouen, in which even this, the utmost degree of fidelity which is possible, has been attained, or even attempted.

The work in Rouen was under the direction of Viollet-le-Duc. Nevertheless, even today, the latter's claim that the intervening hand is permitted to restore a building to a perfection that might never have existed at any time must seem to many to offer the designer or architect a grossly exaggerated authority.[19]

To what condition is it intended that the houses at Pessac are to be restored? Is it the actuality of the buildings at the moment or half an hour after they were handed over by the contractors? Is it when the buildings were occupied some three years later? Of course not. None of these actualities is accessible, along with all other time passed. Thus the aim of the restoration is not necessarily in the realm of actuality, and perhaps it is impossible to accommodate it there (Figure 3.4). The intended restorations are primarily an act of homage to the architect, a man of genius, and not to the houses *per se*; without the architect's reputation in the world, no such restorative pro-gramme would have issued forth. Because of this, the restorations will be measured not against any actuality, but against the discernible intentions of the architect, from his extensive writings. Necessarily this will also invoke guessing or imagining what his indiscernible intentions might have been. Thus all restoration such as these may be fictive.

3.4   Restored house at Pessac

The problem of pressures of conservation was noted by Rem Koolhaas in his recent book *Content*[20] and in a lecture at the Harvard Graduate Design School. After showing a graph of the declining rate of new building against the growth of conservation, and after claiming that the two lines would cross at 'the end of architecture', he proposed as a solution that the city should be zoned in strips within which would be built new architecture which would remain unaltered and be demolished after a century and replaced with new buildings, their timetable syncopated with their neighbouring strips to sustain a sort of urban continuity. In this way the undoubted intellectual and practical problems of conservation, and the threatened inhibition of the architect, might be avoided. Also the architect would not be present to see his work destroyed.

The Festival Hall was the first Modernist building to be accorded Grade 1 listing by the British Government in 1988. Such a listing usually aims to preserve both interiors and exteriors. In so doing the various alterations that the building had undergone since 1951 were indiscriminately enshrined.[21] The hall was the one permanent building to survive the end of the Festival of Britain exhibition on the South Bank of the Thames, built over land previously occupied by various works and a brewery. It was always intended by the planners in the post-war Labour government, and the London County Council, that the hall would be a centrepiece for a major arts and music complex on the site, which it in due course became.

The building was subject to a major refit by the architects' department of the Greater London Council (the successor to the LCC) in the 1960s, on which Nicholas Taylor commented in *Architectural Design* at the time. He suggested that any radical building's popularity reaches a low point in its life after about a dozen years, when its original champions have fallen away or lost their initial enthusiasm, and a new aesthetic is on the rise, and with it a new coterie. Taylor went on to observe that it was the Festival Hall's misfortune to arrive at this major refit at just such a time (Figure 3.5).

The refit of the Festival Hall was part and parcel of the widespread redevelopment of the whole of the 1951 Festival site. The Queen Elizabeth Hall and the Hayward Gallery were built in the same development, as were the walkways. The new works to the concert hall involved major additions to the riverside front to add banks of lifts on either flank, and on the Belvedere Road to add stage door and changing rooms.

The GLC at the time was famously the main barracks for the New Brutalism.[22] The antagonism between the neo-Brutalist architects and the

3.5   The Royal Festival Hall, 1951; architects: Leslie Martin, Robert Matthew, Peter Moro

Festival architects was vivid. It can perhaps be reasonably described in terms of class antagonism, with the rough, tough new boys and girls coming from lower-middle-class provincial backgrounds taking exception to the work of the metropolitan upper-middle-class designers of the Festival; Grammar School versus Public School. In the service of establishing a new identity, differences both political and aesthetic necessarily needed to be explicit. So the Brutalists tended towards individualism and the free market as against the socialist collectivist aspirations of the entrenched party. Brutalists looked towards the United States for inspiration whereas the London avant-garde architects of the 1950s had regard for Scandinavia and socialism.

The work of the Festival was viewed by the newcomers in the 1960s as a paternalist conspiracy to impose good taste on a resistant working class. Thus for the usurpers, the evidence from popular culture, the message from the streets was the primary witness for the prosecution in the case against the attitudes and practices of the recent past. Famously the manifesto for the new phase was broadcast by the *This is Tomorrow* exhibition at the Whitechapel Art Gallery in 1956. The Brutalists' protest was similar to Le Corbusier and Ozenfant's Purist complaint against the Cubists in the 1920s; a complaint against the decorative.

Photographs of the Festival Hall before the 1960s refit show the building to have been extensively clad in many different coloured specified glazed tiles. There may have been many uncertainties about the building, because of the speed of its inception and completion rather than the inexperience of its three authors. For instance, it seems that entry was and remains unresolved, but the nature of the building was evident: it was a decorated box. It underwent at the hands of the GLC architects in the 1960s just that process of scraping that Morris had set out to prevent in the previous century. It is difficult not to read the 1960s work on the Festival Hall as censorious. This would seem to be a temptation that might affect any alteration.

Why freeze the results of such an unsympathetic rehabilitation, especially when the problem of context is so pressing?[23] All attempted preservation seems wrong. Why stop here and now? Preserving a ruin likewise is a very peculiar habit. If the process of ruination should have produced such a valuable result, why would further ruination not increase the value? Or, on the contrary, might not the process be reversed, selectively, intelligently and with scholarship. A ruin, which all buildings might be considered as at certain times, is not a permanence.

An empty building may have its appearance extended indefinitely by certain procedures, as with a corpse, but an inhabited building cannot.

NOTES

1 *Domus*, April 1990, n.p. The continuing schism and four contemporary attitudes to restoration were reviewed in *Domus* 715 April 1990 *On Restoration* pp. 21–27. As the deputy editor, Vittorio Magnano Lampugnani writes, all still spring from the irreconcilable schism between the beliefs of Viollet-le-Duc and John Ruskin. The two camps also include variations regarding the status of work carried out subsequent to the building's initial completion. Rudolfo Machado may be thought to have enunciated at least a poetic or metaphoric attitude to the chronicle of alterations.

This is the deputy editor's introduction to and brief summary of the four different approaches to restoration featured in the magazine, and his own conclusion:

The discipline of architectural restoration has been at any rate since the beginning of our century, deeply torn within. Living cheek by jowl in it are a number of incompatible and quarrelsome, diametrically opposite viewpoints and work methods, from the strictly idealist one which hopes for an improbable return of the built product to an origin which can hardly ever be established with any certainty to the pragmatic one which permissively treats as historical values all the alterations made to the building in the course of time.

Without even aspiring to be exhaustive, we have summed up, with original excerpts from related 'canonical' texts, four of the positions which we feel are among the most indicative of the state of the discipline today. That of Renato Bonelli, who seeks to bring the building to be restored back to its former splendour by ridding it of its superfetations however good they may be, and re-creating its missing parts from the imagination. That of Paolo Marconi, who believes in the necessity for a periodic and total adaptation of 'sacrifice surfaces' and for the renewal of the building's unity and aesthetic appearance through a creative use of analogy. That of Gianfranco Caniggia, who accepts the impossibility of recognizing an 'original state' of the building but aims, through the elimination of added parts and through degrees of restoration that may go as far as total 'period' invention, to lead it back to a typological scheme deduced from its surrounding buildings. And finally, that of Marco Dezi Bardeschi, who refers exclusively to the present reality of the building which he respects and conserves just as it has been deposited, for better or worse, by history, whilst however putting new autonomous and clearly distinguishable projects next to it.

While following these different working approaches with interest and respect, I must confess that I do not personally feel able to espouse any of them. I believe neither in critical, nor in philological, nor in typological restoration, nor in pure conservation. I believe there is less and less difference between a problem of architecture and a problem of restoration; in both a given situation has to be interpreted, a future one thought up and a process of design decisions primed to link one to the next. I believe this process of choices must be founded on a profound and exact knowledge of the history of the building and its context. But it must then be emancipated to the advantage of criteria responding less to a preconceived methodology than to questions more strictly to do with the discipline of architecture. In short, I believe that restoration is neither more nor less than an architectural project.

2 Viollet-le-Duc, *Dictionnaire raisonne de l'Architecture* (Paris, 1854–68), vol. III, first sentence of 'Restauration' essay: 'To restore a building, it isn't to maintain it, to repair or rebuild it, it is to recover a perfection that may have never existed at any given time.'

3 John Ruskin, *The Seven Lamps of Architecture* (London, 1849), extract from 'The Lamp of Memory', Chapters XVIII–XIX, pp. 203–06.

4   See Chapter XV, 'Resulting Forms: Secondly Crests', John Ruskin, *Modern Painters*, vol. IV, *Of Mountain Beauty* (London, 1873, new edition), pp. 199ff.

5   Le Corbusier, 'When the Cathedrals Were White', trans. Francise E. Hyslop Jr., in *A Place of Radiant Grace* (Paris: Reynal & Hitchcock, 1947; English translation. New York, Toronto, London: McGraw-Hill Books, 1964), pp. 74–76.

6   Nickolaus Peusner, 'Scrape and Anti-scrape', in Jane Fawcett, ed., *The Future of the Past* (London: Thames & Hudson, 1976), p. 48.

7   In Ruskin, *The Seven Lamps of Architecture*.

8   Of Ruskin's views on restoration, Morris wrote to him in 1877: 'They are so good and so completely settle the whole matter, that I feel ashamed at having to say anything else about it, as if the idea was an original one of mine, or any body's else but yours.'

9   There is an excellent biography of William Morris, which records his various campaigns throughout his life, including the founding of the Anti-scrape Society, the properly named Society for the Preservation of Ancient Buildings. It also records the troubles he experienced with more politically reactionary elements within the society. One might observe that this clique triumphed after his death, and have reigned unchallenged ever since. Fiona MacCarthy, *William Morris. A Life for Our Times* (New York: Knopf, 1994/5).

10 In actuality Sir George Gilbert Scott carried out many very thoughtful restorations, and was well aware of the conflicting views regarding how to deal with old buildings, churches in particular. In response to Morris's attack in the *Athenaeum* he wrote: 'I do not deserve it, I have lifted up my voice on this subject for more than thirty years, and, though not faultless, have striven with all my might to avoid such errors, and to prevent their commission by others . . . and most of all attack me, who, I am bold to say, am amongst the most scrupulously conservative of restorers.'

    He tried to avoid the dogma of either extremes. As he himself wrote in 1877: 'I have at this moment to fight a double battle. I have, as throughout, to be fighting against those who would treat old buildings destructively, and I have, on the other hand, to defend myself against those who accuse me of the principles against which I contend, and who oppose one's doing anything at all.' His work was often as radical as the French, as at St David's Cathedral in Pembroke in Wales, whose west front had been completely rebuilt in 1789 in a late Gothic manner. He demolished this and replaced it in a Romanesque style, derived from studying old prints of the building.

    He was a master on other restorations at finding evidence 'embedded in later walling' of the original configuration, from which he would ascertain the direction to take in the work. In addition, he was sometimes critical of Viollet-le-Duc. Of the restoration of Carcassonne, he wrote: 'this wonderful genuine specimen of a Mediaeval city' had been changed into 'a (no doubt very learned) model of that which it was the dilapidated original'.

    All Scott quotes from Wim Denslagen, *Architectural Restoration in Western Europe: Controversy and Continuity* (Amsterdam: Architectura e Natura Press, 1994), pp. 60ff

    Scott lacked the deep intellectuality of Viollet-le-Duc, and consequently was prone to allow the pragmatic and personal taste to corrupt consistency and to affect his decisions. But perhaps history should not be too harsh on him, as Stephan Tschudi Madsen pointed out in *Restoration and Anti-Restoration* (Oslo: Universitetsforlaget, 1976), p. 72, he was a man of his age: 'He was a Victorian, for good or evil; he could express ideals, but chose not to follow them himself . . . we glimpse the contours of a moral problem: that of agreement between theory and practice. This is a problem that arises in other aspects of the Victorian community, and should be careful not to form hasty judgements.'

11 William Morris, the Society for the Protection of Ancient Buildings Manifesto (London, 1878). Morris uses as his prime example an English church first built in the eleventh century, and its having been altered every century or so, often radically, as in the change from Norman to Gothic. I'm struck by the thought of how odd it is that a church, which one supposes intends to stand for eternal truths, should need to be re-styled so often. I suspect this phenomenon may be unique to England, or at least more pronounced here than elsewhere in Europe. It would seem to reveal a resident existential uncertainty in the Church of England community itself.

12 Nikolaus Pevsner, 'Scrape and Anti-scrape', in *The Future of the Past*, ed. Jane Fawcett (London: Thames and Hudson, 1976).

13 Ruskin 'The Lamp of Memory', p.205:

'Take proper care of your monuments, and you will not need to restore them. A few sheets of lead in time put on the roof, a few dead leaves and sticks swept in time out of a water-course, will save both roof and walls from ruin. Watch an old building with anxious care; guard it as best you may, and at any cost, from any influence of dilapidation. Count its stones as you would jewels of a crown; set watches about it as if at the gates of a besieged city; bind it together with iron where it loosens; stay it with timber where it declines; do not care about the unsightliness of the aid; better a crutch than a lost limb; and do this tenderly and reverently, and continually, and many a generation still be born and pass away beneath its shadow. Its evil day must come at last; but let it come declaredly and openly, and let no dishonouring and false substitute deprive it of the funeral offices of memory.

14 *Ibid.*, p. 206.

15 *Ibid.*, p. 202.

16 Viollet-le-Duc was far from dogmatic in applying his own dictates, as for instance with the restoration of la Madeleine in Vezelay, where he declines to build a north tower, to match the existing south tower, preferring that the west front remain asymmetric.

17 John Summerson, *Heavenly Mansions* (London, 1949; New York: Norton, 1998).

18 A polemical attack was mounted on British attitudes to restoration and the idea of 'heritage' by Robert Hewison in his book *The Heritage Industry* (London: Methuen, 1987, n.p.): 'a country obsessed with its past, and unable to face its future . . . If the only new thing we have to offer is an improved version of the past, then today can only be inferior to yesterday. Hypnotised by images of the past, we risk all capacity for creative change.'

19 In fact, the positions were not always so black and white on either side of the English Channel: for instance, the western pair of towers at Canterbury Cathedral, where the northern was still Romanesque and the southern late Gothic. Here the Romanesque tower had been demolished and replaced by a copy of the southern tower, because a symmetrical tower front was considered more beautiful. (Quoted from Wim Denslagen, *Architectural Restoration in Western Europe: Controversy and Continuity* (Amsterdam: Architectura & Natura Press, 1994). This is a wonderful book.) Whereas in contrast, as reported earlier, quite early in his career, Viollet-le-Duc preserved the asymmetry of the Romanesque church at Vezelay.

20 OMA/Rem Koolhaas (and Simon Brown, John Link), *Content* (Koln, London: Taschen GmbH, 2004).

21 Since this was written, new work has been completed on the interior of the concert hall in order to improve its notoriously dead acoustics. Function in this case has taken precedent over the building's listing. This is perhaps further evidence that a building must change to remain inhabited.

22 A title I think coined by Peter Reyner Banham for his book on the movement, *The New Brutalism, Ethic or Aesthetic* (New York: Reinhold Publishing Corp., 1966, n.p.). Alison and Peter Smithson stated the intentions of the new movement thus:

Any discussion of Brutalism will miss the point if it does not take into account Brutalism's attempt to be objective about "reality", the cultural objectives of society, its urges, its techniques, and so on. Brutalism tries to face up to a mass-production society, and drag a rough poetry out of the confused and powerful forces which are at work. Up to now Brutalism has been discussed stylistically, whereas in essence it is ethical.

23 The case of the Festival Hall and the South Bank illuminates the affinities between interior and urban design, the building and its context. Apart from the obvious literal difference, what is said about one can be equally applied to the other; they are separated only by questions of scale. The attitudes, abilities and inclinations which apply to one are also relevant to the other. In particular, contextual considerations are integral to both, in a way that is untrue of pure architecture. Various masterplans and competitions have been prepared for the South Bank in recent years, but the apparent disregard that any of these have for the others makes for a pessimistic outlook. The site has become like a ritualized battleground where different generations of British architects scrabble against one another.

CHAPTER 4
PARODY AND OTHER VIEWS

AT ONE POINT IN THE article 'Urban Transformations and the Architecture of Additions', Perez de Arce quotes Louis Kahn: 'When a building is completed it wants to say, look how I'm made, but nobody is listening because the building is fulfilling function. When it becomes a ruin, the way the building is made becomes clear, the spirit returns.'[1] For Kahn, therefore, the spirit or essence of a building is something separate from and perhaps in some cases antagonistic to the function.

When one works on a building one almost always ruins it. The client usually requires it. Rotting elements have to be removed, live plaster hacked off, everything extraneous cleared out. This process of removal from the building prior to or parallel with the work of returning it to a sound condition is usually called *stripping back*. In carrying out work on an existing building, work of repair is inevitably needed, often because of the breakdown of the basic functioning of the building, for instance to stop a leaking roof, as pointed out by both Ruskin and Morris. Work of this kind is commonly called *making good*.

As I understand it, the common ethic has been in recent years that when working on old buildings, works of conservation are permissible, but works of restoration are forbidden.[2]

Advances in many aspects of information technology since the invention of the camera have given unprecedented powers with regard to all aspects of restoration, so that the line between fact and fiction might seem to have become increasingly obscure. It would seem reasonable to assume that we are only at the beginning of an era of similar advances.

Exercises in the popular media that blend the roles of documentary and bibliography are now common-place. All such exercises necessarily invoke the cosmetic, and like the make-up department in a film studio such undertakings require decisions concerning how beautiful or how ugly, how tragic or comic or otherwise, to make the restoration.

Making good may very well be thought to equate to conservation, being a type of common-place procedure, innocuous and unassuming. But any attempt to return a building, if only in part, to any previous condition is not conservation but restoration. Any replacement of the worn by the new is restoration. All work on the existing fabric that is additive is restorative. The continuous maintenance of monuments such as the Villa Savoye amounts to continuous restoration.

The objection may be reasonably put that surely work to prevent further decay cannot be called restoration; it is simply much needed conservation. What is such work? Are only the building technologist, the chemist and materials expert involved in such attempts? Who will make the judgement when judgement is needed?

In 1983, John Richardson wrote an article in the *New York Review of Books* on the treatment by dealers and restorers of paintings by Braque and Picasso.[3] While dealing with aspects of the conservation of paintings, it contains observations which also have resonance for buildings:

> However, varnish is not the only danger to Cubist paintings. Wax relining – a process that most restorers have at one time or another used and far too many consider mandatory – has done even greater harm. By impregnating the canvas from the back with what amounts to an embalming agent, the restorer effects a complete transformation not only of the paint surface but of the entire painting structure. The intention is to preserve the painting from present or future disintegration, but the result is a waxwork, a dead thing. The tragedy is that wax relining, like varnishing, is a virtually irreversible process. Complete removal of wax from infused material is technically impossible, and catastrophic changes often result from heating, infusing and pressing the paint, ground and canvas. (Paintings with a lot of impasto are especially vulnerable. More than one rugose Van Gogh has ended up as sleek as a formica table top.)
>
> What then should be done to protect Cubist paintings (and for that matter any other painting) from deterioration, or to minimize damage that has already taken place? My own somewhat extremist view – one that was

incidently shared by Picasso and Braque, who would rather have a painting disintegrate than undergo plastic surgery – is the absolute minimum.

The idea that works of conservation are ever entirely governed by expediency and necessity is misleading. Consequently, conservation is a falsehood, an attempt at neutrality to avoid the minefields of restoration. There is no neutral ground. Work to existing buildings is of two types: either restorative or interventional. This is not to say that this must lead to full restoration; in making good, these acts are partial and are to be assimilated into the other acts which go to make up the work of intervention. Restoration patently has a great potential for harm and destruction if governed only by good intentions. The physical and the narrative are capable of restoration, the abstract is not, being itself immune from degeneracy. Everything physical ages. An inhabited building is a living thing, and this exacerbates the sequence. Ageing cannot be prevented; in buildings, of course, it can be transmuted, decay can be slowed. As with all things, the process is a combination of the natural compounded by the accidental, which arrives through experience.

These innocent-sounding procedures outlined above, stripping back and making good, may be shown to have extensive theoretical implications for the practice of alteration when considered as acts of examination of the host building rather than physical procedures. It is extremely difficult to say with certainty where the innocence ends and the queasy expanse of restoration and preservation begins. One knows that somewhere within lies the taboo against copying. Navigation in these areas is sometimes further hampered by the practitioners' desire to act instinctively and to avoid the scholarship that such copying would require, even if it were permitted.

Restoration is inevitably discriminate and generally requires imagination, its power to terrify certain sensibilities notwithstanding. To repeat, for Ruskin restoration means 'the most total destruction which a building can suffer; a destruction of which no remnants can be gathered: a description accompanied with false description of the thing destroyed'.[4] Therein, as suggested before, are contained primeval fears, those fears signified in fairy tales: the Grandmother who will devour you, the assassin with the shiny apple. One is reminded as well of the hero in *The Naked Lunch* being interrogated, and being tested with photographs of beautiful girls, some of whom are in fact transvestites.[5]

If, as is claimed, some restoration is inevitable, and since all restoration is at least in part imaginative, however curtailed, where then is the line that separates restoration from parody? It is difficult to believe that it can ever be determined with any accuracy. In addition, where is the line between restorative work and new work, what is interventional work and what new design? The explanation that the designer is at one moment doing one thing and the next day something quite different within the same design process does not bear examination. One might suggest at least an examination of the phenomenon of parody.

Perhaps as a first attempt at definition, one might explain it as a shift in balance between the contrast and the similarity of the new work in comparison to the existing similarity. Is it forbidden that the new work should be infected by the existing? This would seem to suppose a rather safe and remote relationship between the interventionist and the host building.

Here is an example of imitation with a serious political and effective intention. In 1976, the city authorities of Montreal began a huge clearance project in preparation for hosting the Olympic Games. Many Victorian villas were demolished. At a crossroads where three of four villas marking the corner with turrets had been demolished, the architect Melvin Charney, as an act of direct protest, built upon a scaffolding armature two facsimiles of the style of villa, made from 8 × 4 foot boards. Charney described it:

> At the main intersection in the principal zone of CORRIDART, on a vacant lot which was cleared of housing by the Government for some institutional project now long forgotten, I erected a full scale representation of the facades of two typical Montreal grey stone buildings dating from the 19th Century and still standing on the opposite corner. Rough plywood and reclaimed lumber were wired to pipe scaffolding in a manner similar to the display of documents elsewhere in the street – as if it was a physical documentation of a monument to the corporeal substance of the street . . . Their mirror image of buildings on opposite corners aligned the streets on an axis which demarcated the square like significance of the intersection of two streets in the urban tissue of Montreal . . . the Mayor of the city was quoted as saying at the time of the Montreal Expo in 1967: 'The ugliness of slums in which people live doesn't matter if we can make them stand in wide-eyed admiration of art they don't understand.'[6] (Figure 4.1)

4.1   Les Maisons de la Rue Sherbrooke, Montreal, 1976: Melvin Charney

The city reacted quickly and violently to the structures, which they took to be a refutation or criticism of their policy of clearance, and a reminder of loss, sending a team to destroy them in the night.[7] So here is an imitative act that seems to contain elements of homage and of remembrance of things that the city authorities wanted forgotten.

Is the Shinto Temple of Ise in Japan, which is rebuilt every twenty years, a parody of the building it supersedes?

As is well known, the shrine at Ise, the most ancient site of Shinto, the native religion of Japan, is rebuilt every two decades, in a spirit of renewal.[8] This represents an opposite view to Ruskin's, and of something which is akin to copying. This stark difference of attitudes to copying in the East and the West may have caused Gropius, among others, to prefer the Parthenon as a candidate for the world's greatest building over the Shinto shrine. However, this judgement was made several years prior to the discovery that many of the drums which are piled to make the columns of the Parthenon were not in their original positions.[9]

Ise proves that copying can be work of great quality. In the process, myriad crafts are kept alive, for not only the buildings, but also the treasures – the garments, the swords, the carvings – are also renewed. The extraordinary procedures by which this renewal is achieved are well documented elsewhere.[10] Generally, in the renewal of the Inner and Outer Shrines, situated five kilometres from one another, the Inner Shrine, Naiku, sited on rising wooded ground by the Isuzu River, is considered to have the greater status; it is the one that the Imperial Family visits for the rituals of renewal, and at times of births, deaths, marriages and other occurrences of significance.

The central sanctuary and the new buildings must be viewed by the less elevated between completion and consecration; there is a custom where those visiting in this interval pick up white stones from mounds placed outside and use them finally to cover the inner sanctuary ground entirely. On a warm day, the new woodwork scents the air. The reverence for these buildings among architects is formidable and worldwide, and the interval allows photographs to be taken of the newly completed structures[11] (Figure 4.2).

The level of craftsmanship sustained in the rebuilding is generally considered to be unequalled anywhere; this applies to all the treasures that are remade as well as the building processes. It is probably inevitable that among architects and designers, the greatest admiration is reserved for the woodwork, and in particular for the monumental working of the tree trunks to make the structure of the main sanctuary building. The carpenters in the old days used some four hundred different tools; now they will use fifty different planes in the work. An inked snap line (*sumitsubu*) is snapped asymmetrically to mark gentle curves for the carpenters to work to. The renewal is assured by burying the columns untreated into the earth; none of the building materials are treated. (The thatch may be repaired; if this is done, the thatchers wear all black, like the puppeteers in the traditional Bunraku puppet theatre.)[12]

Through these processes and rituals Ise can claim to be both ancient and new. It has been observed that the difference between the approach here and the European attitude to conservation is that in the former:

the Japanese were not interested in preserving old buildings as such. It was the style, not the actual structure embodying it, that they sought to preserve for posterity. Everything that had physical, concrete form, they believed was doomed to decay; only style was indestructible. Fire can destroy a wooden

4.2   The Temple at Ise, the 1953 reconstruction

building in a matter of minutes; the philosophy of the impermanence of all things was a solace to a people who built only in wood. A Westerner would probably insist that style is inseparable from physical, concrete form, but, to go one step further, what the Japanese wanted to preserve was not even the style as such in all its details but something else, some intangible essence within its style.[13]

This intangible would, one supposes, exclude the Western difficulty of talking of style ever since its banishment during the heroic period of modern architecture, and would also eschew the reduced status of craftsmanship that the Machine Aesthetic pretends, and mass production enforces.[14]

Implicit in the whole undertaking of rebuilding are the advantages of copying. To repeat Ruskin, 'the two strong conquerors of the forgetfulness of men' are poetry and architecture, and in contradiction to some of his other views, how potent this becomes with rituals of rebuilding. Certain entrenched attitudes make such benefits difficult for the modern Western mind. It is a question of status; whereas it is difficult for us to say *copying* or *repro-duction* without an implied denigration, at Ise such work is of the highest status.

Other phenomena seriously affect the theory and practice of restoration. One of the problems that is often not recognized is that our view of buildings changes drastically at different times, that an old building is multi-valent, that it will be read in a chosen way, as the result of a particular perception in different ages, governed by the prejudices of the time, and consequently liable to restoration or otherwise according to those prejudices. On a mundane level, eighteenth- and nineteenth-century terrace houses, row houses in central London boroughs and in cities all over the United Kingdom, were demolished in a frenzy of destruction after the Second World War, in order to build Modernist housing schemes in their place. What would one of those houses be worth now?

Such multi-valence is evident in attitudes to the most famous of build-ings, to the Parthenon for instance. When a student of architecture today thinks of the Parthenon, should that ever occur, they must contemplate an actuality deadened by familiarity, as unquestionable as rain in February, some-thing quite inert and impregnable to theoretical questioning. This sense perhaps more than any other suggests a danger and vulnerability, and the need for a fresh apprehension of this paradigm of European architecture.[15]

In the past two hundred years or so, the temple has been seen in quite different ways. In the eighteenth century through the writings of Winklemann, Goethe and others, the buildings were thought of as being pristine and white in their original condition. Following archaeological discoveries by French, German and British antiquarians and architects of traces of paint on ancient fragments of buildings, a proposition was promoted in the first decades of the nineteenth century that the Greek temples were in their prime painted and polychromatic.[16] As a result, it became a common exercise at the Beaux Arts in the nineteenth century, perhaps through some wayward influence of Viollet-le-Duc, to envision Roman and Greek buildings as fully painted as they well may have been. The Parthenon, for instance, in one version of restoration contains a massive polychromatic Athena, with her spear sticking above the

4.3   Restoration drawing of the Parthenon by Eduoard Loviot, Ecole des Beaux Arts, 1881

roof line[17] (Figure 4.3). If now one were to spray the smallest slogan on one of the Parthenon's newly restored columns, the whole of Europe would be aghast. At the moment we wish to think of the temple as being exclusively as white as bone.

Thus the central structure of European architecture came to be viewed in radically different light in the change from the end of Classicism to the emergence of Romantic-Classicism in the nineteenth century. An old building therefore may have different significance for different times; what can be said is that as a ruin, the antique maintains a certain physical and spatial authenticity, but even this is not always as straightforward as it seems. It is not a question of the building alone; the setting is crucial. But then again the Acropolis itself, the setting for the Parthenon, was knowingly landscaped, defences, detritus, a thousand years of 'lesser' buildings and the earth removed back to the bare rock, by archaeologists in the 1880s.[18]

In addition, restoration programmes may set out with widely different intentions, in reference as to which stage the building in question is intended to be restored.

In a fire in August 1989, a large seventeenth-century house, Uppark in Hampshire, was largely destroyed by a fire, although many of the contents were saved.[19] The house had a special place in the collection of the National Trust, because through a set of lucky circumstances it was almost unchanged 'since the year of Waterloo'. The fire burned for four days. It was caused by lead being welded on the roof. After the fire

> the building was open to the sky, the upper floors and their contents destroyed. But while the roofs and ceilings were gone, the walls were standing and the decorative woodwork and plasterwork had survived . . . Heroic work by firemen, staff and volunteer helpers, some carrying on in relays through the night, had saved the bulk of the house's treasured contents. Larger pieces, such as furniture and paintings, had been carried out in the early stages.

A decision was made to 'restore the house to its appearance the day before the fire in "so far as this was practicable"'.[20]

After the fire, the larger pieces were salvaged, and the residue was shovelled into 3,860 labelled dustbins, and panned for smaller remains, right down to picture hooks. Great care was taken to make it appear as though the new house was several centuries old. For instance, new imitative wallpaper was hung and then force faded, except for where the paintings had hung; they were then rehung over these less faded portions. One can imagine the counterfeiting pleasure of the restorers. The work took six years and cost some £20 million, the sum being met by the insurers.

One might compare this scrupulous rebuilding to Ise, and note the differences. Ise is rebuilt as new, and then allowed to moulder over its allotted span; no deception is attempted regarding its age. Uppark sets out to be a deception and one suspects a sustained deception. Lack of certainty regarding the exact state of the house before the blaze is admitted from the outset, apart from any opportunist improvements or desired affects included in the rebuild. The building is to be kept as much as possible as a frozen moment, intended to instil in the paying public a proper reverence for the life led in it in its prime, a confirmation as much of the value of aristocracy as of the progress of equality.[21] In one a reverence for a way of making, in the other restorative skills used to evoke an elite lost style of life.

When compared with the Villa Savoye, one can admit that both cases are deceptions, but with clear differences or contradictions of attitude. The French example restored to a spurious newness, or the English house restored to the state it was in before calamity struck. Who is to say which is the more valid? Somehow or other one thinks that beyond a certain age, a building should show its age but how might one decide what age that is? Is it that the style of building prescribes the approach? Must a Modernist building always appear brand new? Must a pre-Modernist building always appear old? On what would such discrimination be based? Is it that some buildings more than others are suited to ageing, the temple at Paestum compared to the Farnsworth House, for instance? The Villa Savoye, les Heures Claires was rather a beautiful ruin in the early 1960s, as captured in Burri's and other photographs (illustrated in Chapter 2).[22]

NOTES

1 J. W. Cook and H. Klotz, *Conversations with Architects* (from interview with Louis Kahn) (London: Lund Humphries, 1973).
2 Near to the time of writing, the great church by Hawksmoor, Christchurch in Spitalfields, London was re-opened after a comprehensive restoration programme. Initial responses seem muted, which is strange if the restoration of this work by the most talented of English architects has achieved some semblance of the church's original glory.
3 John Richardson, 'Crimes against the Cubists', *New York Review of Books*, 16 June 1983. This brilliant article is referred to again in Chapter 5.
4 John Ruskin, 'The Lamp of Memory', in *The Seven Lamps of Architecture* (London, 1849), Chapter XIX, p.205.
5 William Burroughs, *The Naked Lunch* (Paris: Olympia Press, 1959).
6 Mel Charney and Montreal, recorded in Herb Greene, *Building to Last* (New York: Architectural Publishing Co. 1981) and in 'Corridart: Melvin Charney on Art as Urban Activism in Canada', *Architectural Design* 7–8 (1977), pp. 545–47.
7 Similar mass clearances and demolition are currently occurring in Beijing, in preparation for the Olympic Games coming to the city. Areas that perhaps have been settled for a millennium, that survived all the turmoil of Chinese life during the last century, are being destroyed. See the *Guardian* (London), Saturday, 6 September 2003.
8 Shinto is animistic, that is the belief that things in nature, for example trees, stones, rivers, mountains and rocks, have souls or consciousness. It is thought to underlie the habit of the Japanese saying 'thank you' to a pair of shoes when they wear out. There are no holy texts associated with Shinto, indicating perhaps its ancient origins, but also the ability for the religion to be carried forward by the repeated myth, and also by building practices. It is thought that the first shrine, which has been copied ever since, was built originally in the late seventh century. The founding myth is of Amaterasu the Sun Goddess lured from a cave into which she had withdrawn, tricked into merging with a mirror. The most sacred object at the shrine is the mirror, resting in a wooden receptacle, covered with a brocade in a wicker cage, unseen for generations, and it is this relic which is moved from the old to the new building at the ceremony of renewal every twenty years, 'the transfer of the god-body to the new shrine'. The last renewal was in 1993. The rebuilding involves a protracted succession of thirty-two major ceremonies. The work takes eight years; the 1993 occasion was the sixty-first.

9   These drums were subsequently returned to their original positions during the recent extensive restoration.

10 The books that I have referred to in writing of Ise are as follows: Kenzo Tange, Noboru Kawazoe, *Ise, Prototype of Japanese Architecture*, photographs by Yoshio Watanabe (Cambridge, Mass.: MIT Press, c. 1965); Svend M. Hvass, *Ise; Japan's Ise Shrines, Ancient yet New*, (Holte, Denmark: Aristo, 1999); Yasutada Watanabe, *Shinto Art: Ise and Izumo Shrines*, trans. Robert Ricketts, the Heibonsha Survey of Japanese Art, vol. 3 (New York: Weatherhill/Heibonsha, 1974); William H. Coaldrake, *Architecture and Authority in Japan*, the Nissan Institue/Routledge Japanese Study Series (London: Routledge, 1996).

11 The cost of rebuilding is enormous. The estimated cost of the 1993 rebuilding was $300 million. Since the Pacific War, Shintoism has been disestablished, and as a consequence the work is not eligible for public money. Sources vary as to how many trees are felled, but the lowest estimate seems to be 12,000 cypress, now grown in the Kiso Mountains some hundreds of kilometres from the site, and floated out of the mountains down rivers to the port. It takes five years to grow and harvest 25,000 bundles of grass, 2m long, used for the thatching. The rebuilding takes in total 190,000 man days.

The remaking of the treasures, which consists of some 10 per cent of the total cost, requires five years of fresh drawings and other documentation; the treasures consist of clothing, weapons, horse carvings and trappings, musical instruments, writing implements and everyday items, 60 swords, 932 items of clothing, 55 shields and 4,080 arrows (once 20,000 were made). Three hundred and forty-three ceremonial articles and 199 divine treasures are made, in total 1,576 treasures and articles. A silk cloth is woven with the *motif* of a yellow wagtail, from which in legend the gods first learned how to reproduce on this earth; this bird can readily be seen at the site, living up to its name as wagtails worldwide do, strutting along the river's edge. The bridge over the Isuzu River is rebuilt in a sequence four years ahead of the shrine buildings, to enable access to the site. It was once built in shipyards.

12 The first gateway Itagaki, in the first fence of the western site, which is the primary sanctuary, is offset to the east to belie any suggestion of an attempted perfection, so as not to offend the gods. However, the gateway on the secondary site, Kodenchi, is symmetrical. The first gateway is the usual limit of public access to the sanctuary. Only the mirror and the foundation stones of the alternate Shodens have remained unchanged throughout the sequence of rebuildings.

13 Gunther Nietschke, in a seminar at Brown University, Rhode Island, October 2004.

14 In truth, the buildings of Ise exhibit considerable changes over time. In particular in 1868, with the re-creation of the Imperial household and the consequent adoption of Shinto as the state religion, extensive enlargements and refinements were carried through: the two treasury buildings were moved backwards from being aligned with the Shoden; the large canopy, built to shield the Royal party before the entrance steps of the Shoden, was also added at this time. Most commentators consider this canopy to detract from the overall beauty of the assembly. Photographic evidence shows considerable changes in the design of the balustrading around the raised platform over the years; in the early twentieth century, a copper membrane was introduced into the roof to improve the waterproofing. Thus there are still signs of judgement at work within the processes of replication. Compared with the reconstruction of an original raised-floor granary from archaeological evidence at Toro in Shizuoka Prefecture, the buildings within the sanctuary of Ise are of enormous sophistication.

15 As is perhaps to be expected, a new book on the Parthenon has recently been published: Mary Beard, *The Parthenon* (London: Profile, 2004).

16 According to the most enthusiastic proponents of the polychrome theory, all details were liable to have colour applied to them, including roof tiles (the more conservative sought to argue that the specifically architectural elements, the columns and capitols for instance, remained untouched). These ideas deeply influenced the teaching at the Beaux Arts, and gained acceptance with the volatile student body, unseating the establishment view of the absolute purity of the Classical architecture of Antiquity. In 1826, the *secretaire perpetual* of the Académie des Beaux Arts, Quatremere de Quincey, was 'hooted down and troops had to be called' by the students as he tried to reiterate the established belief in the purity of Greco-Roman architecture. This was one of the ways in which Romanticism began to assert itself in European thought in the second quarter of the nineteenth century. 'But the real significance of Hittorff's campaign, however shallow his archaeological studies,

however facile his arguments and comic his attempts to realize a polychrome decoration, was his demonstration that attitudes to antiquity could be radically revised and revised in a liberating way. He dispelled, virtually single-handed, the torpor into which architects had sunk. It was his very lack of success that inspired others to pursue more thoughtful and sensitive interpretations.' Robin Middleton, 'Hittorff's Polychrome Campaign', in *The Beaux-Arts and Nineteenth-Century French Architecture* (London: Thames & Hudson, 1984), p. 195.

17   The overblown height of these exercises is perhaps best illustrated by the restoration drawings of the Parthenon itself referred to in the text by Edouard Loviot, carried out as a fourth-year *envoi* in 1881. The book edited by Arthur Drexler (*The Architecture of the Ecole des Beaux Arts*, London: Secker & Warburg, 1977) on the Beaux Arts contains several of these masterfully rendered pictures. Marie-Antoine Delannoy, 'The Tiber Island Rome, Restoration 1832', pp. 170–71, Theodore Labrouste (Henri's brother), 'Restoration of the Temple of Vesta at Tivoli 1829', p. 163, and 'Restoration of the Temple of Hercules at Cora 1831', pp. 164–65.

18   Rhys Carpenter, *The Architects of the Parthenon* (Harmondsworth, Middlesex: Penguin, 1972).

19   This property is owned by the National Trust. It seems that lack of water pressure sealed the original building's fate. It burned down in a leisurely manner as a result.

20   Gil Saunders, 'The Sleeping Beauty Awakens', *Sussex Life*, 1990.

21   How the National Trust takes over and runs historic houses (and other buildings and landscapes) is an interesting, one might say typically English solution. The incumbent families are allowed to remain in the property in perpetuity, and a negotiation then takes place regarding public access to the house. The costs of the upkeep of the property then fall to the Trust, which in its turn is supported by government funds, legacies, gifts and members' subscriptions.

22   Rene Burri/Magnum, *Le Corbusier, Moments in the Life of a Great Architect*, ed. Arthur Ruegg (Basel, Boston, Berlin: Birkhauser Publishers, 1999). A similar set of photographs were published to illustrate Nikolaus Pevsner's article 'Time and le Corbusier' in the *Architectural Review*, March 1959. They are credited to Hinks, Hicks and McCallum, Arphot (*sic*). The article is a plea by Pevsner for the adoption of Le Corbusier's villas by the French Service des Monuments Historiques. In it he argues by implication for restoration: 'As regards pleasing decay, the trouble is – to me at least – decay in the case of le Corbusier villas just is not pleasing, either intellectually or visually. Intellectually the shock of seeing recent pioneer-work so patently slighted spoils any possible pleasure in the decay, and one walks away depressed that the battle for modern architecture is evidently lost.' He concludes perhaps a little unconvincingly: 'In spite of all the specious arguments adduced, this essay is intended to take its place in the Ruskin–Morris–SPAB line of descent.'

CHAPTER 5
PARALLELS TO ALTERATION*

THE CULT OF ORIGINALITY INHIBITS treating copying as a serious activity. In other art forms, parody might seem less of a dubious undertaking. Picasso said, 'Copy everyone except yourself.'

In music such practices are widespread: Beethoven's variations on 'Rule Britannia', Bach's transcription of Vivaldi, four violins into four harpsichords, Brahms and Schumann and the small matter of improvisation in music, once fleeting but now made present through recording technology; the bebop habit of using standards by Kern, Gershwin, Cole Porter, Rodgers and Hart and others as a basis for composition and improvisation; John Coltrane repeatedly playing 'My Favourite Things'. One might add to these the different versions of a single work, *The Four Seasons* for instance, or any other work available now because of recording technologies developed in the twentieth century and since.

In the wonderful film of the saxophonist Ben Webster,[1] he is shown near the end of his life in his flat in the Netherlands, his attentive Dutch landlady hovering elsewhere in the room, putting on a Fats Waller record and beginning to blow his saxophone quietly to accompany the record. The recording is the host building and the sax playing is the intervention.

In living memory in London schools of painting, transcription exercises were set where the students were asked to choose a historic painting and paint a transcription, a response in varying degrees of representation according to the individual student's choice. So in parallel academies, practices are encouraged that in schools of architecture are considered delinquent. A recent exhibition at the National Gallery demonstrated a patchy survival of these abilities among established artists.[2] Although possibly the best work in the show was the media installation by Bill Viola, Paula Rego's transcriptions of Hogarth's *Marriage à la Mode* achieved a remarkable success in transcribing the earlier work into contemporary terms, making the emotional complexities of the original suddenly accessible to modern eyes (Figures 5.1a and 5.1b).

5.1a   One of Paula Rego's transcription paintings of Hogarth's *Marriage à la Mode*

5.1b   Hogarth's *Marriage à la Mode*

5.2   Velázquez, *Las Meninas* (detail)

Velázquez's painting *Las Meninas* (the Maids of Honour) has been discussed extensively elsewhere, famously by Foucault at the beginning of *The
Order of Things*.[3] It is a work that on first encounter should convince anyone
of the impossibility of conveying the power and beauty of a painting through
reproduction (Figure 5.2).

In 1957, at the age of seventy-five, Picasso took to his studio in order to
paint a series of transcriptions of all and of parts of the great Velázquez painting.
Whatever triggered this project, there seems little doubt that Picasso was intent
on measuring himself against the achievement of his great compatriot. He was
seeking a contemporary correspondence with his celebrated predecessor. The
output over some six months was phenomenal: forty-five canvases directly
related to *Las Meninas* and thirteen related paintings were produced; the work
poured out of him[4] (Figure 5.3). When inspiration faltered on the main project,
he painted views of the studio and out of the window at la Californie.

Most commentators, in particular John Berger in *The Success and Failure
of Picasso*, are critical of the painter's achievement at the end of the series.[5]
Perhaps the paintings individually are not Picasso's best, although the critics

5.3   Picasso, after Velázquez, 1957

may have been blinded by the other actuality, the profusion of the work. There are great paintings among the total.

But the lesson for the designer contemplating intervention concerns the sustained inspiration that can be available through the act of caricature as homage.

The charge against the parodist is one of heresy.[6] If the original is the orthodox, then any alteration is heretical. The original architect would necessarily object to any alteration, because of an implied criticism of his or her own production. Heresy requires consciousness. The intervening designer must construct a critique of the host building. This is the purpose of stripping back.

Perhaps all alteration needs to be viewed as heresy.

In the Miloš Forman film *Amadeus*, the young Mozart is welcomed at the court of the Crown Prince in Vienna with an anthem especially composed for the occasion by the court composer, Salieri. Mozart is shown taking over the harpsichord and improving as he plays the music written in his honour. This is the ultimate heresy, to work on an original and in the process improve it. And yet, in other fields, in the translation of poetry, for instance, such an occurrence would be less severely condemned.

> *Traduttore, traditore.* (Translator, traitor.)
> Italian aphorism

> The whole subject of translation, for those who are professionally involved in it, is a potpourri of hesitation, exasperation, compromise, headache and occasional thrills and satisfactions.[7]

As the past is a foreign country, introducing new life into an old building is in many ways like translation, the carrying over of the host building from one age to another. As suggested before, the undertaking of making good and new works, including the inevitable incipient restoration, may be thought of as akin to transcription or translation, the carrying across of a building from one age to another, from the past to the present.[8]

Celebrated modern poet translators such as Robert Lowell and Kenneth Rexroth talk of the licence that they and their famous predecessors, Alexander Pope and John Dryden for instance, needed to employ in order to achieve success. Robert Lowell talks of his translations as 'imitations' (the title of a collection of poetry translated by him). In a note at the beginning of *Lord Weary's Castle and the Mills of the Kavanaughs*, he writes: 'When I use the word *after below* the title of a poem, what follows is not a translation but an imitation which should be read as though it were an original English poem.'[9] Later, in 1961, in the preface to *Imitations*, he writes:

> I believe that poetic translation – I would call it an imitation – must be expert and inspired, and needs at least as much technique, luck and rightness of my hand as an original poem.
>
>   My licences have been many . . . I have dropped lines, moved lines, moved stanzas, changed images, and altered meter and intent . . .
>
>   All my originals are important poems. Nothing like them exists in English, for the excellence of a poet depends on the unique opportunities of his native language. I have been almost as free as the authors themselves in finding ways to make them ring right to me.[10]

Here is Kenneth Rexroth, from his essay 'The Poet as Translator':

> When discussing the poet as translator, since time immemorial it has been the custom to start out by quoting Dryden. I shan't, but I will try to illustrate

Dryden's main thesis – that the translation of poetry into poetry is an act of sympathy – the identification of another person with oneself, the transference of his utterance to one's own utterance. The ideal translator, as we all know well, is not engaged in matching the words of the text with the words of his own language. He is hardly even a proxy, but rather an all out advocate. His job is one of the most extreme examples of special pleading. So the prime criterion of successful poetic translation is assimilability . . .

Finally, what does all this mean to the poet himself? What has it all meant to me? Translation . . . can provide us with poetic exercise on the highest level. It is best to keep your tools sharp until the great job, the great moment, comes along. More important, it is an exercise of sympathy on the highest level. The writer who can project himself into the exultation of another learns more than the craft of words. He learns the stuff of poetry. It is not just his prosody he keeps alert, it is his heart. The imagination must evoke, not just a vanished detail of experience, but the fullness of another human being.[11]

Translation then, it is suggested by these eminent writers, is work of the highest calling, requiring creativity and inspiration equal to the writing of new verse, and so conferring considerable licence on the translator, indeed requiring considerable licence in order to avoid the dead hand of literalism.

This kinship might then give useful insights into the aims of interventional design. Translation in poetry is akin to the work of bringing a building from a past existence into the present. This carrying over of meaning in poetry is recognized as work requiring inspiration equivalent to that of the original author, and so similarly, one might come to view restoration as an art equivalent to any other related to building. Restoration that is separate from the literal.

Here is a quote from *Nine Gates* by the poet Jane Hirshfield, from the chapter dealing with translation, 'The World is Large and Full of Noises'.[12]

As George Steiner has pointed out, the practice of choosing archaic language when translating ancient texts, while now rare, can serve a useful purpose, helping to ground the new version within the linguistic history of its new culture. A reader encountering a style of language he had come to expect in literature from the past would feel immediately 'at home' in the new work, particularly if the work in question was already part of his cultural tradition. The King James Bible, surely the greatest translation English has seen, was put into a diction several generations older than that spoken at the time it was made. Creative accident, rather than conscious decision may have played a part in this – the King James translators had been instructed to retain the best of the earlier versions. But however it happened, the result was a translation whose clarity, beauty, and power so overwhelm that its language form remains, four centuries later, a living force.[13]

Here is a description of the use of the archaic in the process of translation, which would seem to have further things to say regarding the language of the translation and the new work. This example contradicts the dictum regarding the need for the contemporaneous as a result of translation. Here is the suggestion too of attaining something out of time by these means, that is something seemingly timeless, by consciously avoiding the contemporary.

There are obvious differences between translation and rehabilitation, most clearly that with translation the original poem can be entirely left behind untouched, whereas the interventionist works directly onto the original, altering it, possibly irrevocably.

Many buildings facing alteration are not 'important' buildings, or even necessarily very good buildings. What is the use of the expertise and the inspiration in these instances? If the parallel with poetry is valid, what is the role of interpretation, so evident in the task of translating poetry, in interventional design?

How does interpretation avoid becoming improvement?

Certain similar issues of restoration and conservation may have been more thoroughly examined in the realm of the restoration of paintings. Similar contradictions may also be seen to be endemic. The territory can be indicated through a series of fables, accepting at the outset that a painting is different from a building, being properly immune to obsolescence, despite the swings of taste and fashion in different ages.

The National Gallery in London has one of the greatest collections of early Italian paintings in the world, housed in the correspondingly primitive Sainsbury Wing, by Venturi, Scott-Brown and Rauch. Amongst them are three panels from the great *Maestà* of Duccio. It is said that the district of Siena which contained Duccio's workshop was renamed the Happy Quarter after the altarpiece emerged in 1311, to be carried and installed in the Duomo. The altarpiece was removed from the high altar in 1506 and eventually sawn into pieces in 1771. The National Gallery came by its three panels from different sources at the end of the nineteenth century.

5.4   Duccio, *Annunciation*

The beautiful *Annunciation* panel had lost paint in strips along the bottom and left sides (Figure 5.4). The gallery's *Guide to the Conservation of Paintings* notes: 'At the bottom it is inpainted with a plain grey and at the side the gilding has been imitated in yellow-orange paint. No attempt has been made to reconstruct the missing forms.'[14]

The uncertainty of approach is more evident in the treatment of the second panel, *Jesus Opens the Eyes of a Man Born Blind* (Figure 5.5). The description of the restoration in the *Guide to the Conservation of Paintings* has an apologetic air. David Bomford, the chief restorer at the National Gallery, writes:

5.5   Duccio, *Jesus Opens the Eyes of a Man Born Blind*

the single major area of damage on *Jesus Opens the Eyes* is a most crucial one. By cruel irony it occurs at the focus of the entire episode: the face of the cured man at the right has flaked away. Here, *a more or less deceptive reconstruction was essential in order not to disrupt the narrative power of the scene* [my emphasis]. However, in order to indicate that this is not original paint, the prominent craquelure [cracking] visible elsewhere in the painting has not been imitated.[15]

An entirely different approach is adopted for each panel, despite their being parts of the same larger work. There is no suggestion of an overall approach based on thoughtful analysis of the issues. The issue of authenticity for instance seems to have been refused in the service of spectacle. Chauvinists may claim this as another triumph of Anglo-Saxon pragmatism over the doctrinaire arguments of the Italians.

Near the Duccios, in the farthest room in the gallery, hang three Piero della Francesca paintings. One of them, *The Nativity*, is thought by many to be the most beautiful painting in the British Isles (Figure 5.6). It has undergone several abrasive cleansings in its lifetime. In the eighteenth century, a particularly energetic arm reduced the three wise men to disfigured wretches. Later cleaning rendered the braying donkey behind the Virgin transparent, and gave the baby Jesus on his blanket the impression of floating slightly above the ground.

It is thought that Piero first formalized the procedures of orthogonal drawing; the late Dr Evans had pointed out that the faces of John the Baptist and Jesus in the *Baptism of Christ* (in the same room as the *Annunciation*) are the same face drawn in strict profile in one and full face in the other. The artist is also believed to have made model heads in the service of exact depiction, and the quartet of angels in the *Nativity* looks like the outcome of some deeply inspired method. Overall, this accidentally acquired intermittent thinness gives to the painting another dimension and radiance. For instance, there is now a transparent head of an ass, seeming to bray in unison with the gorgeous and more substantial quartet of angels. It would have been impossible to paint this now ghostly presence. The painting's coherence can be said to be strengthened by the misfortunes it has suffered. It has a patina which only a long existence can impart. As Pevsner noted in another context, the work of the despoiler sometimes has its own sanctity.

5.6   Piero della Francesca, *The Nativity* (detail)

I refer again to 'Crimes against the Cubists' by John Richardson.[16] There he recounts his censures of MOMA's treatment of its Cubist paintings:

> for MOMA was killing its Cubist paintings with the wrong sort of kindness ... Not that MOMA was the only offender. Many other paintings belonging to American museums and private collectors had their surfaces irreparably jazzed up by well-intentioned but historically ignorant restoration ... 'To subject these delicate grounds to wax relining and, worse, a shine,' I concluded, 'is as much a solecism as frying a peach.'

He laid the blame in part at the door of the publishers of art books. Albert Skira decided to produce a book of Picasso's pottery in 1948, with a high gloss finish applied to the plates in the book in order to simulate more closely the sheen of the pots. Richardson goes on to relate that following the success of this book, Skira subsequently published a three-volume *History of Modern Painting* using this high gloss technique, which by its popularity helped to shape the perception of a generation of students.

Richardson recalled a visit to Braque:

> when a painting of a guitar that had formerly been signed on the back – as was the Cubists' habit – arrived from America to be signed all over again on the front, now that wax relining had obliterated the original signature. The artist's horror at the condition of his recently restored painting was painful to observe. 'Look how the blacks jump out at you,' he gasped. And indeed the black lines that had formerly served as a discreet scaffolding – thanks to glossy varnish – stood out like newly painted iron railings ... No less upsetting to the artist was the awful tautness caused by an aluminium support that stretched the canvas as tight as a drum. 'Why subject it to this racklike torture?' he asked. Why indeed, since it was quite redundant, and the canvas – of almost linen like fineness, as is usual with Cubist works – looked as if it were about to pop.
>
> 'Restorers are amazing,' said Braque. 'They have transformed my guitar into a tambourine,' and he gave a disconsolate tap with his paintbrush.

But sometimes intervention is imperative. Following heavy and incessant autumn rains, the River Arno burst its banks on the night of 4 November 1966 and flood water swept through the whole old town area of Florence. When the waters receded, vast deposits of river mud, in places over two metres deep, indiscriminately covered the entire historic centre of the city, including the doors of the Baptistry of the Duomo, irrevocably destroying two of Ghiberti's panels. 'The damage to the city's art treasures was so great that the entire visual culture of Florence was imperilled.'[17] No greater disaster, natural or otherwise, has beset such a beautiful place since the bombing of Dresden towards the end of the Second World War.

In Santa Croce, the great Cimabue Crucifix[18] was on its supports holding it upright in the Museo dell'opera, the former refectory of the monastery. It had been lowered from its usual position suspended above the nave of the church for a periodic inspection. It was engulfed. When it was recovered from the mud, the gaunt expressions on the faces of the workmen record the keen impact of the tragedy on the Italian nation. Preliminary examination seemed to indicate that the crucifix was damaged beyond recall (Figure 5.7).

The whole of Italian society and other authorities across Europe galvanized their efforts to salvage city and artefact from the ravages of the terrible flood. The polyglot undertaking is prototypically the model for all great pan-European projects in the future. The attempt to rescue the crucifix was under the direction of Professor Ugo Procacci, Superintendent of Fine Art, and Dr Umberto Baldini, Director of the Laboratories of Restoration in Florence. In a unique and perhaps uniquely Italian co-operation between government, academia, industry, scientists, architects and artists, the work was begun.

One particular problem was the extensive and widespread damage to fresco paintings throughout Florence. Using methods which had been largely perfected by the nineteenth century,[19] all the damaged frescoes were lifted from their walls. This in addition revealed under-drawing in many cases, so often through the work of rescue, two works appeared from the feared destruction of one.[20]

The Cimabue Crucifix presented the greatest challenge to the rescuers:

> A picture painted on a wooden panel is . . . a diverse combination of materials co-ordinated with each other in a quite specific way: a wooden support, canvas glued firmly to it, a layer of gesso and size (the so-called priming or ground) and a layer of paint. When covered by water this kind of painting undergoes a number of distortions and metamorphoses.[21]

Patience was central. It was necessary at the beginning to create the same conditions of humidity as when the work was rescued, and from there slowly to

5.7   Cimabue Crucifix recovered from the flood, Florence, November 1966

reduce it, to allow the drying to begin in the most cautious manner; this was achieved through the medium of a layer of sawdust sprinkled on the laboratory floor, which could then be sprinkled or not to maintain the humidity of the air.

> The drying of the support began slowly but surely during the stay in the Limonaia and was completed in the laboratories of the Fortezza di Basso ... Almost eight years after its arrival at the fortress the separation of the canvas, ground and paint from their wooden support had been accomplished; the condition of the support had been stabilized and in February 1975 it was transferred to the carpentry workshops.[19]

The rotted wood was cut away and replaced with a precise and exquisite patching of closely matching small wooden strips, stable, self-effacing and modern in manner, although using only old and consequently dimensionally stable wood in the patching.

The destroyed areas of painting were repaired in the same spirit. These areas were widespread, including large areas of the face and torso. Many painters worked together to devise an equally exact fine polychromatic hatching, the result of a rigorous analytical process of the colour of the original, which was then painted indiscriminately onto all the voided areas of the work.

Through several other processes in which the contributions of technologists and scientists were central, the painting was eventually once more rejoined to its great wooden partner.

The result is a self-effacing work of collective genius, a masterwork of restoration (Figures 5.8 and 5.9).

The outcome proves several different propositions regarding conservation and preservation. The work was carried forward, despite the extreme emergency of the situation, within the strictest intellectual framework, and this is the key to the triumph. Speculation regarding what was lost was forbidden. Despite the urgency, nothing was rushed. No air of apology attaches to the work, it is unsullied by doubt. Such purity of outcome might be difficult to achieve in the built environment.

The procedures parallel William Morris's edicts concerning the treatment of old buildings, including the new work being in a strictly contemporary style. Only the new work cannot be said to be reversible, and perhaps it has no need to be so considered.

5.8   Restored head of Christ, Cimabue Crucifix

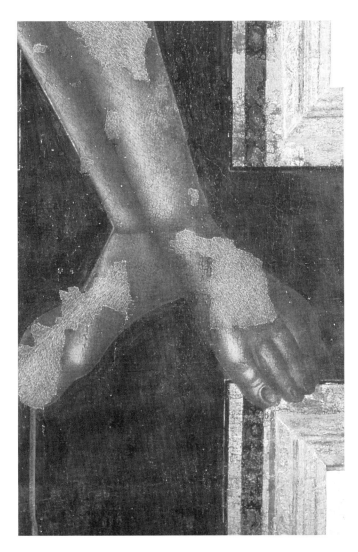

5.9   Restored feet of Christ, Cimabue Crucifix

Here is the question: was the inserted work, the woodwork and the hatching, fortuitously in the self-effacing style of late Milanese Modern, work of the sort that Gio Ponti termed 'without adjectives', or is Modernism itself beyond style? Was Le Corbusier right to demand after outlining the characteristics of the new architecture in *La Ville Radieuse*: 'Where is the style in this?'

NOTES

* Excerpts from this chapter in a slightly different form first appeared as part of the catalogue for *Presences, the Commonplace in Architecture & Art*, the catalogue of an exhibition organized by 5th Studio architects and the artist Paul Coldwell, at the Architectural Foundation, March 2001.

1   *Ben Webster: The Brute and the Beautiful*, a film by John Jeremy for Channel 4 Television.

2   *Encounters, New Art from Old*, exhibition at the National Gallery, London, March–September 2000.

3   Michel Foucault, *The Order of Things: The Archaeology of the Human Sciences* (originally *Les Mots et les Choses*, Paris: Editions Gallimard, 1966. English edition London: Tavistock Publications, 1970). 'As soon as they place the spectator in the field of their gaze, the painter's eyes seize hold of him, force him to enter the picture, assign him a place at once privileged and inescapable, levy their luminous and visible tribute from him, and project it upon the inaccessible canvas within the picture. He sees his invisibility made visible to the painter and transposed into an image forever invisible to himself.'

4   See Susan Grace Galassi, *Picasso's Variations on the Masters* (New York: Harry N. Abrams, 1996). The standard work on Picasso's transcriptions is by his friend Jaime Sabartes, *Picasso's Variations on Velazquez' Painting "The Maids of Honor" and Other Recent Works* (New York: Harry N. Abrams, 1959).

5   John Berger, *The Success and Failure of Picasso* (Harmondsworth, Middlesex: Penguin 1966).

6   Heresy: 'the word means, literally, no more than choice' (*Oxford Etymological Dictionary*).

7   'The Editor's Problem', an essay by Denver Lindley in *The Craft and Context of Translation*, ed. Roger Shattuck and William Arrowsmith (Austin: University of Texas Press, 1961), p. 237.

8   There are more obvious similarities with other topics, for instance set design, installation, performance and collage, which are not enlarged upon in this chapter. These practices usually derive from art schools, so this supports the claim for the art schools to house courses, perhaps postgraduate, on the art and practices of alteration. They contain the potential for interdisciplinary work that intervention is capable of exploiting.

9   Robert Lowell, *Lord Weary's Castle and the Mills of the Kavanaughs* (New York: Harcourt Brace and Co., 1946).

10   Robert Lowell, *Imitations* (New York: Noonday Press, 1990), p. xii.

11   *World outside the Window*, the selected essays of Kenneth Rexroth, ed. Bradford Morrow (New York: New Directions, 1987), p. 29. This essay is the transcript of a lecture at the University of Texas and was first published in *The Craft and Context of Translation*, ed. William Arrowsmith and Roger Shattuck, cited above.

12   *Nine Gates, Entering the Mind of Poetry*, essays by Jane Hirshfield (New York: HarperCollins, 1997), p. 68.

13   The story of the translation of the King James' Bible is told in *Power and Glory* by Adam Nicolson (*God's Secretaries* in the USA) (London: HarperCollins, 2003, p. xi):

> 'but that virtual anonymity is the power of the book. The translation these men made together can lay claim to be the greatest work in prose ever written in English. That it should be the creation of a committee of people no-one has ever heard of – and who were generally unacknowledged at the time – is the key to its grandeur. That sense of an entirely embraced and re-imagined past is what fuels this book . . . The divines of the first decade of the seventeenth-century England alert to the glamour of antiquity, in many ways consciously archaic in phraseology and grammar, meticulous in the scholarship and always looking for the primitive and the essential as the guarantee of the truth.

14   David Bomford, *Guide to the Conversation of Paintings* (London: National Gallery, n.d.), n.p.

15   *Ibid.*

16   John Richardson, 'Crimes against the Cubists', *New York Review of Books*, 16 June 1983, pp. 32–37.

17   The rescue of the crucifix is well described in the catalogue that accompanied the travelling exhibition: Umberto Baldini and Ornella Casazza, *The Cimabue Crucifix*, trans. Michael Foster and Thomas Mackin. The catalogue was published by Olivetti.

18   The crucifix measures 3.90 × 4.33 metres.

19   Cicognara, in an article published in 1825 in the Florentine review *Antologia*, began a crusade against the detachment of frescoes, basing himself . . . partly on the fear that mural paintings . . . might be removed from Italy. The fact, however, was that the techniques of stacco and streppo were pursued with far from unsatisfactory results. In the same year in which Cicognara wrote his bitter invective, the frescoes of Sir John Hawkwood and Niccolo da Tolentino by Uccello and Castagno were removed from the wall of the Duomo in Florence in 1842 . . . By this time such operations were being undertaken all over Italy, so that by 1866 Secco Suardo could write, in a textbook on restoration, that 'at the time at which we live the need to save from certain ruin a quantity of frescoes by great artists, by detaching them, advances by giant steps from day to day'. In the same year Cavalcaselle asserted that 'whenever a wall is attacked by damp, it is essential to detach the fresco if one does not want to see it disappear'.

(Exhibition catalogue of *Frescoes from Florence*
(London: Arts Council of Great Britain, 1969), p. 43.)

20   As quoted in the previous note, this was a wonderful travelling exhibition of murals, designed by Carlo Scarpa, which toured Europe, arriving at the Hayward Gallery in London in 1969. The catalogue (*Frescoes from Florence*) records earlier methods of removing frescoes, some of which reached considerable efficacy by the eighteenth century (see the description of the method employed by Antonio Conti in 1725, pp. 37–41).

21   The authors continue:

The wood swells up, causing the canvas bound to it either to experience a distorting pull or to change independently, detaching itself from the ground. Being made from gesso and size, the ground is more absorbent than the wood and as a result of the pull exerted by canvas and wood it too suffers distortion, causing the surface to swell in various ways. The paint either moves together with the ground it is spread on and its craquelure expands, or it rises independently of the pull beneath or, finally detaches itself from the support, having lost all adhesive power. The painted surface thus alters in size and thickness. Since its causes are multifarious this alteration cannot be prevented, neither can the original state be regained by the removal of moisture. For the latter to be accomplished it would be necessary to counteract each pull with an opposing one that is the same in every respect; and this would have to be carried out at every point of the various individual layers, which, because they are no longer bound together, are incapable of uniform counteraction. Besides, paint, ground and wood do not dry at the same speed.

('The Restoration of the Crucifix', *The Cimabue Crucifix*, p. 26)

22   *Ibid.*

CHAPTER 6
DEGREES OF ALTERATION

IF ELECTRICITY IS INTRODUCED INTO a pre-electric building, it alters it. If central heating is put in to replace local heating via foci of heat, such as stoves and fireplaces, the building is altered spatially. Most markedly, if extensive electric lighting is introduced, the building is altered.[1] The alteration is in the way the building is perceived: to see the spaces fully illuminated by an internal light source during the hours of darkness causes the building to be seen differently from at its inception. The same is true of external lighting. When one considers the work of artists such as Dan Flavin,[2] James Turrell and others, one may be tempted to think that there is an extensive territory regarding lighting, the interior and the exterior that is largely still untried in the fields of environmental design.

Thus a building can be altered without any considerable physical inter-cession, except for some easily concealed wiring. In addition, all advances in servicing will effect changes when they are introduced, both surface and spatial changes. Lutyens is said to have spent the most energy and greatest care in the latter stages of his career planning the insertion of lavatories and other wet services into the houses he had designed, which had been built without internal plumbing. This too indicates that intervention needs to be an art.

Restoring a building nearly always involves modernization of servicing, so it might be noted in passing that as a general rule, everyday restoration does not completely aim at authenticity, even from the outset.

In the question of degree of intervention, one might say that there are two different categories of alteration, surface and spatial, although obviously the latter may include the former. Surface prompts consideration of colour.

Colour sometimes feels to the scholar like an unnecessary and unfair dimension to existence, because of its elusive nature with regard to intelligence, combined with its enormous experiential power. That the act of merely smearing can render such changes, and the magic of it be locked up in the eye and the mind of the artist, seems sometimes doubly unfair to the intellect; its power may even make us feel shallow ourselves.

The results of using colour depend therefore on both the learning and ability of the artist, but perhaps that is little different from any other changes, except perhaps for a greater reliance on artistry. Without this, the outcome is uncertain; thus Viollet-le-Duc's schemes for the interior decoration of the chapels of Notre Dame seem somehow the most shocking of his proposals for the cathedral, despite the depth of learning behind them. At the Villa Savoye, on the other hand, with its many coloured interior surfaces, however like the original scheme they might be (which I believe has been the subject of some discussion), they can be understood to be the result of scholarship and creative judgement. The beautiful colours of the interior of the restored Villa strike many visitors as the most surprising impression, together with, perhaps, when reaching the top of the ramp and the rather perfunctory roof garden, the sudden sense of incompleteness. The villa itself is restored as an unoccupied building, the furniture in the house is merely token, proof of the prowess of the architect as furniture designer. In no sense is the house shown as occupied: there is not a bed anywhere.

Of all the Italian theorists, Paolo Marconi,[3] with the idea of the 'sacrifice surface', has approached the subject of at least paint, if not colour, in restoration:

> One either joins the cause of those that value the macabre valences of disintegration in action on the object and therefore the resorting to transparent varnishes, or one joins the cause of those who don't see the reason for this decadent renouncement or macabre pleasure and so choose the path of cautious, difficult and demanding restoration of the 'sacrificed surfaces'.
>
> In the 70s Marcello Paribeni applied the modern technical concept of 'sacrificed surfaces' to those more or less thin layers of perishable and renewable material (plasters, stucco, varnishes, paint) that universal tradition had used to cover the exteriors of buildings in order to both protect the materials underneath from atmospheric deterioration and to periodically 'restore' its complexion. In fact the concept not only includes that of

superficial protection but above all alludes, with lapidary conciseness to the necessary perishability of that protection, the sacrifice of which guarantees the greater duration of the construction, on the condition, of course, that this sacrifice befalls a prompt restoration, and that is the chromatic and physical remaking of the preceding layer.

You need a lot more skill, sensitiveness and culture to carry out a good limestone paint job rather than to impregnate a wall with miraculous varnishes that, what's more, would give it the permanent appearance of a biscuit soaked in oil.

One might feel that this piece more than ever confirms the fugitive and potentially treacherous nature of paint, and the need for the highest discrimination in its use. It sounds suspiciously like another attempt to disguise restoration as conservation. The surrender to the cosmetic of course sounds strange to more Calvinist ears, but this may be the honest implication of using any paint, whether inside or out. Perhaps it says little more than that painted surfaces will need repainting, but by doing this, the initial use of paint on every surface is thrown into question; the proposition that an originally unpainted surface should have applied over it a 'sacrifice surface' sounds at least ill advised. What would a 'good limestone paint job' be?[4]

Ruskin and Viollet-le-Duc[5] were united in their prohibition of obscuration through paint or any other means; they both believed in 'reality' in architecture, and yet since Jasper Johns made his painted bronzes of two ale cans, it is difficult not to be intrigued at least by the painted object;[6] also Braque's habit, learned as a house painter, of simulating wood grain on paper to incorporate in his Cubist period paintings, would seem still to be more than just illusionistic. One may associate the choice of colour with a certain neurosis, particularly as related to fashion design, and perhaps it is the case that colour is an agent of temporality, in the tension between that and timelessness in matters architectural. All colouring to a lesser or greater extent is fugitive.[7] The tussle surrounding polychromy and ancient buildings at the Beaux Arts in the nineteenth century, described earlier, was just such a contest between the establishment and those wanting change. To most people still, white will signify timelessness, or an indifference to the passage of time. Because of this, colour's more active association with the traditions of interior design should seem only proper.[8]

The simple matter of surface would seem to remain in many ways unconquered by theory, so leaving it unable ever to be entirely prescribed. Colour shares with music the quality of elusion from language, and perhaps because of this, they share keywords, such as tone, harmony, clashing and blues. They both are developed from an infrastructure of seven parts. Probably as much as any other factor, the choice of range of colour for setting up correspondences between the existing and the proposed has a great and unexplored potency. This is, one would suppose, prevented from fuller expression by the established conventions of conservation, but abetted sometimes by the wilful individuality of the designer. The entanglement made possible between old and new by the lifting of these conventions must be enticing to most. One thinks of the Surrealists and their choice of palette.

Spatial alteration involves the plan and section. At its most simple, the alterations will involve either enlarging or subdividing the existing spaces, sometimes combining two or more spaces together. Either of these may retain the original spatial organization, with its sequence of entry, circulation and spatial hierarchy, in the classic sense of served and service spaces.

Changing the existing spatial organization is a further extension of intervention. Whereas the former conceivably may be achieved, and the building made inhabitable with small use of restorative techniques, making good with seemingly innocuous imitation, changes in spatiality can only be affected by new works, either in the style of the original or in contrast to it.

In doing this, in changing the entry point and consequently the building's circulation, in removing or inserting staircases and other alterations, the building is broken by this process.

When one works on a building one inevitably ruins it; it is a requirement of the job; one does it at the behest of the client if for no other reason. Old plaster, rotten floorboards and other degraded parts must be removed. But this can be made good through imitative work. The full realization of interventional work requires that the building be broken; this is the test of the possibility of alteration. The process of ruination is intrinsic to the art of intervention, and not merely as an expedient required by building practices and client requirements.

The nature of ruins might be said to be this: the physical remains of an obsolete building, a building which in this ruinous condition can speak of itself, no longer obscured by its original use or function, which is to paraphrase Louis Kahn, as quoted by Rodrigo Perez de Arce.

This definition would seem to have something in common with Aldo Rossi's definition of the role of buildings as acting as silent monuments in the city.[9] Rossi suggests the idea of a building having an unchanging and monumental quality, regardless of the uses to which it is put at different times. One can think of it like a rock, basically unchanging, as at different times, different uses wash over it.

Both descriptions assume a separation between function and being, between the temporal and the timeless.

The ruin is the building that, according to Kahn, is able to speak, to say how it is made. The common result of ruination is loss of enclosure. A ruin then has qualities of transparency, of becoming incidental in a spatial continuum, as is a transparent structure.

The quality of transparency suggests an affinity with Modernist theory and practice. In addition one might comment that decorated architecture is tectonically generally made up of cover-strips that carry the ornamentation. Cover-strips are among the most vulnerable parts of a building, the parts generally destroyed or displaced during the process of ruination. Modernist aesthetic intends to abolish the cover-strip and to become, by this, tectonically explicit. In many ways a Modernist building strives to become an exquisitely detailed structure that is explicit in the way it is made, a quality shared with ruins in Louis Kahn's definition. In this respect there is thus a further affinity between the ruin and Modernism.

The ruin is something in process, belonging to the past, present and future,[10] and consequently is an aspect of temporality, contrasted with the preserved building, which is a corpse, a product of the mortician's art, preserved and maintained in an attempt to keep it beyond the reaches of time: the Villa Savoye. It is the difference between the living and the dead.

The ruin allows privileged views from previously inaccessible viewpoints, and from these it offers a fresh explanation of itself. A building in this respect may show itself in a way only previously available as drawings, or other depictions, sometimes making evident the plan and section within the structure (Figure 6.1). A ruin may be said to give, in certain circumstances, a more complete expression of a building than when it was newly completed. A ruin is not merely surface; it is also structure.

But above all else, a ruin may be thought of as incomplete.

A building is usually altered because of a change of use, which may be

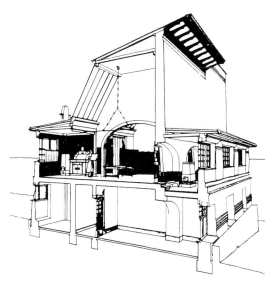

slight or radical; it is in either case a change in style of occupation. It often accompanies other related changes in the surrounding urban context. Such a brood of changes is the manifestation of socio-economic changes in the wider society, as we said at the outset. In this as in other ways, the alteration of buildings has affinities with the alteration of the city. There is an affinity between urban design and interventional design.

Buildings change as the city changes.

After a long, cruel and bitter guerrilla war of independence against Spain, the Dutch gained independence in 1648, finally as part of the conclusion of the pan-European Thirty Years War. The Protestant victors initially forbade Catholic worship, but after some five years, in an act of tolerance that one has now come to think of as typically Dutch, Catholic worship was allowed to revive, but the building of explicitly Catholic churches was forbidden. In an ensuing compromise, the Catholic community was allowed to convert houses for religious services or to build churches that looked like houses.

Amsterdam has three of these. The most celebrated is Our Lord in the Attic, now the Amstelring Museum, in the red light district. It is embedded in two adjoining traditional merchants' houses. Behind the façade of what appears to be a typical, large, canal-side Amsterdam house, the new visitor mounts the usual exterior steps to the front door, and through to climb up following a complicated route, to discover unsuspected an ornate miniature Baroque church, miraculously insinuated into the top two and attic storey. From the beautiful organ loft one can watch through the window the business of the quarter going on in the streets below. On the back stair, descending one comes upon two adjoining linen cupboards which have had their doors removed and replaced by a curtain. A grille has been inserted to connect the two spaces. In one cupboard is a kneeling stool and in the other a grand chair with a priest's sash thrown over it. It has become a confessional (Figure 6.2).

6.2 Linen cupboards as confessional: the Amstelring Museum, Amsterdam

Here is an example of that radical degree of alteration which converts service spaces into served spaces.

In changing the Palazzo della Pilotta, Parma, into the National Art Museum in 1987, the architect Guido Canali introduced a ramp into the disused theatre of the palazzo, on an axis running from the stalls cleared of their seats, and landing into the backstage, deeply through the line of the proscenium.[11]

This rupture of the hallowed separation of the original, the separation between the audience and the performance, shows the potency of breakage (Figure 6.3). One now moves as in a ruin, in a way previously accessible only to the intruder or the thief, seeing the building from new and privileged points of view. The Norman Foster insertion to give access to the new Sackler Gallery that was built on the roof of the Royal Academy in London has similar qualities.

In such cases remnants of the previous hierarchy will remain, now detached from one another, like ghosts of the previous inhabitation.

Both Rodrigo Perez de Arce and Aldo Rossi refer to the Diocletian Palace in Spalato (Split in former Yugoslavia) in their respective writings.[12] Through the centuries, dwellings have been built within the palace, and the original spaces adapted. Houses were constructed which encroach upon the

6.3   The subverted hierarchy: National Art Museum, Parma

6.4   The Diocletian Palace in Split (Spalato), repeatedly emptied and re-colonized

main hall, so that they now fill in between the columns of the original grand order, forming the walls of a new enclosure. As a combined result of these different occurrences, the palace has been transfigured in the classic manner described previously, as if digested by the emerging town. And yet the extent and grandeur of the original is still easily read within the common-place of the present town (Figure 6.4). This is Rossi's description of it:

> The most telling example to be seen even today of continuity in architecture is undoubtedly the city of Spalato . . . This example repudiates any distinction between building and city, it carries urban values into architecture and proves that the city itself is architecture. Over the millennia man has been repro-ducing the palace at Knossos. But within this persistence of a unique experience the answers are always different: this is the progressive character of architecture. The transformations in Spalato, of a vestibule into a square, of a nymphaeum into a covered square, teaches us to use the old city as a formal structure, which can become part of our planning.[13]

In contrast, Rossi describes the building kept from change, the preserved building, removed from the processes of life and the city as 'the pathological primary element' attempting to freeze time and as a consequence life also in its context. But more of this later.

The city changes as buildings change.

How much alteration can a building survive? Where is the point when the host building becomes as limp as a sack, in Giancarlo di Carlo's words, into which anything can be thrown?

There may be some discernible rules, which may relate to proportions and materials.

At Audley End in Essex, one of the finest examples of what Summerson[14] calls the Elizabethan prodigy houses, in the main hall, its one end closed by the typical giant wooden screen containing the minstrel gallery above, through which the hall is entered, at the other end in the eighteenth century the Adam brothers inserted a stone screen through which one mounts a staircase to their new sequence of rooms running down the south wing (Figure 6.5). The Adams' insertion is in stone, in the manner of a Veronese set piece in architectural style, and so doubly contrasted with the context. Yet through an adoption of the geometry of the hall, the new piece makes a fresh conclusion to the space.

Such houses are unique to English architecture. They are too wayward to be called a contribution to European architecture, for so it has proved, but they are an extraordinary backwater in the history of the large European house or palace. They contain several features unique to themselves; the previously mentioned giant carved screen and panelled great hall, the strange long gallery, the succession of rooms and the plan they all tend to share.

In adapting New England farm buildings to be used as an art centre,[15] the architects imposed an auditorium within a barn, which to gain sufficient space breaks through the envelope of the barn on the side and the back, and employs a foreign geometry (Figure 6.6). However, the work is carried through in the material and using the built features of the original: for instance, using external shingle cladding. This, too, makes a new satisfactory entity (Figure 6.7).

Perhaps it is the case that one may insert in a foreign style and adopt the host building's geometry, or vice versa.

In 1921 Mondrian returned to Paris after his sojourn in his homeland, having been trapped there by the First World War. Now with his mature style, he took a studio close to Gare du Montparnasse, at No. 26 Rue du Depart.[16] There he lived and worked until 1936. Over the years of his occupation Mondrian slowly and intermittently worked to bring his studio space into balance. His process was to place rectilinear painted boards within the space.

6.5   Audley End House, Essex, the stone screen inserted by the Adam brothers

6.6   Interior, Rock Arts Center, Connecticut; architects: Hardy, Holzman and Pfeiffer

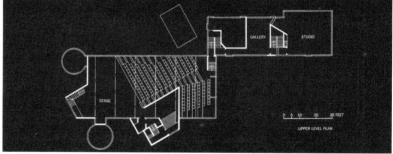

6.7   Exterior and plan, Rock Arts Center, Connecticut; architects: Hardy, Holzman and Pfeiffer

De Stijl, as was said earlier, is part of the general utopian tendencies within European Modernism in the early decades of the twentieth century. Common assumption would have it that the world as it is must be swept away, as with Le Corbusier's Plan Voisin, before Utopia can be realized. This tendency to totality inherent in Modernism was instrumental in its eventual fall from public favour. The suggestion of the studio in the Rue du Depart, which may be no more than a whisper, is that Modernism can work into the world as it exists, that there is no need for the present to be abolished to achieve the promise of Modernity, that Utopia might lie hidden within the existing world, attainable without the total destruction of the existing (Figure 6.8).

The case of Mondrian's studio would seem to solve certain dilemmas regarding intervention, particularly, for instance, the central question of the

6.8   Model of Mondrian's studio, Montparnasse, Paris, in 1936

relationship between the provenance of the new work and the style of the host building. One is reminded also of the installation works of Daniel Buren in this respect.[17]

NOTES

1   There is an excellent study of the lighting of buildings by Dietrich Neumann, *Architecture of the Night: The Illuminated Building* (Munich, Berlin, London, New York: Prestel, 2003).

2   Dan Flavin retrospective at the National Gallery in Washington, DC (curated by DEA), October 2004.

3   Paolo Marconi, one of the four theorists quoted in the 'Restauro' article in *Domus*, April 1990.

4   I live on a listed public housing scheme, which has, following the listing, undergone a quite scrupulous project to restore the original colours of the 1950s buildings. The one very difficult aspect in this has been the repainting of the *in situ* concrete balustrading that was originally unpainted, but at some time was painted cream. At the time of writing some four colours have been tried on

different blocks, each only serving to contradict the 'authenticity' of the others. Once painted, a surface such as these would resist ever being returned to its original condition, and so once painted, it is embarked upon the unending cycle of periodic repainting.

5 Viollet-le-Duc in *Les Entreteins*: '*Croire qu'on peut atteindre à la beauté par le mensonge est une heresie*'. Ruskin in 'The Lamp of Truth' (in *The Seven Lamps of Architecture*) writes: 'Do not let us lie . . . the painting of surfaces to represent some other material . . . the marbling of wood', quoted by Nikolaus Pevsner in the first Walter Neurath lecture, *Ruskin and Viollet le Duc* (London: Thames & Hudson, 1969).

6 'The cans of ale were not found but were made . . . Evidently these bronzes are here in the guise of works of art, but as we look at them we go out of our minds, transformed with respect to being.' John Cage, 'Jasper Johns: Stories and Ideas', in G. Battuck (ed.), *The New Art: A Critical Anthology* (New York: Dutton, 1973), n.p.

7 Someone is sure to point out that glass and mosaic have a permanent colouring, but my remarks deal with surface, with painting and staining, rather than with intrinsic colour.

8 There are many notable interior designers who characteristically make extensive use of colour in their work. In particular one thinks of the work of Ben Kelly Design in various projects, including at the Science Museum and the offices for the Council of Industrial Design in Bow Street, both in London. In the discussion regarding the preferred locus for schools of interventional design, whether in art or architecture schools, it is not only tradition but the more vigorous attitudes to such aspects as colour that argue for the art school.

9 Aldo Rossi, *Architecture of the City* (Cambridge, Mass.: Opposition Books, MIT, 1982). Rossi's statement marks the decisive break in architectural thought with liturgical Modernism and the mantra of form following function. In *Architecture of the City* he states, drawing from Marxist and Jungian roots, that this monumental character of buildings exists in the collective memory of the citizens, as if to form elements of a dream cityscape, like one of de Chirico's paintings of cities, to which he often makes reference.

10 I am grateful for this insight to Wei-Fu Kuo, a student in Interior Architecture at RISD, who first mentioned this to me during a tutorial in 2000.

11 Philippe Robert, *Adaptations: New Uses for Old Buildings*, trans. Murray Wyllie (Paris: Editions du Moniteur, 1989; Princeton: Princeton Architectural Press, 1991). This is still the best survey of alteration projects; they are mainly European examples.

12 Rodrigo Perez de Arce, 'Urban Transformations and the Architecture of Additions', *Architectural Design*, 4 April 1978.

13 Aldo Rossi, 'Architettura e citta: passato e presente', first published in *Werk*, September 1972, n.p.

14 John Summerson, *Architecture in Britain 1530–1830* (dedicated to Sir Giles Gilbert Scott, senior trustee of the Soane Museum) (Harmondsworth: Penguin Books, Pelican History of Art, 1954). Summerson writes (p. 28):

> Supreme among the buildings of Queen Elizabeth's reign are the great houses built by the ministers and political servants who surrounded her. Elizabeth herself built nothing of great importance. Her improvements at Windsor and the few official buildings executed in her time were inconsiderable in extent and in quality compared with such adventures as Longleat or Kirby or Wollaton – the adventures of private gentlemen living remote from the Court. To call Elizabethan architecture a Court art would be misleading; and yet no architectural effort has ever originated more decidedly in the prestige and personal influence of a sovereign. Much of Elizabethan architecture is the expression – conscious and deliberate – of a cult of sovereignty. Most of the greatest houses – Burghley, Theobalds, Holdenby, and many more – were built or enlarged specifically as places in which to receive the Queen, as tributes and as monuments of loyalty.

15 Farm buildings, Great Barrington, Mass. Converted into a school's art centre. Architects: Hardy, Holzman, Pfeiffer Associates. Published in Sherban Cantacuzino, *New Uses for Old Buildings* (London: The Architectural Press, 1975).

16 Frans Postma (ed. Cees Boelraad), *26, Rue du Depart* (Berlin: Ernst & Sohn, 1995). This book contains the results of scrupulous research and beautiful models that re-create the original interior of Mondrian's flat, overlooking the railway lines.

17 See 'Deconstructions of an Artwork: Installations at Mies van der Rohe's Krefeld Villas', in *Daidalos* 26 (special issue on 'The Art Interface') (December 1987), pp. 40–45.

CHAPTER 7

STRIPPING BACK

It is a mistake to apply ornament fit for a public building to a private one or vice versa, to use that for a private building on a public, especially if the latter are smaller buildings of that sort; if they are ephemeral, then these small, trivial, expendable things may be painted with pictures that are inappropriate to public buildings. For public buildings should be built for eternity. And in truth I often perceive a grave error among people who burden or overlay a building still under construction with a false exterior made of paintings and sculpture. This is why such trifles often have aged even before the building is finished. Thus a building should be built naked, before it is clothed.

Alberti's *De Re Aedificatoria* (c. 1452) on the 'Omission of All Purposeless Decoration'

ATTITUDES TO THE HOST BUILDING are those that most clearly distinguish the work of intervention from the work of pure architecture.

If the arguments and discussions of the previous chapters hold true or at least are not entirely erroneous, then one may start to suggest an outline anatomy of the work of intervention, that which might form a basis for establishing proper procedures for the work. As we are at an early stage of considering theoretical aspects of intervention, then the terminology will be closely related to everyday practice, springing so to speak from existing procedures in the building process, rather than from literary sources, for instance.

This is an attempt to see what can be said generically regarding the alteration of architecture.

Works of alteration usually in practice proceed in distinct stages: firstly, stripping back as alluded to earlier, which entails the stripping out of rotted fabric, mainly plaster and wood. The installation of new work is usually preceded by two procedures: making good, where original fabric is repaired and replaced, usually replacing much of what has been removed in the first stage; followed by enabling works, that usually involve the demolition and removal of those parts that would prevent the implementation of the new work if they were to remain. New works are the implementation of the proposed changes to the existing building, as a way of achieving change of use for the new occupation. Each of these involves general qualities of all work of intervention, which can be written down as an outline strategy for the task.

The following are proposed developments of the everyday stages of building, so as to form a more generic basis for the activity; this is an appropriation of common-place building terms for theoretical purposes.

Stripping back in its extended manifestation is the process by which the interventional designer acquires an understanding of the host building with which she or he is engaged. It is to the end of developing a structured affinity, as a preparation for the correspondence between their work and the existing. The host building needs to be understood intrinsically and in terms of its setting, and to be looked at in terms of actualities and provenance. This is an enquiry that will have both architectural and socio-economic aspects.[1] It is proposed here as the foundation for all consecutive procedures.

Stripping back is the process of delineation of the qualities of the host building, an analysis of the given.[2]

Above all of these is the view that needs to be found regarding the style of the host building. It should be remembered that the original condition of the building is inaccessible, as with all things past, even for a building that is only a few years old. The object of stripping back may appear then to be obscure or difficult to read. While surviving actualities will of course give much evidence of the building's original condition, the fuller understanding requires a wider enquiry, otherwise the procedure may degenerate into a ragbag of assumptions.

The building needs to be understood in terms of its architectural style, and this will be necessarily derived from an exemplar, a paradigm or model of that style. A particular building may or may not of course be a good, or even a competent, example of a particular ideal, and must be recorded as it is, but the idea of stripping back centrally depends on the idea of a supposed ideal form, from which one's own host building is derived. This needs to be understood. Thus one is intending to comprehend the direction of the original builders' intentions as well as their surviving production as embodied in the given structure. The idea therefore proposes that any building that can be considered as architectural has a relationship to an ideal form, which will be obscured in reality by usage, or some failure in execution on the part of the architect, and also to a lesser degree by later additions.

Perhaps all the key buildings in the history of architecture have attributes of being ideal or are as a first crystallization of a new architectural style; one may think of the Tempietto by Bramante and the Unite de Habitation in this respect. One may think that this hypothesis holds good only for buildings that have a pure geometry and are rhythmic, rectilinear and proportionate, such as buildings that are of Classical or Modernist derivation. But if one thinks of the great Gothic ruins of the monasteries, of for instance Rievaulx and Fountains Abbeys in Yorkshire, then one can see it has a more general application. In actuality the best theoretical writings on this matter stem from a familiar nineteenth-century source.

Viollet-le-Duc is of course the great analyst of the Gothic, but it is sometimes under-emphasized that from this work he derived a universal rule of architecture, which was that any true style of architecture is rational.[3] From within his great work *Le Dictionnaire*[4] the author proposes a deeper definition of 'model'. In a later important commentary by Hubert Damisch on *Le Dictionnaire*,[5] in response as much to a problem of Structuralism[6] as to a commentary on building, the latter-day critic wrote:

> The first of these difficulties . . . relates to the status that should be assigned to so called 'structural' logic, and to the degree of objectivity found in the *models* that linguists, anthropologists and aestheticians build in order to reveal the structure, the system of connections and variables, underlying

the phenomena which they seek to explain. Does this logic reside in the things, the facts themselves? Or in the mind which knows them and intends to discover their disposition? And in the preparation and application of systems, which aim, at least partially, at the study of meaning, or at receiving and conveying meaning (a category to which architecture obviously belongs), what part should be given to the various processes of the conscious or the unconscious mind? Viollet-le-Duc was convinced that systems of this type are not necessarily the result of one clearly expressed thematically defined intention: his model of the Gothic cathedral, 'ideal', 'complete', and 'perfect', had not been envisaged by any one architect at any one time. If it appears in the *Dictionnaire* it is precisely by virtue of its existence as a *model* as a conceptual instrument, designed to reveal the structural link which connects the numerous and various representations of the Gothic age, to show what common ground they shared, and to create a comprehensive synthesis of the problems encountered in individual experiments. The architects of the Gothic Age worked at a task which was beyond them; their only model was the buildings, and they had no precise notions of the objective towards which all their efforts were directed.

Thus the idea of the *model* here proposed is something that is of potential and of inevitability; its continual imminence is perhaps like the perfectly circular ripple that is harboured or suspended somehow within any amorphous body of water.

One can think that the often stated but rarely proven affinity between music and architecture is most evident, in that the pattern of lines and dots which make up the score of a piece of music are traces of the ideal,[7] of the model, and any consequent performance of the score is akin to a building in that particular style, with all the variation and scope for interpretation that a musical score allows. For this reason conversely it is known that certain virtuosos will refrain from recording or performing music that they most revere, as for instance the Russian pianist Evgeny Kissin recently admitted, regarding the keyboard works of J. S. Bach.[8] Anyone, however, who loves music will also know that the strength of a score is often made clearest through the most *louche* of performances. As Dr Kinsey once remarked, there are only variations, satellites as it were of the model. Variation and the ideal are thus inseparably twinned one with the other.

Damisch writes that none of the medieval masons knew what the model was, of course not:

The architects of the Gothic age worked at a task which was beyond them; their only models were the buildings they erected, and they had no precise notion of the objective towards which all their efforts were directed. They never took the trouble – or even had the chance – to place their undertaking on a theoretical basis. However . . . no-one could possibly doubt the existence of a logical spirit which pervades their work, endowing it with its sense, its finality and its *reality*.[9]

All that perhaps needs to be added to this is to ask if the logical spirit referred to is in some way the model, or is it more a sense of direction towards a model that is different and separate? Either way, this one knows from experience to be the source of the exultation within the process of designing, uplifting, and freeing one of all doubt in the design, however hard won it has been. One would also add that the successful direction in designing is typically triggered by a glimpse of startling clarity of the finished scheme following exhaustive analytical work, a sighting which is then immediately lost and cannot be accurately recalled.

There are of course other issues involved in all of this, in particular the issue of authenticity.[10] Ruskin's argument, which is that this is the stone put there and worked by the medieval mason, and its lost surface is because it is as old as it is, and so should be sacrosanct, would seem unquestionable. It is also, however, a type of blindness, which can perhaps be shown by referring again to his great French contemporary. To quote Damisch once more:

If he [Viollet-le-Duc] denounced the academic teachings of the time, it was because it stopped at appearances, at the envelope that encloses the building, and because it enunciated the basic rules of composition, while totally ignoring the *real* logic on which the art of building is based. The *Dictionnaire*'s method resembles that of the establishment in that the visible aspects of architecture constitute its starting point, but it is distinguished by its refusal to recognize the conventions of a game of tactics whose rules are found partly on the acceptance of transcendent principles.[11]

Damisch goes on to say through his approach that Viollet-le-Duc makes the building the *scientific object*.

One might use the same quotation in respect to the above that Roberti Venturi used in *Learning from Las Vegas*,[12] from Herman Melville: 'Not innovating wilfulness but reverence for the archetype.'

Such theories would seem to suggest that all possible models of archi-tecture, both of the past and of the future, are perpetually existent but hidden, in a similar manner that the laws of gravity reflect a reality that was undetected before Newton. In a similar way, are creative works also discoveries? Are the cello sonatas of Bach an echo of something outside of time? This strange idea lies at the heart of the primary purpose of stripping back, of making an acquaintance with the building, in order for this to support a notion of *model*, abstract, ideal and complete, as the thing from which the building is derived and the thing to which all conditions of the building, past, present and future, in some way bear allegiance.

It is possible to claim that with the adoption of the idea of *model*, of an ideal, as being able to aid direction, projects of restoration are changed from the retrogressive to the progressive, and so able to address a correct approach to the future of the host building, rather than one mired in the sentimentality of the past.

This is not the complete story, however. Wren suggested that there are two sources of beauty, which perhaps can be typified as the formal and the colloquial.[13] A building may have, is even liable to have, particularities or peculiarities, which may be due to a variety of things. They may be the result of eccentricities in the original, difficulties of the site or later impo-sitions. They may be intelligent and inventive. They may be overall in nature or specific and isolated; for instance there may be a general heaviness in the ornamentation, or there may be a fine later addition in a different style from the original; both might be thought of as valid components of the host building. In addition, other aspects of the host buildings, for instance various contexts, social, spatial and temporal, are liable to be particular rather than general.

The point of stripping back consequently is to establish a means by which the designer can begin a negotiation between the ideal and the actual, and also to begin the process of intervention by which other disparate parts must be made to cohabit. The aims of intervention are similar to the aims of the painter Sean Sculley, when he said that 'things must fit together'. The pro-cedures are therefore intended to locate the tension between the idiosyncrasies particular to the host building, acquired at its inception and afterwards, and also its derivation from a paradigm or archetype, the clearest indication of the model or the ideal.

Stripping back is here proposed as the theoretical basis for the work of intervention and alteration. The work requires both intellect and intuition; the investigation must be one of feeling as much as of analysis. It is an understanding that is cultural, physical and spatial. One should adopt the Zen attitude, recommended by Walter Gropius to a group of Japanese architects in an inn near Fujiyama: 'Develop an infallible technique, and then place yourself at the mercy of inspiration.'[14] The designer seeks to establish empathy with the subject of his or her enquiry. The work is bipartite, concerned with the paradigmatic and the material evidence. The enquiry needs to be emphatic, as in Ezra Pound's comments about translation: 'The question of using another man's manner or "style" is fairly simple. Good writing is coterminous with the writer's thought, it has the form of the thought, the form of the way the man feels his thoughts.'[15]

Literalism as ever is to be treated with caution; the most convincing photographic evidence of a building's past should perhaps be treated with the most suspicion.[16] It is a procedure to determine the characteristics that are irreducible regarding the host building. These qualities are those that the work of alteration aims to carry over from the past into the present, while seeking clarification at all stages of the process. From this it is intended that strategies for the work of alteration can begin to be derived for both the host building and its context.

Stripping back is quintessentially a work of interpretation.

NOTES

1   Stripping back may be thought of as consisting of an examination of four aspects: firstly, material, of the servicing, structure and construction of the host building, of what and how the building is made; secondly, spatial, concerning entrance, circulation, hierarchy and proportion; thirdly, the style of the building and the exemplars from which it derives; and fourthly, the building as palimpsest (after Rudolfo Machado), being the marks of previous successive occupations. An understanding of the previous rituals of inhabitation, of how the building was occupied, is also an important component of stripping back. I have had a recent discussion with a friend concerning the role of drawings, if extant, in the analysis. Of course they are primary evidence, to be compared with the resultant built form, but I don't think they are definitive. The way that buildings are described prior to construction is not as encompassing as, for instance, how a piece of music is set down on paper prior to performance.

Musical notation seems to me to be superior to how buildings are formally described, as instruction for execution, in several ways. Of course the one will suffice any number of performances, whereas architectural drawings usually serve a once-only undertaking, and it may be my lack of familiarity with musical notation that causes me to appraise its ability to set down without prejudice the deepest meaning of the work it describes. It is perhaps worth noting also that in music, as far as I know, the question of authenticity seldom if ever arises despite the variety of interpretations to which a classical work is unavoidably exposed. This topic is addressed in an article in *AA Files* 53 (Simon Shaw-Miller, 'Notation–Composition–Event: The Architecture of Music', p. 41): 'Though the score is never a blueprint – a vehicle for guaranteeing the production of identical or predictable performances – the visual identity of music in notation came to embody the notion of the musical work itself. The score became a cult object, touched by the hand of genius. Between its pages, the work existed more tangibly than in the ephemeral space of performance. Notational representation became not simply the signifier of the musical idea, but its embodiment.'

2 The nature of context in interventional work is almost always more complicated in everyday practice than in pure architecture; working within any existing building obviously throws up more problems of context than preparing a new building for a cleared site. One might also note a certain indifference to context regarding much in the history of architecture; the Tiempetto by Bramante, for instance, whatever else it establishes concerning High Renaissance architecture, a certain independence of context seems to be one of them. Conversely the top floor of the nineteenth-century terrace house, beneath which the Maison de Verre was inserted, was regularly painted out in the early publication of the building, so that the Modernist piece appeared to stand alone and unhindered by context. Pure architecture is often more akin to a system of belief, and consequently abstract, and because of this is largely indifferent to place, or even sometimes antagonistic to it. Context to the interventionist is a nurturing and more complex issue than it is for the pure architect. The architect often must consider it as the enemy (as manifest in legislation, conservation, and resistance to the new). Different attitudes to the issue of context may clearly delineate the work of alteration and that of pure architecture. The more common attitude to context was made clear by Rem Koolhaas in a recent lecture in London when, talking of the proposed CCTV building in Beijing, he said that new buildings make their own context.

3 For the artist unconscious reasoning is not enough. He must analyse what pleases him; he must be conscious of the logical process that lies behind the successful result. The architect's education, therefore, must proceed in two stages. First he must learn to analyse the master-pieces of the past; then he must learn to make his own synthesis, serving the conditions and using the materials dictated by his age . . . This is as different as can be from the Gothic beliefs so ardently cherished by Viollet-le-Duc's English contemporaries – men like Pugin, Butterfield, Gilbert Scott, Street and Pearson. All of them were as deeply imbued with a love of Gothic architecture as Viollet-le-Duc but not one of them was man enough to think his way through the romantic attraction of style to a philosophical point of view applicable to all buildings at all times.'

(John Summerson, *Heavenly Mansions*, New York: W.W. Norton, 1963, p. 141)

4 Viollet-le-Duc, *Le Dictionnaire raisonné de l'architecture française* (Paris, 1854).

5 Hubert Damisch, 'The Space between: A Structuralist Approach to the Dictionary', first published in 1964 as an introduction to *Viollet-le-Duc, l'architecture raisonné* and reprinted in a special issue of *Architectural Design* 3/4 on Viollet-le-Duc (ed. Charles Jencks) in 1980, pp. 84–89. It is a brilliant piece of writing; its value to my arguments is immeasurable.

6 In the article (*ibid.*, p. 86) Damisch defines Structuralism thus: 'One of the clearest tenets of Structuralism is that it is possible to recognize a philosophical system – or at least the main elements of its structure – from any one part, and the way that part reacts to the other constituent unities and defines itself in relation to them. This principle is particularly productive when applied to the study of architecture. A single expression, one element of an architectural narrative, has no intrinsic value – or even meaning unless it is in its rightful position in the system.'

7 I am reminded that fashion designers each have (or perhaps had) as their most treasured pos-session standard patterns for arms, legs, backs, etc. from which all other pattern sizes and variations were worked up. Those in a way were representations of an ideal from which other work was derived. They were called, as I remember, 'blocks'.

8 Evgeny Kissin interviewed on BBC Radio 3, Saturday, 6 March 2004.

9 Damisch, 'The Space between', *Architectural Design*, p. 88.

10 Peter Blundell Jones pursued the issue of authenticity in a series of four articles in the *Architects Journal* in November and December 1991 ('In Search of Authenticity'). Some of the discussion in these pieces has already been referred to in the analysis of functionalism earlier. In the third

article, entitled 'Social Authenticity' (*Architects Journal*, 4 December 1991, pp. 22–25), he suggests that the truest authenticity, if such a phrase may be ventured, resides in the social programme of the building, and the clear reading in the form of the specific 'social rituals' it houses. This would seem to confirm what was earlier proposed, that functionalism was and is a cover for political commitment, which necessarily requires a codification of everyday life. This may be a truism dressed as lamb; perhaps all architecture requires this to an extent. As stated earlier, buildings such as this would defy alteration, but not demolition. Blundell Jones quotes from Pugin's *The True Principles of Pointed or Christian Architecture*: 'Pugin . . . discusses the question of propriety. He compares Magdalen College Oxford, in which he claims that ". . . every portion . . . had its distinguishing character and elevation", with "Modern collegiate buildings" in which "all is concealed within one uniform mass, unbroken either in outline or in face, undistinguishable from other buildings which surround it. As to its purpose", Pugin continues, "it might be taken for a barrack hospital or a lunatic asylum".'

11   Damisch, 'The Space between', *Architectural Design*, p. 88.

12   The chapter headed 'Some Definitions Using the Comparative Method' Robert Venturi, Denise Scott Brown, Steven Izenour, (*Learning from Las Vegas: The Forgotten Symbolism of Architectural Form* (Cambridge, Mass.: MIT Press, 1977), p. 87) begins with two other quotations in addition to Herman Melville: 'Incessant new beginnings lead to sterility' (Wallace Stevens),'I like boring things' (Andy Warhol).

13   Sir Christopher Wren:

> There are two causes of beauty – natural and customary. Natural is from geometry consisting in uniformity, that is equality and proportion. Customary beauty is begotten by the use, as familiarity breeds a love to things not in themselves lovely. Here lies the great occasion of errors, but always the true test is natural or geometrical beauty. Geometrical figures are naturally more beautiful than irregular ones: the square, the circle are the most beautiful, next to the parallelogram and the oval. There are only two beautiful positions of straight lines, perpendicular and horizontal; this is from Nature and consequently necessity, no other than upright being firm.
>
> (Quoted by Colin Rowe at the beginning of his essay 'The Mathematics of the Ideal Villa', in *The Mathematics of the Ideal Villa and Other Essays*, Cambridge, Mass.: MIT Press, 1982)

14   Walter Gropius, quoted in Kenzo Tange, *Katsura: Tradition and Creation in Japanese Architecture* (New Haven: Yale University Press; Tokyo: Zokeisha Publications Ltd., 1960), p. 5.

15   Ezra Pound, *ABC of Reading* (New York: New Directions, 1960), p. 113.

16   The potential duplicity of photography was a subject once commented on by Kafka:

> When I took a series of photographs of Kafka I said light-heartedly: 'For a couple of krone one can have oneself photographed from every angle. The apparatus is a mechanical Know-Thyself.
>
> 'You mean to say, the Mistake-Thyself,' said Kafka, with a faint smile.
>
> I protested: 'What do you mean? The camera cannot lie!'
>
> 'Who told you that?' Kafka leaned his head toward his shoulder.
>
> 'Photography concentrates one's eye on the superficial. For that reason it obscures the hidden life which glimmers through the outlines of things like a play of light and shade. One can't catch that even with the sharpest lens. One must grope for it with feeling.'
>
> (From Gustav Janouch's *Conversations with Kafka*, quoted by Susan Sontag in *On Photography*, Harmondsworth: Penguin, 1979, p. 206)

CHAPTER 8
THE PROCESS OF INTERVENTION

THE WORK OF INTERVENTION IS therefore based on an analysis, of thought that must be both intelligent and intuitive. The work of intervention then proceeds, founded upon this initial analysis.

Making good in its general usage means the process by which a building is repaired, rotten elements replaced, damaged architraves and mouldings restored. Usually no interventional intelligence is invoked in such work, but it may be appropriated to assist the purposes of definition and the development of a strategy of alteration. Making good expands the task of repairing in accordance with the previous proposition that all repairs contain restorative implications.

On a visit to Bolsover Castle in Derbyshire, one spring not long ago, I was struck by the considerable amount of renewals of battlements, finials and balusters, and new carving in the courtyard of the Little Palace (Figures 8.1 and 8.2). I'm not sure what instruction the stonemasons were working under, but the level of carving throughout was excellent. Because one is able to make such a statement, it begins to reveal the nature of this work, which I am sure one was supposed to consider as innocently making good normal wear and tear of the old building. What if the original masons had been less skilled or more careless than the present-day workers? The question is rhetorical; it has no answer. It is impossible to know the nature of the original work; it has probably been replaced several times by the pretended innocence of repair. It is lost. The same might be said of any building more than a few years old. There may be photographic evidence, but the physical evidence will be worn, and perhaps repaired.

8.1   Repairs and renewal: Balustrade, Bolsover Castle, 1988

8.2   Repairs and renewal: Pinnacles, Bolsover Castle, 1988

The second uncertainty, already implied, equally elusive, is the condition to which the building is being maintained or returned, as mentioned earlier, to the day it was built, or to a year ago last Tuesday; both conditions are beyond accurate recall; both would require guess work.

Thirdly, what is the idea of maintenance? As argued earlier, and with the example of Bolsover, maintenance is new work, which is restorative.

Of course the ancient should be preserved as a key signifier to the building's longevity, and the surviving fragment must be sacrosanct, one assumes. This still allows in the mind a model to be constructed of the specimen building; both can co-exist. The model serves as a gauge to what discriminate partial restorations might be carried through on the host building. In building, the usually assumed innocuous processes of repair are often responsible for the widespread destruction of the original fabric. It is at this often under-supervised stage of building that the role of the armature needs to be considered in a true work of alteration, that ways of supporting the authentic fragment need to be considered, or how otherwise to embed the fragment within the new.[1]

Concerning the role of the armature, both of the great English writers thought that a prop or crutch was a legitimate means of conserving a structure. Despite their censure of all other new work on ancient buildings, both Ruskin and Morris refer to such means as a legitimate insertion to shore up a part of a building in danger of collapse.[2]

A prop or a crutch aims to maintain certain spatial relationships that would otherwise be under gravitational threat. It aims to do this in a straightforward, honest and non-rhetorical manner. The prop is like the armature that maintains the surviving pieces of a Greek sculpture group in their original position, one to the other. It is also an indication, a measure of what is missing.

One might easily agree with Ruskin and Morris, but also be attracted by the prop, and expect of it an integrity and distinction of its own that is separate from the part it supports. The pleasure of looking at reassembled antique sculptural groups, such as the east and west pediment groups in the museum at Olympia, is added to by the self-effacing and direct design of the armature that now holds the disparate pieces of the group in their original spatial relationship to each other. It has an importance; the armature cannot help but be a reminder of loss, which in itself is a heavy purpose (Figure 8.3). The support is a stoic record of absence, so the life of the fragment is entirely

8.3   Fragments and supports: the west pediment at Olympia

dependent on the thing that must be attempting to represent absence; the armature is at once a model of self-effacement and of the impossibility of this ever being completely achieved (Figure 8.4).

The skill that makes an American teenager's tooth brace would also suggest that there is a requirement for fine engineering, in particular so as to be as unchallenging as possible to its context, despite and because of its inevitable visibility. One definition of 'authentic' is 'true and trustworthy': this would properly apply to the role of the armature in stabilizing a fragmented structure. Possibly the most skilful of examples on the larger scale of building is the work by the engineers Ove Arup and Partners in the 1960s to stabilize the Minster at York.[3] The completed project is inspired engineering throughout, and an exemplary integration of the modern with the ancient; in particular the system of taut cables and brackets employed to stiffen the east end and its great Gothic window is work to be considered of exceptional quality, and at which to wonder.

As with the clear plastic bra strap, armatures are also things that signal that they aren't really there. Similarly the presence of the puppeteers on stage in such companies as the Treblisi Marionette Theatre, and in classic Japanese puppet theatre referred to earlier, Bunraku, dressed entirely in black, where one might say that they must perform dynamically just as the building prop does statically, in an identical manner to give life to the parts. They achieve their goal through an absence of self-expression.

The survival of the fragment and the suggestion of the lost whole are familiar to restorers of ceramics, pots and urns in particular. In looking at a

8.4   Prop or armature: bridge on the Mincio River

museum exhibit of original fragments of pottery, embedded in a neutral form
which follows the shape of the original, one can be convinced for a moment
that this solves all the problems of restoration. The Archaeological Museum
on Ischia, which is where this idea first struck me, has many excellent examples
(Figure 8.5).[4]

8.5   Repaired Hellenic pots

The armature is here considered as part of making good, but it can be seen as a bridge between this and the actual intervention of the new works. It must make no claims beyond its clear purposes, and the directness and perhaps elegance by which these are achieved; in this it tends towards a true functionality. The prop or armature is the quintessential functional piece, in the sense that in Modernist thought, function replaces style. It is support for Modernism's claim of being styless, through its espousal of functionalism.[5] The armature is without style.

Gio Ponti said he strived for design 'without adjectives'. The previously described work on the Cimabue Crucifix is a shining example of intervention without adjectives. In particular, in the repair of the great wooden cross, the intervention at once becomes part of the cross and at the same moment can be recognized for itself, as a wonderful example of Milanese minimalism, collective and self-effacing.

Once while I was walking around London with a Swiss painter, he remarked as we gazed at a small early nineteenth-century house in Pimlico that the English alone could make such a small house seem grand and upstanding;

it is a genuine quality of architecture to carry out such illusions, to sway the spectator away from the actual nature of the building.[6] All architecture contains a conceit; 'architecture begins when you bring three bricks carefully together.[7] One may wonder therefore why architecture should become entangled with problems of the authentic.[8] It would seem to be the most fugitive of qualities, so much so that the temptation is to give it no regard. Architecture, along with all the other arts, is, in Picasso's words, 'a more or less credible lie'.

The recent French adulation for the copy, the simulacrum, and its elevation above the original, however, does not entirely dismiss the necessity for a clear view of the original in order satisfactorily either to make or embrace the imitation. The devotion of the model maker or counterfeiter requires an idea of the ideal or the model in the first place in order to proceed at all, a devotion which may be dogged or inspired.[9]

One of the great American popular composers, it may have been George Gershwin, was a dreadful pianist. He would arrive at his publishers and give an appalling rendition of his latest song for their approval. The two publishers would look at one another, and then one would say: 'It must be good; he wrote it.'

The designer contemplating restoration is like a later performer of the original work of architecture, as innumerable singers have been of the great American songbook. It is a matter of interpretation.[10]

Similarly there are questions of execution that can be raised in deciding how to make good. It may be that there are aspects of the host building, or even overall treatments, which the interventionist might judge to be less than skilful. When this is so, how is an intelligent person to proceed? The designers are required to be good, and in addition they are required to make any addition *at least* as good as the original. Is this a limiting requirement?

These are questions that apply to both making good and to new work. They concern issues of improvement; the idea of improvement therefore is not to be banished. The taboo against improvement may also be misleading in other ways. It is clearly an attribute of the general vow of chastity that typifies Ruskin's approach to the existing built form. Such vows are rarely maintained. The phantom that haunts restoration is in part the threat of 'improvement', which in its turn is a fear of dilution of authenticity. This may sometimes be a confusion between the actual and the authentic. The constant companion of improvement is deterioration. If this too is to be avoided, works of intervention are expected to strike a fine balance. If one should err, which direction would be preferable? It may be that improvement is merely a myth attached to that other idea that conservation is different from restoration.

With regard to stripping back, the question of improvement may come to be considered as an act towards the clarification of the host building.

Why should a building be frozen, for that is surely what is intended, as it was a week ago or three hundred years ago? What thinking lies behind such decisions, beyond an incipient unease regarding our own mortality?

No work of restoration should be attempted without knowing all that there is to know of the host building, materially, spatially, historically, archaeologically, anecdotally. Even then any such restorative work will be arbitrary, that is needing judgement and imagination as well as learning to be carried through. All investigative and analytical work will only take you to this threshold where decisions are needed. It is work for the informed imagination.

The objection to such a definition would stem from the concern for the authentic and the taboo against improvement through any restorative work; it relies on a belief that no mistakes happened in the past, or that such mistakes are indiscernible in the present. One might wonder if there is a similar censure against detrimental work, and one can assume that there is. It is difficult to think of anyone denying this, but for some reason one believes that it doesn't carry the moral weight of the first prohibition. If the original or particular actuality of a building is lost to us, which it is in all cases, how then might anyone judge what is or is not improving work? This is of course a discussion aside from the understandable desire of the client to welcome and encourage whatever improvements the designer can deliver.

We talk here of the responsibility of the designer, perhaps the primary one, to carry a building over from the past and through the present, so that it will survive into another age. That is, the requirement of the designer who works on an existing building not to damage but rather to elucidate its essential nature. For such work to be considered self-effacing, so as to attempt to walk an imaginary line between detriment and improvement, can only lead the designer to delusion, of their self, of others or of both.

Should mistakes if confirmed be repeated? One might argue, not without reason, that there are never true mistakes in the way that things come to be as they are, but it requires a certain balance of mind to claim it. It is also a consciousness, similar to Morris's attitude to an old English church with its later additions, that its realization carries a prohibition on any further engagement in the present or in the future. One cannot consciously make new mistakes, but they can be copied. If so, is the copy also a mistake?

All restoration requires interpretation and consequent judgement; it might also absorb work of genius. In the seventeenth-century, Bernini was often employed to replace missing parts of newly discovered and newly revered incomplete Roman statues for the Museo Archeologico in Rome. It can be agreed after a moment's consideration that if it is to be permitted at all, then it requires the keenest attention. Over and above all, in approaches to making good, the delusion of the difference between conservation and restoration should be borne in mind. There is no difference; John Richardson's cautionary tale from the attempted conservation work on Cubist paintings should be remembered.[11] Everything changes, strategies and attempts to prevent it may equally destroy that which one intends to save unchanged. Restoration needs to be either candid or forbidden.

Francesco Veneziana rebuilt the neo-classical Palazzo di Lorenzo, wrecked in the terrible earthquake in Sicily in 1968, in a most beautiful manner[12] (Figure 8.6). The façade was incorporated into a new museum for Gibellina Nuova, which replaced the town also destroyed in the earthquake. It seems to me there are admirable elements of copying and parody in the completed project.[13] Much of this is achieved by rebuilding against the fragment with freshly cut stone from the same source as the original, although this suggests some automatic programme which the finished work clearly confounds. Such matching is one of a set of decisions with which the project was realized. In addition, as the architect writes, because of the seismic conditions, this led to a new form of play 'separating that which belongs together, and joining what was separate. Between the freshly cut stone slabs and the irregularly chipped edges of the old façade fragments runs a clearly visible four-centimetres-wide joint'[14] (Figure 8.7). He presaged the description of the project with the following comments:

> Moulded stone blocks lying scattered on the grass at the foot of still standing sections of a building. A well known or even familiar sight – the picture of a fragmentary world testifying to the passed presence of a great architectonic unity. On a construction site this image may come full circle: here the chaos

8.6   Ruin of the Palazzo di Lorenzo in Sicily, 1968

8.7   New museum for Gibellina Nuova incorporating the ruined palazzo; architect: Francesco
      Venezia

of the different building materials, also a fragmentary world by analogy, is brought to a new architectonic unity through the power of design . . . In the present state of the art of architecture the idea of creating a unity through the composition and recomposition of the fragmentary elements only appears to be paradoxical: actually it is one of the few possible ways of counteracting the omnipresent fragmentation by resorting to techniques which contribute to the extension of that poetic duration of a building that grows out of the combination of elements which are heterogeneous or belong to different periods in time – thus creating a feeling of remembrance. And a sense of resonance.[15]

From this key work and from other observations, the definition may be proposed that works of intervention are concerned with inhabiting ruins; the inevitable ruination of the actual work on the host building and the degree to which the ruination survives the transformation are within the remit of the designer. An altered building is as an inhabited ruin. The ruin is the means by which a building addresses its past, present and future.

Wei-Fu Kuo's and Louis Kahn's observations on the nature of ruins allow one to arrive at a definition of a ruin stripped of any trace of sentimentality; in a ruined condition, a building may speak of how it is made, and in this condition it refers to the past, the present and the future. It is what has survived; it is the limit of guarantee that the designer has regarding the physical and spatial nature of the host building, past and present. A ruin will have qualities of transparency.

Enabling work equally rises from the regions of the pragmatic in conventional building to the level of thoughtful strategy in works of intervention. Whereas in straightforward architectural work the site must be readied for the footings of the new building, existing structures demolished, the ground stabilized sometimes by draining a pond or suchlike, work that needs the least instruction for the builder, with intervention such work requires a surgical precision. The partial demolitions of and removals from the host building are in one sense like a shadow being cast of the new work to come. The making of such absences can be understood to be equal to the insertion of new works. These removals have also potencies of their own in revealing the Khanian spirit of the built spaces and structures.

Demolition can therefore be as new works. Enabling works establish the configuration of the altered spatial relationships and hierarchy of the new occupancy. It is the process by which a carefully made ruin is prepared, which is then to be made inhabitable by the new work. Making the ruin in interventional work is a precise and creative undertaking, equal in many ways to the installation of the new work. They are twinned operations, with equal requirements of skill and attention, fused together as the outcome of the work. It is this act of breaking the host building which will be seen to be crucial later in the proposed full process of alteration.

The cliché of the wall stripped back to bare brick in the newly converted building is familiar to everyone, being a deeply accepted and implemented aspect of ruination, and cheap to achieve too. Such work is concerned with surface, but this is not to say that such work can only be clichéd. In particular, the sculptor Terry Smith, working entirely within the limits of removal, has made numerous engaging site-specific intercessions related to surface.

The true potency of ruination, however, is spatial. If one thinks of a building being broken in a manner other than through mischance or neglect or disaster, if one thinks of a building broken programmatically, one thinks of the work of Gordon Matta-Clark. No-one has shown so eloquently the breaking of existing built form through the exactness of geometry, and the consequent strength of such acts in revealing the nature of the building. Even the mundane is transformed by these processes. In an early work, a modest abandoned New England house becomes an object of wonder by being sawn in half, and the two halves jacked to reveal the split.[16] All his works were carried through in buildings due for demolition, which is our loss (Figure 8.8). The attempts to save his *Office Baroque* work in Antwerp posthumously are chronicled by Pamela M. Lee in her book on Matta-Clark.[17] He was under-valued when he was alive, and he died young, so it is too late to make it up to him now.[18] His twin brother had committed suicide earlier, and perhaps the two boys were both undermined by the absence in South America of their famous Surrealist father, Roberto Matta.

His later work became progressively explicit in geometric terms. This is the artist's description of *Office Baroque* in 1977, using a plan of two interlocking semicircular areas of slightly different diameters:

> These began on the first floor providing the constant motif as they were cut up through floors and roof. Where these circles crossed, a peculiar, almost boat shaped hole resulted and was mutated from floor to floor as structural

8.8 Gordon Matta-Clark, *Circus or The Caribbean Orange*, Chicago, 1978

beams and available floor space dictated. In this project . . . the disposition of spaces (large open offices near the ground, small interconnecting rooms towards the top) determined how the formal elements transformed from uninterrupted circular slices to shrapnel-like bits and pieces of the original form as they 'collided' with partitions and walls.[19]

One of the late major interventions was in the last Hausemannesque mansion standing on the site next to the Centre Pompidou in rue Beaubourg,[20] the site on which later was to be built the IRCAM studios. For this project, there exists a Matta-Clark drawing from which the work was done and from which it is named, *Conical Intersect*.[21] This perhaps reveals something of the magic of these works: they are like accidents which are realized programmatically, a destructive force smashing into the building which, instead of increasing disorder, makes order, so suggesting a world that might be our own except that here accidents decrease entropy. The work proposes that a ruin may be neither accidental nor imprecise.

Such works allow the occupant a privileged view of the building, one which when a building is complete is unavailable except in the form of a drawing or model, a view or glimpse of the usually hidden section and plan of the building. In an early work, *A W-hole House: Atrium Roof*, in 1973 in Genoa, Matta-Clark intended to 'defunctionalize' an abandoned office for engineers. He said he wanted 'no longer a building to separate owners from workers but [to be] a hub around which nothing but light worked'.[22] This is the other consequence of such acts of precise ruination: by breaking down the compartmentalization of the building, by making unhindered paths for light, the built form gains a transparency.

There are now new technologies related to rapid prototyping that have great potential for use in intervention; they use projective geometry.[23] The relevance of these techniques is, in the first place, that the programme will give a large number of possible cuts through the object or building; and, in the second place, a separate geometry, such as for instance the removal of a conic form or a cube or a sphere (all of which are easily expressed mathematically) from the building can quickly be tested in an almost infinite variety of orientations, to find the correct fit that the designer seeks. They are the most potent way of testing spatial fit of the new and the existing. In the matter of intervention, this is of very great potential, and offers the interventionist a tool of enormous potency, so care will always need to be exercised in its use. This is a means by which Matta-Clark's cutting art can come within reach of us lesser mortals (Figure 8.9). By these techniques, the exact delineation of the demolition desired of the host building can be rapidly sought, and as with such matters, very slowly found. In particular these techniques are unrivalled in

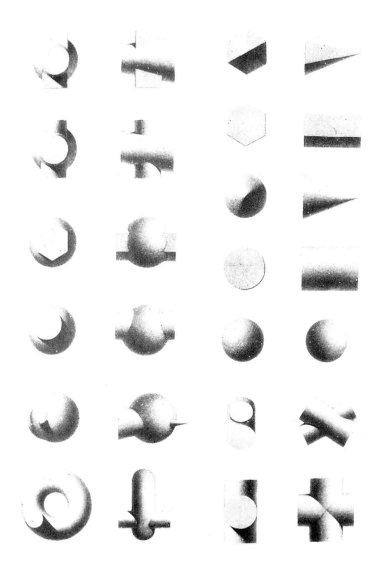

8.9   Nineteenth-century projective geometry exercise for engineers

discerning occasions of spatial coincidence occurring while fitting one spatial set to another. All of us look upon coincidence as affirmation in our work.

As was suggested earlier, with Mondrian's Paris studio as reference, Modernist formal vocabulary can act as the universal medium of alteration; the purity and impartiality of pure form and smooth surface can be introduced and integrated into any existing context, acceptable anywhere. As said earlier, many problems would be solved if this were so. The interventional designer could become licensed in these prescribed operations. In the art of intervention, then, Modernism might prove at last to be somehow a supra-style, a quality often claimed for it by its founders, and so able in its transcendence to be placed in any context, regardless of the resident style.

An oblique confirmation of this rule of the general applicability of pure form is contained in an elegant investigation using projective geometry into the origins of the strange cylindrical penetration through the corner of a seventeenth-century chapel in Rome, the Sacristy of San Carlo ai Catinari.[24] This was a project by Preston Scott Cohen to analyse the origin of a passage struck diagonally across the external corner of the chapel, passing behind the corner pilaster to emerge on two façades, one on Via del Monte della Farina and the other on Via di S. Anna (Figure 8.10). The purpose of the tube is to admit diffused light into the interior through another elliptical opening, made by the collision of the upper wall of the interior of the chapel with the tube. The chapel was built between 1650 and 1660. Scott Cohen created a sequence of drawings to show how, 'given the circumstance of the corner, this particular mutation of form was the optimal solution that could both perform well, by providing diffuse light, and be disguised as an embrasure by conforming to classical imperatives – congruency, symmetry, seriality and co-axiality'.[25]

Although this is an investigation of a building built as a piece rather than a later alteration, the tube acts as an insertion, an unexpected move using an unusual form, the cylinder, to complete both an interior and exterior organization with the one action. In this it is akin to how a successful later insertion might act, and a seeming example of the supra-style qualities of pure form.

In an article on projective geometry,[26] referred to by Preston Scott Cohen and others, Morris Kline writes:

> The key to three dimensional representation was found in what is known as the principle of projection and section. The Renaissance painter imagined

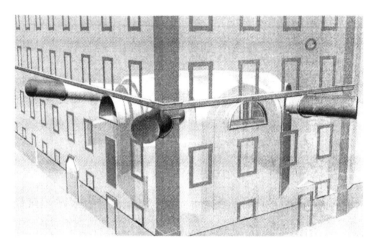
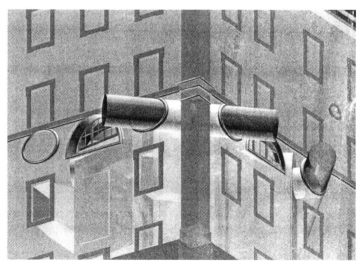

8.10   Analysis of cylindrical element connecting interior and exterior

that a ray of light proceeded from each point in the scene he was painting to one eye. The collection of converging lines he called a projection. He then imagined that his canvas was a glass screen interposed between the scene and the eye. The collection of points where the lines of projection intersect the glass screen was a 'section'.[27]

It is reasonable to claim that the discovery of perspective, the rationalization of sight, is the phenomenon that most clearly delineates the Renaissance from the medieval.[28] It is interesting to see here a scientist give credence to the proposition that fifteenth-century perspective is the seed of architectonic transparency in the twentieth century. The unexpected deep penetration of light from the outside world may be the formal component of transparency, but it has also a social or deviant dimension.

The idea of the section made visible and evident brings to mind again the work of Gordon Matta-Clark, and as well the idea of ruin and precision being twinned in the work of alteration, to allow, in Louis Kahn's terms, the building to speak of itself. This is how the designer is licensed to practise precise ruination with regard to the host building, beyond the expedient requirements of the client, and why such decisions are integral to the proper conduct of alteration. By this means, transparency can be introduced and become integral to the altered condition of an old building.

With the example from seventeenth-century Rome and with the work of Matta-Clark, one dealing with presence and the other with absence, one with insertion and the other removal, one might be persuaded that here are the makings of a comprehensive strategy of intervention.[29] This may be true for enabling and new works, but in making good one will inevitably stray into the territory of imitative work and the complex issues of 'work in the manner of'. Therefore, to suggest that the interventionist needs only a commitment to Modernist forms alone is misleading.

In making good, both imitative[30] and repetitive new works may arise as part of the overall strategy of intervention; the pleasure of copying and showing it to be a copy is not to be overlooked, like an echo, or an imitative bird-call. One might also note the numerous cases of mimicry in the natural world, particularly among moths and butterflies.

One can return to the idea previously discussed mainly in the realm of painting, of *work in the manner of*. Picasso, when painting his *Las Meninas*

8.11   Imitation in (a) art and (b) nature

series, said: 'copying is not possible, even by working hard. You copy a corrida, a painting of Velasquez, a photograph: you concentrate yourself and finally you are filled with your subject. Still there is always something that resists and which you lose control of: yourself.'[31] I suppose one must read this as a qualification of his injunction to copy everyone except oneself:[32] One might set out to examine what is meant by copying. In any case, one might set out to copy something; this is certainly within the realm of possibility. That this might lead inevitably into analysis and interpretation is not entirely regrettable, as intelligence and creativity will have also been invoked by the process. No two things are the same, but still things can be classified (Figures 8.11a and 8.11b).

The purposes of mimicry may be both reverential and light-hearted, or more solemn, but should be the outcome of learning, of structured knowledge of what is to be copied. No-one today is prepared for such work, for it is easier said than done; however, the history of architecture of course is laden with examples of such undertakings. One immediately thinks of Gothic in the nineteenth century, and the early Renaissance buildings were at least partially work in the manner of the Greeks and the Romans. There is one style or aesthetic that can be reproduced today; present practice would feel no inadequacy or embarrassment at reproducing Modernist work, which possibly indicates the continuing prevalence of Modernism in architectural design, if nothing else.

In recent times, it is little more than a rumour that work in an imitative manner in building has a potential for success[33] (Figure 8.12).

One would assume that to set out to copy something requires the copyist to be in many ways as good as the originator. In regarding the recently completed restoration of Hawksmoor's Christchurch Spitalfields,[34] is it assumed that the restorative architect is at least the equal of the original architect in a variety of respects?

Philippe Boudon published an explorative project in *Daidalos.* He writes: 'Since copying is impossible, why not try it? What is it, in this process, that the doctrine of modern architecture would like to conceal? How can the copy be caught out? What is the nature of its depreciation?'[35] Such a project, he insists, must always be diachronic, contrasting with the synchronic[36] assertions of the Modern Movement. Later he adds:

8.12 The uncertainty of imitative work: New finial (1930s) for the Grote Kerk in Alkmaar, Holland

The terms *copy*, but also *pastiche*, *imitation*, *mimetism*, *quotation*, *influence*, *homage* and finally *model*, are somehow related to the *manner*. One should consider the project *after the manner* as such . . . Apart from the usual type of programme, such as 'an art school' or 'a tourist information office' for instance, the operations which directed the most complex ones were: *translation*, *transformation*, *extension* and *interpretation*.[37]

On studying the illustrations of the work produced in the project, one might be inclined to say that these are ambitious claims for the work. That may be due to several reasons, but the interest of the work is not entirely dismissed by the results; it may merely prove the difficulty of attitude, approach and execution of such work as *in the manner of*, and the need for considerable talent to tackle such work, or for a more conducive pedagogic environment. As stated earlier, this would go against the shibboleth of originality, and individual genius, tending to subsume these into a more general cultural objective.

In the eighteenth century, Sir Joshua Reynolds, as head of the Royal Academy Schools, considered copying to be the most demanding task for the artist, requiring the highest intelligence, 'a perpetual exercise of the mind, a continual invention'. As there is to be imitative work with a role in intervention, it needs to begin with a proper respect for the processes of copying. And copying itself must be undertaken with at least curiosity, or something stronger. In all these matters, the example of Ise needs to be borne in mind.

To suggest that a designer must be able to work in an imitative manner at one point and then go on to work with pure non-referential insertions is to introduce a fatal schism into the process of alteration; this is disconnected formulae, and no designer can work in this way. There is probably a double misunderstanding buried here, the first being that the sequence on site of making good, enabling works and new works is somehow reproduced in the designer's own work methods, accompanied by an ordering of relative importance. Of course this isn't so. As with all such work, in designing, everything must be considered at once equally somehow, none has precedence over the others. Designing occurs in flashes, where seeming contradictory elements will suddenly alter into close allies, and where synthesis must be approached, if at all, from every direction at once. All design relies on the unlikely coincidence for resolution; only good designers have the skill or art of sensing them and where they might lie.

The second misunderstanding is that the designer aims to make his or her work coherent. How else can one judge its progress? In alteration the task is to seek out such a coherence while working with disparate elements, the intended and the existing, as with composing a collage.[38] Intervention, like collage, is the assimilation of disparate elements into a resolution where the parts work together while maintaining their own identity. While concerned with purity of style at certain points, the activity is more akin to assemblage and bricolage; and as with collage, the coherence must derive from this.

So the easy acceptability of pure form as a general solution to the work of insertion and alteration may be merely a palliative, and a further enquiry must be pursued for a more satisfactory proposal to appear.

NOTES

1 This idea crystallized as I was looking at restorative work to Dieppe Cathedral in August 2004. Something which I have since forgotten of the work being carried out there prompted me to this conclusion, marrying the intelligence of vase restoration with building works. It had something to do with the preservation of the profile, of a fragment and of the whole, which the restoration of vases achieves.

2 John Ruskin, *The Seven Lamps of Architecture* (London, 1849), p. 205: 'Take proper care of your monuments, then you will not need to restore them . . . bind it together with iron where it loosens . . . do not cry about the unsightliness of the aid; better a crutch than a lost limb.' William Morris, Society for the Protection of Ancient Buildings Manifesto (London, 1878): 'put Protection in the place of Restoration, to stave off decay by daily care, to prop a perilous wall or mend a leaky roof by such means that are obviously meant for support or covering, and show no pretense to other art, and otherwise to resist all tampering with the fabric or ornament of the building as it stands'.

3 York Minster's architect was Bernard Fielden and his engineers were Ove Arup and Partners. The main work, to build a concrete raft to replace the original medieval raft foundation and to make a near invisible tension-wire system to strengthen the building, was carried out in the 1960s. After a fire in the roof in 1984, Arup again worked extensively on the minster. See Ove Arup and Partners, *Engineering the Built Environment* (Basel, Boston, Berlin: Birkhauser Verlag, 1994), David Dunster, *Arups on Engineering* (Berlin: Ernst & Sohn, 1996), and Ove Arup and Partners, *Technology in Architecture* (intro. Peter Murray) (Milan: Tecno, 1986).

4 As I write this, a marvellously repaired Tang vase has appeared in the *New York Times*, in an article by David Colman (Sunday, 21 November 2004, Section 9, p. 8): 'The starkly elegant vase, about 14 inches tall, with a faintly carved surface of peonies, was probably used to pour wine and is emblematic of the Tang court, a peaceful time when a studied cultivation of simple pleasures reached new heights. Sometime in the 19th century, it was broken, most likely falling onto the floor. It was painstakingly repaired by a Japanese craftsman using molten bronze as solder to mend the seams and fill the gaps.' The vase belongs to Tobias Meyer, Sotheby's principal auctioneer in New York City. The Tang dynasty ruled from AD 618 to 906. In a recent conversation with Angela Heskett, she told me that Lorenzo de' Medici had his collection of antique vases repaired in a similar manner, usually mending the damaged rim, using gold, and also that he inscribed his initials into the body of the vase itself. She went on to say that the whole issue of mending and repairing was worth a book of its own, a thought which had somehow managed to evade me while writing this one.

5 The late Modernist phenomenon of high-tech buildings may be thought of as making entire buildings as far as possible from such armature-like elements.

6 More usually nowadays an opposite skill is needed: the architect is more likely to be asked to 'disguise the bulk' by planners and clients in the modern world.

7 Peter Smithson quoting Mies van der Rohe in Peter Smithson, Catherine Spellman and Karl Unglaub, *Conversations with Students* (Princeton: Princeton Architectural Press, 2005), p. 24.

8 The most concerted attempt to pin down the subject that I know of is by Peter Blundell-Jones, with his four articles on 'In Search of Authenticity' in the *Architects Journal* (13 October, 6 November, 4 December 1991 and 15 January 1992) referred to earlier.

9 Alison Smithson once observed: 'Reconstruction is often touchingly faithful – take for example, the desks and chairs of Alexander Rodchenko's Workers' Club reading room that recently turned up in London.' Article on the occasion of the remaking of the Smithsons' *Patio & Pavilion* of 1956 for an exhibition at the ICA in 1990, *AA Files* 47 (2002), p. 37). One should also remember here the remaking of the maquette of Vladimir Tatlin's Tower (*Monument to the Third International*

1919–20) by Christopher Woodward and others for the exhibition on Soviet architecture organized by the Arts Council of Great Britain at the Hayward Gallery, London, in 1978.

10 Classical music equally contains many different performances, none more famous perhaps than the broadcast performance (on CBC) of Brahms's piano concerto no.1 in B minor, for which Glenn Gould, playing with the New York Philharmonic, had devised a very personal interpretation, particularly with regard to tempi, and which caused the conductor Leonard Bernstein to come out and forewarn the audience, and also to state amiably his doubts concerning the authenticity of what they were about to experience. One should also mention the two recordings of J. S. Bach's Goldberg Variations that Gould made, at the beginning and at the end of his career, in 1955 and 1981.

11 John Richardson, 'Crimes against the Cubists', *New York Review of Books*, 16 June 1983.

12 Francesco Venezia, *Transfiguration of the Fragment* 'The Architecture of Spoils: A Compositional Technique', *Daidalos* 16 (1985).

13 Venezia (*ibid.*, p. 12) proposes four historical precedents for his project for the reconstruction of the Palazzo di Lorenzo, introducing them thus:

> This valuable technique [the architecture of spoils] has been refined in centuries of experience. The Great Mosque at Cordoba, the Tempio Malatestiano in Rimini, the Palazzetto of Pius IV and the Villa Giulia in Rome are just a few of many examples. All of these buildings convey a sense of unity. And yet they were all born of the transfer or integration of pieces which either existed at the site or came from demolished or derelict buildings in other regions. The metaphorical aspect of architecture: transfer of material or transfer of reference.

14 The architect goes on (*ibid.*, p. 103):

> A second joint subdivides the fragment of the old façade into two different areas and restores some of the lost symmetry. Both joints find their continuation in the pavement of the court, ending at the opposite wall with its single aperture. Just for a short moment at sundown, one can experience the dance of the moving joints of light with the fixed joints of shadow which the sun stages in the court. This moment is the highpoint of the architectonic spectacle.

15 *Ibid.*, p. 124.

16 *Splitting*, 1974, 322 Humphrey Street, Englewood, NJ. The house belonged to Gordon Matta-Clark's dealers, Holly and Horace Solomon, and was awaiting demolition at some point to allow redevelopment of the plot. Fortune then seems to have stepped in.

17 Pamela M. Lee, *Object to be Destroyed: The Work of Gordon Matta-Clark* (Cambridge, Mass.: MIT Press, 2000).

18 He was by choice an outsider. His hatred of the Manhattan architectural avant-garde is revealed in the incident described by James Attlee and Lisa Le Feuvre (pp. 55–56) in their catalogue for an exhibition of Matta-Clark's work (*Gordon Matta-Clark: The Space between*, Glasgow and London, 2003):

> In December 1976 he was invited to contribute to an exhibition at the Institute for Architecture and Urban Studies in New York entitled Idea as Model, curated by Andrew McNair. Matta-Clark was to take part alongside three members of the so-called 'New York Five', the architects Michael Graves, Charles Gwathmey and Richard Meier. Another member of the group, Peter Eisenman, had founded the Institute. These architects were heavily involved with the teaching of architecture . . . and, thanks in no small part to the writings of critics such as Colin Rowe, their work was entering the canon alongside the giants of modernism. Academic, apparently uncritically modernist, allied to institutions and big business; in short, everything that Matta-Clark had come to detest in the architectural profession.
>
> Matta-Clark . . . decided to submit 'Widow Blow-Out', a series of photographs of social housing projects in the South Bronx. The broken windows of the apartments in the photographs signalled their inhabitants' rejection of both their containment and the modernist cell blocks they had been assigned to. On the day before the show was to open, Matta-Clark turned up at the Institute with an air gun that he had borrowed from the artist Dennis Oppenheim. Andrew McNair . . . reluctantly agreed to his proposal that he shoot out a couple of windows that were already cracked; the empty casements were to serve as frames for the photographs of the Bronx

apartments. For whatever reasons Matta-Clark did not stop at two, but blew out all the windows on the floor of the Institute in one cathartic liberating session, shouting abuse at the members of the Institute and their ideologies as he did so. 'These are the guys I studied with at Cornell,' he reportedly yelled, 'these were my teachers. I hate what they stand for.'

The best book on Gordon Matta-Clark's work is probably another catalogue for an exhibition of his work: *Gordon Matta-Clark* (Valencia: IVAM Centre Julio Gonzalez, 1993).

19 Matta-Clark quoted in Lee, *Object to be Destroyed*, p. 223

20 Gordon Matta-Clark, *Conical Intersect*, 1975, 27–29 rue Beaubourg, Paris.

21 Lee, *Object to be Destroyed*.

22 *Ibid.*, p. 12.

23 Stereolithography is used for the manufacture of thinly laminated models. As with drawing, the section plane removes material to make the hidden visible. Rapid prototyping uses the section itself as an element. This is used in the manufacture of laminated objects, and is reached with software specializing in description by means of a sequence of closely packed sections, which can then be used to grow a three-dimensional model of what has previously only existed in two. Typically, a base LED stencil is projected into a bath of photopolymer, that is a polymer that is cured or solidified by light projected onto it, followed by the next stencil, which is in its turn cured, and so on. Thus the model is grown by a series of planes, deposited one on another. Typically the stencils advance 0.1 mm at a time; each time a surface is deposited which will then be rendered more or less invisible by the next precipitation or growth, until the model is complete. I am indebted to Russell Lowe, who first made me aware of these techniques in a lecture in the Interior Architecture School at RISD, and in later conversations with him. The lecture contained a project by the lecturer for fitting Aldo Rossi's *Memorial to the Resistance* within the Pantheon Dome, which at least shows the diverse capabilities of the software. This latter exercise was exhibited in the *Drawing the Process* exhibition at Kingston University, England, in 2003 (curator Leo Duff).

24 Preston Scott Cohen, 'Regular Anomalies', *AA Files* 42 (Summer 2000), pp. 46–55.

25 *Ibid.*, p. 48. Scott Cohen continues (ibid.):

> Though the tube is necessary, it responds not so much to function as to a necessity for the classical language to adapt a decorative or symbolic programme for a particular context. Fortuitously, as the classical language mutates in the Sacristy, the tube transmits even stealthier and more beautifully diffuse light than would a more conventional embrasure. This kind of perverse functionalism – in which the adaptation of form was not seen as fundamentally necessary to an essential function but was considered nevertheless to produce 'more beautiful' results than a normative form – was an idea, according to Daston and Park, particular to an early modern (eighteenth-century) view of wonder as it regarded the marvel of monstrous births . . . Oddities in this sense were no longer admired for their singularity (or were no longer of interest in themselves), but exemplified malformations that, because they were explained in terms of function, could be considered extraordinary (rather than naturally erroneous or novel), and thus revelatory of a more elaborate normative system. Thus, to the extent that the tube is perversely functional, it is like the anatomical marvels of the eighteenth-century – not aberrant but extraordinary.

26 Projective geometry and perspective have been twinned since the beginning. Other ages have demonstrated a fascination with this double phenomenon, as with the sixteenth-century development of anamorphic projections.

Probably the best general survey of the uses in art of projective geometry is still *The Science of Art* by Martin Kemp (New Haven, Conn.: Yale University Press, 1990). Dr Robin Evans also wrote extensively on the subject of perspective, which he was in the process of summing up in his book *The Projective Cast: Architecture and its Three Geometries* (Cambridge, Mass.: MIT Press, 1995) at the time of his death.

David Hockney's recent book *Secret Knowledge: Rediscovering the Lost Techniques of the Old Masters* (London: Studio Books, 2001), a sort of optical detective story, is a valuable contribution to the subject. Another interesting piece is 'The Cutting Surface: On Perspective as a Section, its Relationship to Writing, and its Role in Understanding Space', by Gordana Korolija Fontana Giusti in *AA Files* 40 (1999), pp. 57–64. A recent use of projective geometry can be seen in the elegant work of Torres and Lapena for the rehabilitation of the Rondo Promenade of Palma de Majorca's city walls (published in *El Croquis* 61 (June 1996), pp. 28–45).

27 Morris Kline, 'Protective Geometry', *Scientific American*, January 1955, pp. 86–88.

28 Kline writes (ibid., p. xx):

> With the Renaissance came not only a desire to paint realistically but also a revival of the Greek doctrine that the essence of nature is mathematical law. Renaissance painters struggled for over a hundred years to find a mathematical scheme which would enable them to depict the three dimensional real world on a two dimensional canvas. Since many of the Renaissance painters were architects and engineers as well as artists, they eventually succeeded in their objective. To see how well they succeeded one need only compare Leonardo da Vinci's 'Last Supper' with [Simone] Martini's 'Annunciation' . . .
>
> The work of projective geometers has had an important influence on modern physical science. They prepared the way for the workers in the theory of relativity, who sought laws of the universe that were invariant under transformation from the co-ordinate system of one observer to that of another. It was the projective geometers and other mathematicians who invented the calculus of tensors, which proved to be the most convenient means for expressing invariant scientific laws.
>
> It is of course true that the algebra of differential equations and some other branches of mathematics have contributed more to the advancement of science than projective geometry. But no branch of mathematics competes with projective geometry in originality of ideas, co-ordination of intuition in discovery and rigor in proof, purity of thought, logical finish, elegance of proofs and comprehensiveness of concepts. The science born of art proved to be an art.

29 It will be obvious from this double exemplar that the author considers a knowledge and love of projective geometry to be an important quality in a designer. This is also referred to elsewhere.

30 Copying was ever present if unrecognized in the practice of altering buildings, and it needs now to be raised up, and considered paradoxically as a true component of alteration. Restorative work is imitative and interpretive; of course all 'conservation' work involves imitative work, but this somehow is considered the realm of the workmen or craftsmen, and so is relegated to beneath critical consideration. However, when considered critically, the impossibility of an exact copy opens the discussion onto the realm of imitation and parody and works *in the manner of* in the composing of new work and the existing. Imitative work is an important project within the *work* of intervention, which *will always* require an awareness of the dangers of mimicry and the consequent potential for destabilization. It should be considered as an interpretation, which is central to reaching an equivalence. Imitation is concerned with what is possible today, and imitative work and its associate, variation, constitute a central project of intervention.

31 Quoted by Phillippe Boudon, 'Project in the Manner of . . . Notes on a Pedagogic Concept . . .', Daidalos 8 (June 1983), p. 68.

32 The famous exception to all this is of course Marceld Duchamp, who perhaps spent more time in the latter part of his career on copying his own work than on anything else, in order to make editions of various kinds. The production of what became finally three hundred *Boites* is probably the best known of these, although not all were by his own hand. His obsessive dedication to exactitude at the outset is recorded by Calvin Tomkins in his *Duchamp: A Biography* (London: Chatto & Windus, 1997; Pimlico edition, 1998):

> 'It was important to Duchamp that his original notes be reproduced exactly as they were, with crossings out and revisions, second thoughts, incomplete phrases, contradictions, marginal scribblings, ink blots and pencil smudges. In later years Duchamp admitted that some of the notes had deteriorated so badly that he was obliged to re-copy them, but even then he went out of his way to make the reproductions conform in every detail to the originals, some of which were tiny fragments torn from envelopes or bits of wrapping paper. 'I wanted to reproduce them as accurately as possible,' he told Michel Sanouillet in 1954, 'So I had all these thoughts lithographed in the same ink which had been used for the originals. To find paper that was exactly the same, I had to ransack the most unlikely nooks and crannies of Paris. Then we cut out three hundred copies of each lithograph with the help of zinc patterns that I had cut out on the outlines of the original papers.''

As pointed out elsewhere, mistakes cannot be consciously made twice, but it seems they can be copied. So copying is a peculiar realm where sometimes meanings tend to reverse.

33 The late nineteenth century is littered with cautionary attempts at *work in the manner of*. Gilbert Scott's Hereford screen, for instance, originally intended for the cathedral and now in the Victoria and Albert Museum, is surpassingly ugly.

34 The claim that this is a complete restoration, and that it undoes the damage done by the nineteenth-century alterations is disingenuous. As Kerry Downes says of Christchurch in (*Hawksmoor*: London, Thames & Hudson, 1969), the original condition of the church is compromised in many other ways. I have recently visited the newly restored church, with in my mind the wonder of the magnificent part-ruined interior prior to restoration, to which the public had had occasional access. The loss of magnificence in the new interior is striking. All works of restoration are works of the imagination, or else they are not, that is they are works of part-dead literalism and part guesswork. The work at Christchurch falls into this second category. The changes require a longer commentary, but the process by which a grand haunted masterpiece has been rendered into something akin to a provincial town hall surely will require some explanation.

Without vision, restoration is a disaster, matching exactly Ruskin's censure. After leaving the church, I called into the Society for the Protection of Ancient Buildings, whose offices are near by, to ask if it had an interest in the work. I was referred back to the charity that has responsibility for Christchurch itself. This perhaps is the most surprising: the absence as far as I can tell of discussion of this work. It suggests a shocking want of interest or concern within the architectural community. What if a major painting in the National Gallery were planned to be restored, if for instance it was planned that the damaged trio of male figures on the right in Piero's *Nativity* were to be repainted? Some people probably would give their lives to prevent this happening. I'm prompted to think from the example of Christchurch, and from the example of Uppark previously discussed, that the contemporary practice of restoration in Great Britain is similar to the condition of English painting in the early twentieth century, compared with Continental Europe, that is mired in realism, unconscious of its illusionistic component, and consequently enmeshed in a sterile literalism.

35 Boudon, 'Project in the Manner of', p. 70. See also by the same author 'Kopie, Imitation, Interpretation', *Werk-Bauen & Wohnen* 12 (December 1994), pp. 4–9.

36 Diachronic: 'involving or relating to the study of, the development of something, especially a language, through time'. Synchronic: 'relating to or studying something, especially a language, as it exists at a certain point in time, without considering its historical development'.

37 Boudon, 'Project in the Manner of', p. 71.

38 The similarities between works of intervention and works of collage are discussed elsewhere in the book.

CHAPTER 9

PROHIBITIONS AND DIFFICULTIES

ONE WOULD EXPECT THAT THE work of alteration must take account of the context of the undertaking; of course any procedure is impossible without considering the nature of the site for the intervention. One can see that such considerations stretch over a considerable range of topics, from the essential physical, spatial and structural understanding to a response to any characteristic of the host building, as determined through the processes of stripping back. The degree of infection is a decision of prime importance for the designer, the degree to which the new is informed, affected or sets out to respond to the setting, the degree to which the setting might be considered contagious, is the crux of the engagement with the host building, within and without.

The *Shorter Oxford Dictionary* defines 'context' thus: 'construction of speech' (1645), 'a continuous text or composition' (1641), 'the connection of the parts of a discourse' (1641), 'the parts which precede or follow any particular passage or text and determine its meaning' (1568). Context derives from the word meaning to weave or knit together, so the use of 'context' to apply to the built environment can be thought of as the return of the word to the physical realm after its exclusive sojourn in the linguistic. In the physical world, context will have a dimensional and a historical dimension, both of which go to make up the layering of a place. Context is inescapable for the interventionist; the work is clearly inseparable from its context.[1] It is almost always a more complicated matter than context and pure architecture. It is a cause of the intimacy that the designer must cultivate with the given building, and this equally has no limit of scale. It relates to the intrinsic qualities and conditions of the given, and to its setting.

A building is either one that must appear unchanging, an exemplar from another time, removed from the everyday, or it is a building that is available for alteration, generally but not always for the assimilation of a new use. If a building is altered once, it becomes generally a candidate for other future changes. It becomes an element within the continuity of the city. Such a building therefore may be properly considered as being in process, in contrast to the unchanging chosen paradigm. It will need properly to carry evidence of its provenance, of its contemporary affiliations, and not to be sealed against future alteration.

Alteration has no limit of scale. Groups of buildings, and their context, may be considered in a similar manner to the individual building. The significance of context at an urban scale is made apparent by the paucity of a single building surviving, like an impostor, within a comprehensive redevelopment (Figure 9.1). Because of the context, the work in a way is never quite complete: it is more like a stage reached in a process which is slower than life itself. The architect and the furniture designer on the other hand might be said to be

9.1   Survivor becomes impostor: St Giles, Cripplegate and the Barbican, London

linked by the desire for completion, the impulse to make a totality; this may suggest why so many of the greatest furniture designers have also been architects.[2]

Alteration comes about as a function of the general strategies of conservation, particularly in urban areas. It comes about as a consequence of a general wish to keep things as they are. This then is the paradox of change, which at least invites synthesis. Its justification, beyond the limits of sentimentality, is one of change of use or occupation being required in order to give new life to a building or a quarter, and so to ensure their vital continuance within the fabric of the city. In serving the purposes of apparent conservation, such change is expected to be implemented so as to leave clear – and, as has been argued here, to clarify, to make more explicit even – the nature of the host building or district. This clarification is the shift argued in the previous chapters, in comparison to historical arguments regarding conservation and restoration. In addition, supporting arguments propose that such purposes are best served by radical strategies of intervention, degrees of alteration that previously only careless casual history has wrought on the city. So at the outset, let it be said that caution should accompany any enthusiasm prompted by what has been written herein, but equally courage also.

Interventional design contains a set of natural antagonisms, which must be recognized and dealt with in the work of alteration and the approaches to it. The antagonisms are contained within the installation of the new use into the existing. They range from the practical to the problems of style, and will include the clash of established and intended hierarchies of use and space, of entrance and circulation. Buildings will resist alteration in several respects; these will be made clear by a contemplation of the limits of alteration for any given subject.

The assumption that Modernist interventions using pure forms are universally applicable regardless of the style of the host building, as hinted at in the project in Rome described in the previous chapter, tends to meet other objections at a slightly larger scale. There are several oppositions between the nature of Modernist and Classical buildings that are not easily dismissed if a successful mutual integration of one with the other is to be considered. Kenneth Frampton seems to refer to these difficulties in the title of his essay in *Five Architects*, 'Frontality versus Rotation'.[3] This duality can perhaps stand for a series of others that contrast Classicism with Modernism in architecture.

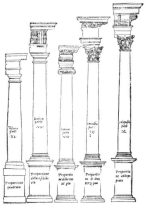

The Five orders. Pl. 1 (above): Serlio's woodcut of 1540, the first presentation of the Orders as a complete and authentative series. Pl. 2 (right): Claude Perrault's version, 1676, engraved on copper, reflects the greater precision and scholarship of its time.

9.2a   The persistence of the Orders: the five Orders, by Serlio (1540) and by Claude Perrault (1676)

9.2b   The Persistence of the Orders

One might add to this: symmetry (on one or more axes) versus asymmetry; axial planning (linear or co-axial) versus open plan; façade versus transparency; seriality versus abstracted elevations;[4] and the altered status of the ceiling in Modernist buildings compared with the Renaissance (Figures 9.2a and 9.2b).

Frontality itself equally implies both a front and a back, whereas Modernist composition aims to deny such a hierarchy, and instead tends to give an equality to all sides, which, because of this, then wants to be free-standing whenever possible so as to make this evident. The façade in a building, as implied in the title of the essay just mentioned, is also a contrast of supposed viewpoint, comparing the static square-on view of the Classic with the perambulatory, cinematographic, moving viewpoint, the eye moving unencumbered through space, as advocated by Le Corbusier and others, sometimes referred to as the *promenade architecturale*.

The potential conflict and discomfort between rectilinear and curvilinear plans and elevations should also be noted, when imposed one upon the other.

The Classic plan is ordered, axial, sequential and tending towards symmetry where space allows, composed of discrete spaces, of rooms, with a distinct hierarchy matched to its circulation[5] (Figure 9.3).

The Modernist free plan, as propounded by the great man in the Five Points, is akin, as suggested earlier, to being able to draw the plan with the freedom of an artist (Figure 9.4). The free plan from Loos onwards[6] is to be essentially wandering, open and indeterminate, and ambiguous regarding spatial conclusion and division.[7] As much as the elevation, the plan is an agent of the transparency that Modernism requires of the built form, of a diminished difference between interior and exterior.[8] The Classic plan has a hierarchy of entrance, circulation and spaces; the Modern plan tends to dilute or diminish this formality.

The blatant contrast between Classic and Modern is the tendency to symmetry in the first and the commitment to asymmetry in the second.[9] One would think that it would be wiser to devote oneself entirely to one or the other than attempt to work them together. The topic of symmetry, in that the designer must sometimes try to reconcile it to its opposite, is one that the interventionist cannot afford to dismiss, as sometimes the contemporary architect is tempted to do. It needs to be studied.[10] Immanuel Kant in 1783 realized while studying his hand in a mirror that space introduces a difference between two similar and equal things.[11]

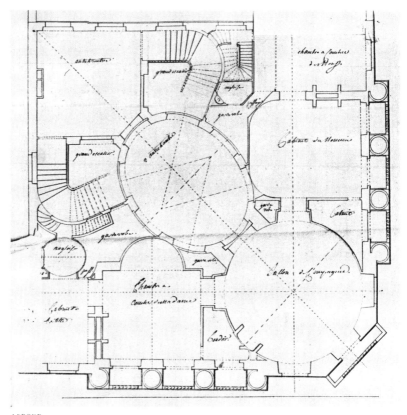

LEDOUX
164 Hôtel de Montmorency, 1770: plan, original
design.

9.3   The Classic plan: Ledoux, Hotel de Montmorency, Paris, 1770

It might also be said again that there are certain affinities between the nature of ruins and Modernist aesthetic: for instance, in both there is an explicit architectonics, a loss of decoration, and an inherent transparency. A ruin, however, may also contain the traces of a Classic plan, composed as it is of axes and rooms. In a ruin, therefore, they both may co-habit. This might suggest that the idea of ruination may be a key element in allowing a deeper integration of new and existing built form, and that transparency may be, in an important way, a medium for the resolution of the conflicts outlined above, of the assimilation that the act of intervention must seek.

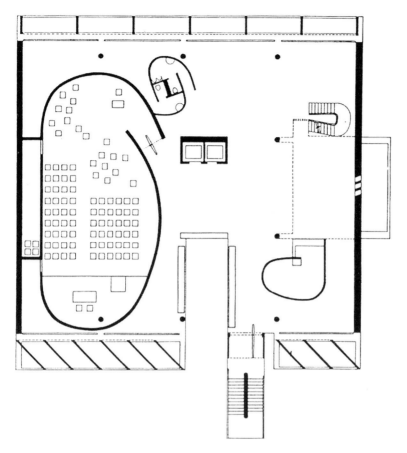

9.4   The free plan: the Millowners Association building by Le Corbusier in India, 1954

The attempted conflation of the contemporary and the Classic is the common-place work of alteration, and perhaps one can detect the possibility of a rich potential complexity if this is achieved.

The answer to how much a building can be changed is contained within statement by Giancarlo di Carlo.[12] It must not become 'as limp as a sack' into which anything can be placed; this is primary admonition to the designer. The work of alteration that always involves destruction can claim to be legitimate only through the act of carrying over a building from the past to give it new life in the present. Works of intervention are inevitably violent; the designer must make legitimacy for his or her work in the same way that the poet makes truth in poetry.[13] The sources of legitimacy are found equally in reference to the prototype, archetype, paradigm or model from which the host building derives, and also from the particular, the host building's distinguishing characteristics, acquired at its inception and subsequent to that.

Any building can be considered as ascertained by five aspects: its footings, plan, section, elevation and profile. These can be guarantors of the building's continuance if they can be reconstituted from what survives in the alteration. One may think that this is a straitjacket, but if one thinks that if only half a mono-axial symmetrical building survives, then reconstitution would still be conceivable.[14] Looked at in isolation, this would seem almost the opposite of restraint, offering, it would seem, too great a licence. However, if taken as one of a set of requirements regarding the five aspects, a programme of potential alteration comes about which allows for rich and complex new work to the host building.

Taking the combination of footings and profile, it seems that alteration needs to be contained roughly within the volume of the host building, that any disproportionate extension either vertically or horizontally breaks out of the envelope of alteration. I believe this to be true: alteration as an art is not a means for enlarging buildings. However much I try to appreciate famous extensions, for instance the extension to Gothenburg City Hall by Gunnar Asplund,[15] such projects seem to be incapable of attaining the degrees of assimilation and fusion of the new with the existing that must characterize a true work of alteration.

One might object that there are other famous additions that radically alter one or other of the five aspects, and one has to admit that above the line of the cornice has habitually been treated as unregulated territory. One must concede that new work can be rested upon an existing building with interesting consequences. The roof has been the site of extreme invention that would not fall within any of the limits set out above. The work of Coop Himmelblau in Vienna springs immediately to mind, in particular the extension for the lawyers' offices,[16] as does the addition to the Villino Alatri Sacri in Rome by Mario Ridolfi (1948–49)[17] (Figure 9.5).

The most revered of additions, the twin towers by Nicholas Hawksmoor added to the Gothic Westminster Abbey in the eighteenth century, might be put forward as an exception to the rule proposed above. But this is just the

9.5   Above the cornice: Villino Alatri in Rome, 1948–49; architect: Mario Ridolfi

point: the towers make a version of the intended original profile; towers on
the completed bases at the west end were certainly planned by the original
masons, only their exact nature is forever lost to us. By working to this schema,
one might say Hawksmoor was working towards a *model* that was other than
an actuality. The towers are works to an uncompleted building, so do indeed
lie within the strictures laid out above and elsewhere, and in so doing they
establish a truth through the genius of the architect regarding the origins of
the abbey.

The addition of the two towers on existing Gothic bases at the west end of Westminster Abbey are the culmination of Hawksmoor's strange quest to marry the contemporary Baroque with the departed Gothic, started while working for Wren and continued thereafter. One might say that this peculiar impulse becomes the singular characteristic of the English Baroque. The calm grace and quiet beauty of the two towers, which require a second look even from the most knowing to see them as additions, mark an extremely rare level of synthesis. These were his last executed work; they prove the possibility of the project of self-effacement leading to the clearest, most lucent evidence of genius.

One might contrast Hawksmoor's work with the crude siting of Henry VII's chapel, and the manner in which it is banged onto the east end of the abbey. In itself, it is undoubtedly a masterpiece of the English late fascination with the Gothic, but as an addition to the abbey it is assertive and corrupts one of the original building's defining characteristics, the run of buttressing which once fanned around the east end of the choir. The chapel, in its over-assertiveness, was added in an almost opposite manner to the addition of the towers at the west end 235 years later.

It is also certain that the original masons were intending to construct a tower or steeple on the crossing: there is a model in the abbey, once kept in the north wing of the crossing, of a proposal by Sir Christopher Wren for a spire on the crossing. I was once told that the building has only ever moved significantly at the crossing, and that the weight of a structure above it would have probably prevented even this. At the moment, the roof here is closed by a shallow pyramid, which makes one doubt the claim of the universality of pure form. The idea now of adding a tower, a spire or anything else at the crossing would I think be met with disdain or dismay by the establishment; this is an indication of strictures within our own times which clearly did not apply in Hawksmoor's day.[18]

All forms of environmental design are a compendium of the formal and the social. In many ways, style mediates between the two.

The relationship between interventional design and architecture is as the relationship between temporality and timelessness, while one takes note in passing that temporal is different from temporary. The interventional designer is an agent of temporality, of change and of altering styles of inhabitation. Therefore, he or she needs to be fully conscious of such changes, and if possible ahead of their full expression. This is the business of the designer; for generations it has been the art student's special province. Fashion, with its imbalance of extremes of acceptance and rejection, is the quickened context upon which the designer must gaze and acknowledge, more so than the architect. It is that which will test the designer's discrimination and control to withstand the mood swings of fashion in order to make work of lasting value. The temporal is in response to the needs, habits and desires of a particular age, which through our careful art must affect the building but not diminish its role in Rossi's terms, as a 'silent monument' of the city, or damage its dumb inimitable presence. Old buildings mean different things to different ages; it is the meaning that is transitory. Alteration may be described then as being the agent of temporality, of the re-colonization of the existing, but equally the agent of the abiding.

If a building is to be altered, the chances are it will be altered again. The designer therefore has responsibility for a building's past, its present and indirectly its future. The interventionist makes a contribution to a continuum, which is the life of the host building.

The old adage of interior design – that it introduces new life into old buildings – seems to me to be still a relevant description of the activity. Buildings are taken over in the recurrent victory of the living over the dead, new ways of life replacing the old. The object of alteration is to translate a building into the present, in so doing making it suit a modern way of life. The new organization imposed on the building in the course of its being changed for new uses is in part guarantee of this transformation.

Occasionally there have been building restorations that seek to reinstate the life once lived there, including the restitution of dress, manners and conduct of life. In the light of alteration being a form of translation, from the past into the present, however, these would seem to be delusions.[19]

In the pursuit of the re-colonization of an altered building, it is easier to understand that, within limits, function will fit to space in a way that is an inversion of the founding law of functionalism, of form following function. The imprecision of fitting space to use is of course a necessary condition of any change of use being visited upon the built environment.

As a consequence of alteration, it must often be the case that the clarity of the spatial organization is disrupted by the new work. This is not always detrimental, as described earlier, for new ways of moving through the building will allow for one of the chief pleasures of intervention, a previously unavailable experience of the spaces, perhaps in a new sequence and allowing new points of view. Such an imposition of a new spatial and circulatory hierarchy will allow the same privileges previously available only to thieves or ghosts, that is a novel view of the original hierarchy, which will now be a relic and memorial of previous occupation.

New use is a transgression of the original use, and the new occupant is therefore like a thief or an adulterer on the verge of exposure.

One may wonder if this is the whole story, if there is no contagion either between the host building and the new conduct of life introduced into it, if this new life is antiseptic, untouched by the context, if the pleasures of colonizing the existing are limited to this detached voyeurism.

Winston Churchill once said, 'We make the buildings, and then they make us.' Having at another time considered the relationship between spatial arrangement and sociability,[20] certain things can be said about the consequence of certain spatial arrangements (Figures 9.6 and 9.7). Transparency[21]

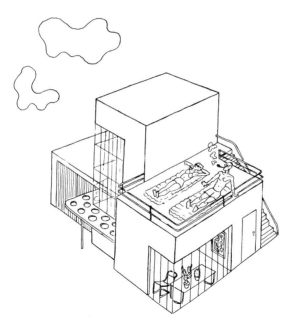

9.6   Styles of life and architecture 1, as observed by Osbert Lancaster, *Here of All Places* (1959)

9.7   Styles of life and architecture 2, as observed by Osbert Lancaster, *Here of All Places* (1959)

in application tends to make open, unhindered vistas that in consequence need a supporting cellular arrangement of spaces, small separated rooms, to become habitable. This causes a certain inhibition of conduct in the first, because of the casual surveillance endemic there, and a very private behaviour in the second, which will tend towards the furtive and secretive.

The sequence of rooms of the Classic plan, for instance in the plans of the houses by Robert Adam in central London (Home House in Portman

Square, the Derby House, the William Wynn House in Berkeley Square[22]), is a matrix and support for a more complex sociability; an arrangement of discrete spaces, which are then formally related axially, an arrangement of vistas, conclusions and fresh vistas. Might it not be true, therefore, almost as an echo of functionalism, that the occupation of old buildings affects how we behave one to another.[23]

The similarities between collage and intervention make available to the designer a range of practices and strategies common to the artist, especially the use of the accidental and the improvisational[24] in carrying through the work. Both are the processes of making a composition from disparate elements, old and new, found and given. The similarities between interventional composition and the work of the Synthetic phase of Cubism must be apparent (Figures 9.8a, 9.8b and 9.8c).

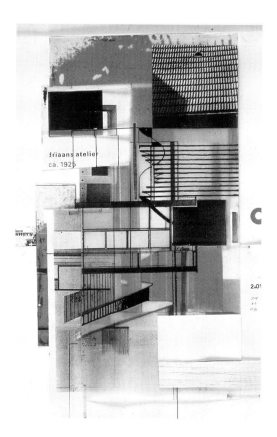

9.8a   Collage as a compositional tool for intervention: Collage by Richard Blurton

9.8b   Collage by Vivi
        Saveras

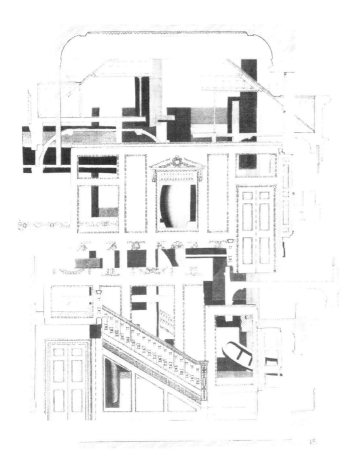

9.8c   Collage by Andy Bate

The connections in another way, in terms of content and new meaning generated by unpredictable encounters, may be less obvious. This is of particular significance to the new occupation of the existing. A re-used building is one that was once considered obsolete. In this way, architecture is unlike machines: it is made of ideas, whereas the machine can be taken and trashed following obsolescence. Re-colonization of existing buildings has similarities to the collage work of Max Ernst.[25] Alteration may always contain an element of the surreal (Figure 9.9).

9.9   *Loplop ivre de peur et de fureur*, Max Ernst: 'the complete act, as that of love, will make itself known naturally every time the conditions are rendered favourable by the given facts; the coupling of two realities, irreconcilable in appearance, upon a plane which apparently does not suit them'

Degrees of change are questions of style rather than quantity. The existing hierarchies of a host building may be completely overturned by alteration;
the survival of their legibility, however, is another matter. The elements of intervention might be said to consist of selective partial restoration and surviving
fabric, new and worn parts, precise ruination, the armature and the new work,
additions and removals (Figure 9.10). The precise destruction which alteration
requires is akin to dissection. All of these acts are based upon a view of the
host building gained from the processes of stripping back.

Leon Krier proposed a 'creative (forward looking) restauration' of a
derelict Modernist masterpiece in contrast to a 'conservative restauration
(nostalgic)' (Figure 9.11).[26] There are two aspects of the outcome as proposed,
one might say two new taboos of alteration which are indulged. The first is a
question of style, although this is a reversal of the more common practice, as
here the neutrality of Modernism has been changed by Classicism. If one
assumes that this rule of 'creative restoration' is a generic proposition, and
consequently does not forbid the opposite translation of a Classic building
through such a process of restoration into a Modernist finished work, one can
see the damage visited on the existing through such an approach. The style
of the original has been replaced by another. It is then a transgression; the

9.10   Partial restoration and the existing

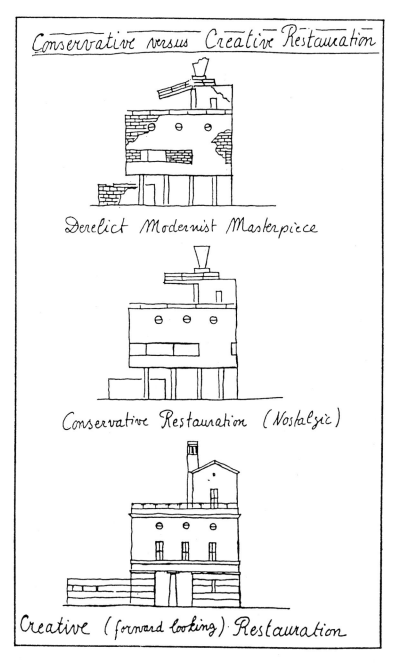

9.11   *Architecture or Fate* by Leon Krier

style above all must survive (as at Ise), and even be clarified by an act of alteration. This proposal is the destruction of the host building's very being, the corruption of an urban artefact, the wrecking of presence, that which a proper work of translation will be intent on carrying over from one age into the next.[27]

Perhaps an equal transgression is that this is a project of completion, one that aims to remove the building from the cycle of alteration that will see it into the present and also allow for later translations to ensure its continuing active existence.[28] A building must not be changed beyond recognition, its essential nature has to be assured by the work of alteration, discerned by the act of alteration; its poetic duration depends upon it.

NOTES

1 One should note in contrast the tendency in world architecture of recent years of making signature or iconic buildings, which, like the first Guggenheim, are intended to stand free of or to contradict their various contexts; or, as Rem Koolhaas recently said, to make their own contexts.

2 One should add also that great furniture designers have been architects, most famously Gerrit Rietveld. When I first visited the Schröder House in Utrecht, I was surprised to see it attached to the flank wall of its neighbour. My feeling is that early illustrations of the house set out to disguise this context. This would have been only proper, as the house represents a universal solution, an archetype, and is consequently detached theoretically from any actual positioning. The drawings of De Stijl, notably those by Theo Van Doesburg using axonometric projection, show structures as if they are floating in space; no context is suggested or indicated. In this way, pure architecture, in its claim to a universality, rationally has as a result an antipathetical stance towards context.

3 This is taken from the introductory piece to *Five Architects: Eisenman, Graves, Gwathmey, Hejduk, Meier*, ed. Arthur Drexler (New York: Wittenborn, 1972). Although this is the title of the essay, the topic is not explored to any degree in the text; it feels more like a comment on his fellow contributor Colin Rowe's earlier essay comparing Le Corbusier and Palladio's villas ('The Mathematics of the Ideal Villa', in *The Mathematics of the Ideal Villa and Other Essays*, Cambridge, Mass.: MIT Press, 1976). That essay sought to establish certain similarities between the Mannerist and Modernist villas. The conflict of 'frontality and rotation' was perhaps thought by Frampton to be an oversight or an omission, an obvious difficulty that had been ignored by Rowe in the earlier comparison.

4 It seems to me that issues concerned only with surface, such as decorated versus pure surface, are not the obstructions to resolution that the preceding list might be; in fact, the chance of any truth attaching to the proposition of the universality of Modernist insertions relies four square upon the easy co-habitation of pure with decorated surfaces in the finished work. The phenomenon of the triumph of the pure surface over the articulated Classical surface at the beginning of the twentieth century probably deserves a book of its own. A contribution to understanding the Classic order can be found in Frances Yates, *The Art of Memory* (Chicago: University of Chicago Press, 1966), which investigates in part the use of Classical architecture as a device for lodging specific facts at specific places as part of a spatial matrix of memory, at once in the mind and in the world. It can be understood that this is an ability of the Classical façade which would be found missing in the plain undifferentiated Modernist façade. One is tempted to say that the non-referential nature of undecorated Modernism is the clearest sign of its progressive nature; it is an allurement to forget the past.

5 Any designer who has unwittingly wandered into the iron grip of axial symmetry while seeking a resolution to a plan will know its unforgiving power, the mirror-image insistence of a move on one side being matched with an answering equal move on the other.

6 The two contrasting approaches of Loos and Le Corbusier are explored by Werner Oechslin in 'Raumplan versus Plan Libre', *Daidalos* 30 (1988), pp. 42–45.

7 In fact the Modernist plan, in needing to cope with the usual activities of any building, tends to make arrangements of minimal compartmentalized spaces to accompany the swaths of unencumbered open planning. When teaching at the Architectural Association with Robin Evans in the 1970s, we came to typify the Modernist plan as being a combination of all open and all closed, of the very big or the very small, as manifest in the minimal dwelling fixation of Modernism. Thus the Modernist prescription for spatial division seems to lack a middle scale somehow, such as was proposed by Palladio when he said a house is composed of large, small and medium-sized rooms.

8 Transparency was discussed in Chapter 1 as being one of the founding qualities of Modernism in architecture. One seminal text dominated discussion of this subject from the date of its publication in 1963 (Colin Rowe and Robert Slutsky, 'Transparency: Literal and Phenomenal: Part I', *Perspecta* 8, pp. 45–54). Only in recent years has anyone pointed out the numerous contradictions in the piece. The work sets out to compare modern Cubist, Leger and Purist paintings with certain key Modernist buildings. In particular, in comparing the Bauhaus of Gropius and Meyer (1925–26) and the Villa Stein-de-Monzie of Le Corbusier (1926–27) the piece seeks to establish a superiority for the latter over the former, in terms of both complexity and intention. The writing suggested that the architect might work in the same manner as the fine artist, and this may have been a reason for the reverence accorded it on both sides of the Atlantic. It may also account for its longevity.

Detlef Mertins, in 'Transparency: Autonomy and Relationality', *AA Files* 32 (1996), pp. 7–8, set about chasing down the contradictions in the text. In particular, although the analysis of Rowe and Slutsky uses as its prime reference post-perspectival paintings, the buildings are analysed from a central static viewpoint, including the final reference to the unbuilt League of Nations project of 1927 by Le Corbusier. Mertins quotes one of their key sources back at them:

> Kepes' opening section on 'plastic organization' laid the theoretical foundation (interpolated from Gestalt theory) for his claim that these other forms of representation – at once more primitive and more modern – were also more natural. He suggested that, like the anatomist, the perspectivalist achieved knowledge as well as optical and scientific mastery of nature only at the expense of the living, moving aspects of the body, 'the flux of the innumerable visual relationships that the visible world has for the spectator'. For Kepes, perspective 'froze the living, fluctuating wealth of the visual field into a static geometric system, eliminating the time-element always present in the experience of space, and thus destroying the dynamic relationships in the experience of the spectator' (G. Kepes, *The Language of Vision*, Chicago, 1961. First pub. 1944).

The Rowe and Slutsky piece seems to dismiss out of hand Le Corbusier's principle of *la promenade architecturale*, adopting instead the fixed central viewpoint, in the case of the Villa Stein somewhere down the end of the garden. The authors were clearly disengaged from the experiential aspects of transparency.

This note touches on the formal nature of transparency in architecture. A note on its significance regarding sociability appears elsewhere.

9 Symmetry acquired a bad reputation in the twentieth century, and is consequently little referred to or understood now. In a special issue of *Daidalos* (15, March 1985) Dr Robin Middleton begins 'Symmetry: A French Obsession' (p. 71), which is his contribution:

> 'The great formal gardens of Vaux-le-Vicomte and Versailles that Andre Le Notre laid out in the seventeenth-century are not exactly symmetrical, yet they provide an image of symmetry, indeed they provide the symmetrical image of French architecture and landscape design. Symmetry has long been something of a French obsession; it embodies all their notions of grandeur, magnificence, order and even grace; it constitutes perhaps the Frenchness of their architecture. Just as the picturesque, whatever its origins, serves to epitomize the English sensibility . . . In 1673, Claude Perrault, translating the only full-scale treatise on architecture

to have survived since classical antiquity, Vitruvius' ten hallowed books, made bold to denote the Greek term 'symmetria' – a harmony derived from proportional relationships – by no more than 'proportion', and to take over the term symmetry for the French.

In the Editorial (p. 13), Bruno Reichlin records: 'It is the same sense of admiration that caused J. F. Blondel to praise the "wit, taste, and intelligence" of a Françoise Franque who successfully created a regular lay-out of rooms and perfectly symmetrical interiors even on extremely irregular plots.' The French brilliance at fitting axial plans to awkward sites is well documented in the book *Forme et Deformation, des Objets Architectureaux et Urbains* by Alain Borie, Pierre Micheloni, Pierre Pinon (Paris: Ecole nationale superieure des Beaux-Arts, 2nd edition, 1984).

The axis gained notoriety as the chosen plan-type of the Third Reich, as described in the same issue of *Daidalos* by Anna Teut ('Axis and Symmetry as a Medium of Subordination: Nazi Architecture Redivivus'). The article is headed with two quotations: 'The new architecture has utterly destroyed the axis of symmetry, and has as a result placed front and rear, left and right and even, where possible, up and down on a par with each other. Neither the one nor the other predominates (Theo van Doesburg, 1922)'; 'The greater the demands which the modern state makes on its citizens, so much the mightier must the state then seem to them . . . Our opponents may suspect it, our supporters must know it as a fact: our buildings are erected to underpin this authority (Adolf Hitler, 1933)'.

In other fields also the issue of symmetry, the reflected sameness about axes, the strangeness of right and left, is of equally critical importance. On the back cover of *The Molecule and its Double* by Jean Jacques (trans. Lee Scanlon, New York: McGraw-Hill, 1993) is this statement:

> Science is haunted by an enigma: Amino acids, which make up living matter, are able to exist, chemically speaking, in two forms, a left and a right, like our two hands, yet strangely enough they are all found to belong to the same 'hand'. Pasteur said that these natural molecules were 'dissymmetrical'. Another discovery has just re-opened the question. The Universe itself, we find, is characterized by a decisive break in symmetry, one that has given matter the upper hand over antimatter.

10 Laurie Anderson, in a recent performance at the Barbican Theatre, London, referred to the 'claustrophobia' of symmetry.

11 Immanuel Kant, Prolegomena to Any Future Metaphysics (1783), quoted in Jean Jacques, *The Molecule and its Double*, trans. Lee Scanlon (New York: McGraw-Hill, 1993), p. 7.

12 'If a building is changed too much, it becomes as limp as a sack' (*Space and Society*, 1988, n.p.). This way of treating buildings will be familiar to all. In London, notoriously the Nash Terraces in Regent's Park were demolished except for their façades, which were carefully kept in place while being backed up with new buildings. This approach was extensively used in the recent rebuilding of Beirut. All cities will have similar examples.

13 The idea of legitimacy struck me while visiting the Unite d'Habitation in Marseille, in August 2003, where it seemed apparent that interventional work in any post-war housing block needed at the outset to look at, to visit and to study this prototypical, archetypical example of the genre, the huge, tranquil Unite, this closest approximation that exists of an ideal form, of the model. Reference to the model then is an act of validation for alteration.

14 In the nineteenth century, a Romanesque tower on the west front of Canterbury Cathedral was demolished in order to complete the symmetrical front implied by the Gothic remodelling, with a new tower to mirror the one left standing. It is difficult not to feel that something was lost by this, that was not quite compensated for by the resultant symmetry. This illustrates the dangers of the desire to complete.

15 Peter Blundell-Jones has published excellent essays on this building and its architect (*Gunnar Asplund*, London: Phaidon, 2005). I am still not convinced that it is not a rather different exercise, very demanding for all that, of placing a new building next to an existing monument. It is included in a very good book *New Buildings in Old Settings* (an exhibition catalogue by the Bayerische Architektenkammer & Die Neue Sammlung, Munich: State Museum of the Applied Arts, 1978), as is Scarpa's work at Castelvecchio in Verona, which is quite a different kettle of fish. This book is one of the very few that deals with issues of urban context; the non-contextual urges within pure architecture have been noted earlier. From the work published in the book, it would appear that

certain Italian architects are most accomplished at this subtle and difficult art; it contains clues as to how the contagion between the existing and the new, through the application of a scrupulous craft, might be advanced.

16   Co-op Himmelblau, roof extension containing a conference room for lawyers' office, Vienna, 1988–89.

17   Illustrated in Marco Frascari 'Some Mostri Sacri of Italian Architecture', trans. Alan Sheridan, *AA Files* 14 (1987), p. 46.

18   Standing at the foot of Whitehall, looking out at the wonderful assemblage of the Palace of Westminster, St Margaret's church, Westminster Abbey and Middlesex Town Hall, one can be persuaded that this is the best view in all of London. It is the compiled work of centuries; that it might now be considered untouchable is a characteristic of our time, not of its history.

19   In recent years, a house was restored in Spitalfields, London, back to the reinstatement of levels of servicing and methods of lighting as were in use at the time the building was built in the seventeenth century, and the occupant then lived out a life as dictated by this level of amenity. The house was opened as a museum on certain days of the week during the resident's lifetime. This strikes me as being similar to the historical quarter in Williamsburg, Virginia, where a population of actors is employed to act out during working hours, in costume, speech and practices, the life of two or three hundred years ago. Nobody lives there. The actors are entreated to project the air of nonchalance. One may visit, move among the populace, converse and wonder whether you or the ersatz populace is the interloper. This too is an echo of the 'hermits' employed by the English landowners of the Enlightenment, who were engaged to live in grottos on the newly landscaped estates and were given strict rules of conduct. There is a brilliant and frightening parody, written by George Saunders (*Pastoralia*, New York: Riverhead Books, 2000), of the lives of employees playing 'authentic' cavemen in a fictional theme park in the near future.

The tenuous link between architectural style and dress and behaviour is largely virgin territory. One of the few pioneering pieces is by Ernst Gombrich ('Styles of Art and Styles of Life', *Domus* 744 (December 1992)). At the beginning the author makes a well-deserved acknowledgement:

> I can best explain what I mean by the title of my essay with two plates from the late Osbert Lancaster's satirical survey of the history of style, which I consider the best textbook on the topic ever published. The first illustrates the style of life and of art known as the Rococo; the other is entitled 'Twentieth-Century Functional' and I must leave it open whether it represents the style of a vanished epoch or one of the future.

20   Work carried out by the author and Dr Robin Evans while teaching together at the Architectural Association, Diploma Unit 4, London, in the 1970s, on an architecture of conviviality, of living together. The work is the background to Evans's article 'Figures, Doors and Passages', *Architectural Design* 4 (March 1979) and my own 'Pictorial and Sensual Space', *AA Quarterly* 8, No. 4 (1976). We took the view at the outset that Modernism was a sometimes uncomfortable alliance between an aesthetic and an intention to reform society. Before we worked together, Bob had, as part of his Ph.D., looked into the origins of the built form as a tool for social change and control in the eighteenth and nineteenth centuries. In particular his work on Jeremy Bentham's Panopticon is brilliant and original (see Dr Robin Evans, *The Fabrication of Virtue: English Prison Architecture 1750–1840*, Cambridge: Cambridge University Press, 1982). One should also record here the work of Stephen Willats, who since the 1960s has continuously worked to codify the relationship between modern monumental buildings and their inhabitants, concentrating mainly on housing blocks (Stephen Willats, *Between Buildings and People*, London: Academy Editions, 1996).

21   Transparency is the architectural response to the scientific understanding of space as infinite; it first gains expression in the post-Revolutionary projects of Boullee in particular, especially in his *Monument to Sir Isaac Newton*. From its inception, space as infinity, as without limit, began to marginalize the role of the room or any other form of discrete enclosure in architectural theory. It is a consciousness which dissolves the corporality of the built form, arriving in the twentieth century, through advances in glass production, with the ability to give unfettered expression to the idea of space as continuous, within and without, visually dissolving the divide between interior and exterior. The socially inhibiting qualities of transparency must be apparent to most, yet they are rarely discussed. Only an insomniac exhibitionist could be entirely pleased with a transparent house. The limits to such a type in an urban setting became clear with Mies van der Rohe's design for a house for the Berlin Building Exposition of 1931. In order to achieve a sense of consistent

infinitude, the boundary is walled and the spatial sequence is returned onto itself, chasing around the house, making an endless circuit. That the greatest icon of transparency, the Farnsworth House, should have to stand in an empty landscape should perhaps come as a surprise to no-one.

22 This is how Robin Middleton describes Robert Adam's style:

> Something of this more dynamic approach to internal spaces suffuses the architecture of . . . Robert Adam. Adam composed his interiors as a succession of related spaces, one counter-pointing the next, together making up an organic whole. His volumes, though geometrically related, were designed to be approached from oblique and unusual angles. The most celebrated example of his diagonal planning is the relationship between the second and third drawing rooms on the first floor of Derby House, London of 1773 to 1774, which he commissioned Benedetto Pastorini to record for the second volume of his *Works in Architecture* (1779). This view, showing the extension of space beyond the third drawing room into the Countess of Derby's dressing room, is unparalleled in contemporary architectural publications. The drama of the view, depicted in all its richness of light and shade, is new to eighteenth century conventions of domestic decorum. Other examples might be adduced, such as the arrangement of rooms on the first floor of Home House, 20, Portman Square, of 1773 to 1776, where the rooms form a circuit.
>
> (Robin Middleton, 'Soane's Spaces and the Matter of Fragmentation', in *John Soane, Architect*, ed. Margaret Richardson and MaryAnne Stevens, London: Royal Academy of Arts, 1999)

23 The Architectural Association itself occupies two large co-joined eighteenth-century houses in Bedford Square in London, which have retained a close semblance of the original spatial hierarchy, or at least the main component of it, from street into the ground floor, and up to the arrangement of grand rooms on the *piano nobile*. Much of the rest of the school is cellular, chaotic and in constant flux, but it is this spatial survival as the heart of the place upon which the famed sociability and informality of the school depends.

24 Improvisation: the art of improvising, to fabricate with what is to hand, combining disparate elements to create a whole; working with the accidental and the coincidental.

25 The late nineteenth-century interior was the setting for numerous strange and disturbing scenes in Max Ernst's collage 'novels': *La Femme 100 Tetes* (1929), *Reve d'une Petite Fille qui Voulot Entrer au Carmel* (1930) and *Une Semaine de Bonte* (1934). The last of these appeared in five booklets throughout 1934. Ernst had been born in the Rhineland in 1891, and the mood of catastrophe of the *Semaine* has been said to echo the events in his homeland at the time. The 'novel' was completed in three weeks while he was visiting friends in Italy.

On commenting on *La Femme 100 Tetes* (phonetically in French 'The Woman without a Head') Siegfried Giedion said:

> What can this be but a symbolic name for the nineteenth century and its restless meanderings? Here irrational images unmask the devaluation of symbols at work . . . Almost always the atmosphere is of violence and death. From a glassed bookcase of the 1850s, La Femme 100 Tetes in the guise of a plaster bust will perhaps fall out onto a learned bystander, while the stamped lion heads of the chairs come to life grimacingly changed into a giant ape, which the caption designates with Dadaistic impudence as 'the monkey who will be a policeman, catholic, or stockbroker.'
>
> These pages show how a mechanized environment has affected our subconscious. I once asked Ernst about the origin of his novels, and he replied: 'They are the reminiscences of my first books, a resurgence of childhood memories.'
>
> (Siegfried Giedion, *Mecanigation Takes Command*, Oxford: Oxford University Press, 1948)

26 This is contained in *Architecture: Choice or Fate*, Krier's most extensive exposition of his convictions and work (Windsor: Andreas Papadakis, 1998; the book is dedicated to *Mon Prince*). It comes at the beginning of the chapter 'Critique of a Modernist Ideology' (pp. 72–83), which contains the most virulent expression of his hatred of Modernism, in addition to outlining principles of 'restauration'. It begins with a dismantling of the restoration principles of the Charter of Venice, formulated during the second International Congress of Architects and Technicians of Historic Buildings in Venice in 1964; his robust manner of argument sets the scene for his proposed 'creative restauration'. The second part is an attack on Modernism. A mere half century ago Modernist movements claimed to have definitive solutions to all the problems of the built environment.

'Today, one truth is evident: without traditional landscapes, cities and values our environment would be a nightmare on a global scale. Modernism represents the negation of all that makes architecture useful: no roofs, no load bearing walls, no columns, no arches, no vertical windows, no streets, no squares, no privacy, no grandeur, no decoration, no craftsmen, no history, no tradition. Surely, the next step must be to negate these negations?' The chapter contains several examples of Krier's restorative projects at an urban scale; the project for the radical restoration of the Belvedere of San Leucio, Caserta, is a particularly convincing exercise.

27 As I write, the fate of Edward Durrel Stone's Huntingdon Hartford Museum at Columbus Circus in New York City hangs in the balance, with a proposed scheme of alteration that would destroy the unique cranky Mannerist Modernist character of the building, in particular by replacing the deeply considered white marble elevations. This in its turn would affect one of the most charming views in Manhattan, where standing on the sidewalk at 61st Street and 6th Avenue, looking south one can see Broadway and the avenue separate around the seemingly petite building, and looking down Broadway as it heads for the towering chasm of Midtown see a unique sequence of increasing urban scale. After the museum is the nineteenth-century New York Athletic Club on the left in this progression.

28 Some may object that this proposal is as proper as Alberti's conversion of the Tempio Malatestiano in Rimini, one that must be considered by all to be a work of genius. However, I think this is a reading only of the most famous photograph of the Temple, the black-and-white image from the three-quarter front view, the one that has to my knowledge been used exclusively to illustrate the double-natured compilation, to represent a purity of composition that is almost absent in actuality. Alberti's work partially encloses an earlier Gothic building, and the two fold assembly is also gloriously unfinished. This is Francesco Venezia speaking of the work in 'Transfiguration of the Fragment: The Architecture of Spoils', *Daidalos* 16 (1985), pp. 97–98:

> Does the unfathomable secret of this building lie in the integration of the marbles of Sant'Appolinare into the impressive structure of the blocks of Istrian rock? In the flash of a moment, the concrete presence of the material in the geometry of the rhythm brings together images far removed from each other. This building, which might give the impression of only trying to evoke the lasting, comforting greatness of a newly envisioned imperial age, also presents a subtle impression of dissolution resulting from the combination of the huge, unhewn stone blocks and the finely veined slabs taken from a building which reminds us of the decline of the very period thus evoked. A state of melancholy enters the picture as a variable reflection of two different states of consciousness.

CHAPTER 10

SOME RESOLUTIONS

TO DEMOLISH AND BUILD SOMETHING better is the legitimate purpose of architecture, in perpetuity, but this presupposes an assumption that not everyone can manage. On the other hand, the symbiotic or dependent nature, the feeling of subservience that infuses alteration, regularly provokes a sense of claustrophobia in many architects. It is possible that two contrary imaginations are involved. The paradox of architecture is that the adored city must in part be destroyed to allow for the new. The enigma of intervention is that one sets out to alter, but at the same time to be the advocate for a building.

All buildings are in an imperfect state, they are made of reflections of a model, which has generic status, and of particularities, or peculiarities. A purpose of alteration is to move the building in the direction of its model as discerned through the processes of stripping back. The outcome will properly have temporal qualities, from the overlay of changes on the original, but also will have, through the interest in archetype, timeless qualities. The work is a mediation between the processes of accretion and purification.

Two taboos of alteration are rendered obsolete by the realization of the lack of difference between restoration and conservation. They are the taboos against improvement and against copying.

All works to existing buildings related to their original condition are restorative, including those that are now generally considered to be conservation. As the original condition of the building is lost from the moment of its inception, works of restoration are imaginative, or a matter of judgement if a more sober description is required. The aims of restoration have been historically uncertain in most cases; it has been usual to assume that such work has been carried forward with some extraneous goal in mind, some precise knowledge regarding the original condition. At what exact moment was this certainty supposed to have occurred, when the last workman withdrew from the site, when the building was handed over to the client, or the Tuesday after that? It is illusory.

Intervention must aim to be always equal to the host building in some respect, and better in others, or else it is a failure. It is incontrovertible that the interventionist may be more talented than the original builders, as it is equally true that the opposite will also occur. Their effort in resuscitation[1] of the host building is akin to transcription in poetry and music.[2] The designer has it within his or her scope to clarify the intentions of the original builders through their intervention; this is a question of licence, and as with all creative undertakings, there can be no preordained promise of the excellence of the outcome.

Copying was ever present if unrecognized in the practice of altering buildings, and it needs now to be raised up, and considered paradoxically as a true component of alteration.[3] Restorative work is imitative and interpretive;[4] of course all 'conservation' work involves imitative work, but this somehow is considered the realm of the workmen or craftsmen, and so is relegated to beneath critical consideration. However, when considered critically, the impossibility of an exact copy opens the discussion onto the realm of imitation and parody and works *in the manner of* in the composing of new work and the existing.[5] Imitative work is an important project within the art or conscious craft of intervention, which requires awareness throughout of the dangers of mimicry and its potential for destabilization.[6] It should be considered as not of equivalence, but rather as an attempt at interpretation. Imitation is concerned with what is possible today; and imitative work, and its associate, variation, constitute a central project of intervention.

These two taboos are in actuality reflections of the same issue: the key to both is the status of the copy. As it is impossible to make an exact copy, both in terms of physicality and in undertaking, and as an equivalence is a misty destination, does the copy set out to be inferior to or an improvement on the original? What is set out here might through a proper reticence lead to nothing being attempted, but if the work of alteration is to go forward, and the client will usually have a view about this, then a programme of improvement may begin to be defined from the status of the imitative work.

Because of this, one may question if every intervention needs to be in a contemporary style, as suggested by William Morris. The argument today would surely be the same as the situation in the second half of the nineteenth century, which was as stricken with idiosyncrasy in matters of style as the beginning of this new millennium. The admonition relies on there being a single contemporaneous style, established beyond counter, and it falters in the absence of such a condition. In addition, as Modernist belief has space-making matched to specific uses, the fitting of new uses into existing spaces would seem to preclude this deeper motive for the implementation of Modernist form.[7]

The universality of Modernist work,[8] as suggested by Mondrian's work to his Paris studio,[9] might more properly be seen as an aspect, and confirmation, of a commitment to the abstract, and in particular geometric abstraction. Geometry, with its close correspondence between the ideal and the actual, the point without dimension, the line without width, it is an apt component of interventional work. Being without style, it stands outside of time and so can act as a trans-temporal medium for composition.[10] As Colin Rowe set out to explain in the 'Mathematics of the Ideal Villa',[11] there may be geometric correspondences between very different styles of building, and so geometry may also act as a medium for the blending of the new with the existing (Figures 10.1 and 10.2).

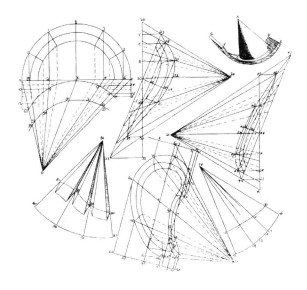

10.1   Guarini, *Architettura Civile* (1737)

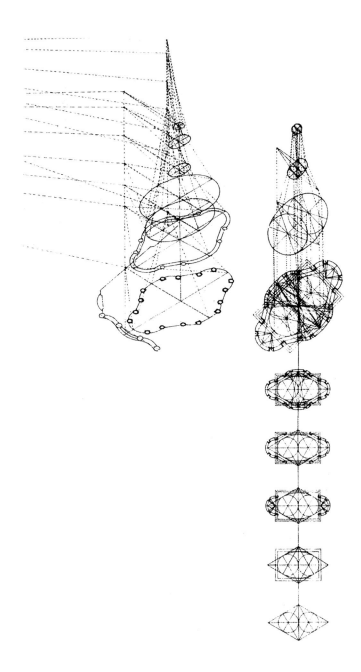

10.2   Project work at the Architectural Association (Peter Beard, Unit Master) 1996

To an altered building and the time-lapse camera, the occupants are like spirits, transitory and passing magically through what had once been floors and walls.[12] For the occupants, the new circulation of the altered interior may be like a journey through ruins, taking previously impossible routes, and having new, almost aberrant viewpoints as a result. An altered building explains itself; it is in this way an inhabited ruin. The ruin may, however, be neither accidental nor imprecise, as is made evident by the work of Gordon Matta-Clark. The altered condition may have qualities of exposure that previously one thought of as confined to drawings, such as sectional perspectives.

Alteration is breaking and entry, the precise cut, the strategic section exposed. It makes absences as well as additions. An over-reverent and potentially tiresome regard for every aspect of the existing can clog the creative mind. A clear diagram of intention, however radical, is more likely to lead to an effusive absorption of a new occupation into the host building.

The two conflicting types of spatial articulation, which seem destructive one of the other, need to be conflated in the work of alteration. Symmetry assumes completeness, and asymmetry suggests incompleteness, with the chance of addition and subtraction. This marriage of opposite styles requires that the remains of a symmetrical plan imply the complete; this need not be too restricting, for as noted elsewhere, half a symmetrical building can describe the whole (Figure 10.3). The use of transparency to unify and to integrate the new programme with the host building has been explored earlier in Chapters 7 and 9; the classic and the modern[13] can be worked through geometry and transparency, which are together the strongest tool for the work of intervention.

Change of use[14] almost always requires spatial and physical changes. Unlike Ise and the Villa Savoye, most alteration occurs as a result of change of use; this is the source of the new life of the building. The new use is one usually derived from expediency, from needs that may be outside of formal considerations. Unlike the making of a new building, the question of fit is different and more complex in re-use than in pure architecture. This disjuncture has its value.[15]

The aptness of the new occupation within the existing is derived from coincidence; such intersects are often not clear at the outset, and the search for them is commonly the longest phase of the design process. The process of insinuating new use into the given building is coloured throughout with reappraisal and reinterpretation. The fitting of the new into the existing is ever

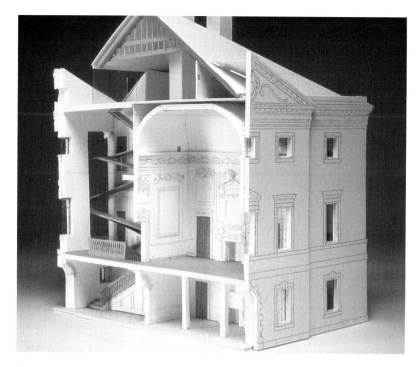

10.3   Marble Hill altered (project by Johanna Ahl, Kingston University, 1997)

a negotiation, and so the fit is likely to become less clear than the more explicit requirements that can be made of a new building, and of course the new identity often needs to be made explicit within the old context. The work will always provoke divided loyalties in this way. The designer needs an acute eye for the poetry of the everyday, of the play between the fleeting and the fixed, as this is how the success of the new colonization can best be appreciated or judged. The play between the new occupation and original use contains meaning for the overall work; use, re-use and seeming misuse are rife with significance, which may be other than spatial. The terminology of the plan contains an encounter between the past and the present, a contrast of form and function, a play of temporal differences, the salon and the boardroom, the inspection pit and the sacristy (Figure 10.4). Encounter is the essence of surrealism, and composition in interventional design is fired by unexpected encounters.

10.4   The poetry of the everyday: garage in Ferrara, 1967

New life is made manifest through new materials and new techniques of building; this is how a tenet of Modernism becomes a part of intervention, the strength of the new materials, as image and actuality. James Gowan has written that when it comes to details,[16] time is meaningless, the purposes of detailing remaining the same regardless of the age, whether for instance to cast off water or to ensure an enclosure or to give adequate support. While this is true, the choice of new materials will give it a temporal twist. This will apply to any age, as with the Adam brothers' insertion of the stone staircase in the Elizabethan wood-panelled Great Hall at Hatfield House. The designer is more inclined than the architect to experiment with new materials[17] (Figure 10.5).

The programme of intervention has the same aim as that of certain contemporary painters: to quote Sean Scully, the proposition that 'things must fit together'.

Regarding composition, allegiance to a particular style is usually the source of cohesion, consistency and coherence in architecture, and in other things. Such an allegiance can be almost religious in its intensity, and to stand outside of it might be considered heretical. One might reasonably claim

10.5   The designer's love of new materials: Ben Kelly's studio, 2005

that the great developments of architecture and design in the last century were manifestations of just such allegiances.[18] Such purity of production is unavailable to the interventional designer. She or he must seek other paths to composition, among which is collage, a means to engage confrontation and contradiction in composition.[19] This is a territory of real difficulty. The usual reliance on purity of style for coherence is familiar to all, but the results of its absence are far less certain. Alteration is best considered as a postmodern project, in that 'post-modernism acknowledges and ascribes importance to content, context, and to eclecticism, and considers appropriation one of its fundamental strategies'.[20] It is difficult on the other hand for the pure architect to celebrate eclecticism in other than words, as Robert Venturi was to find out, in contrast to working with the found or given as in interventional work.

An altered building is a complex thing, a set of co-habitations, where one style may emulate, parody or paraphrase another. It is the outcome of an encumbered struggle towards a norm, having regard for both the idea of paradigm and for the otherwise vernacular qualities of the host building or buildings. It will therefore contain comparative elements. If even through the most conscientious analysis some aspect of the host building remains unfathomable, whether in planning or in detail, abstract or material, such a feature then needs treating with special circumspection. The old push and pull between what Christopher Wren described as the two ideas of beauty[21] is the designer's constant companion in the difficult work of alteration.[22]

The ideal in alteration is the same as how Dr Kinsey[23] considered the normal in his work: it exists only as an idea, and as such it is suited to only allusion and is inimical to realization (Figure 10.6).

The existing needs to be broken in a manner to allow for a resolved inter-vention; greater dangers may lurk in doing too little. The work of intervention requires a certain savagery, otherwise a confused mélange of petty changes will result from a too reverent approach to the host building, and this will surely ultimately destroy it.[24] An altered building is not old fashioned, that is in the sense of being in Lionel Trilling's phrase 'inauthentic for the present time'.[25] There is necessarily something speculative in the nature of an altered building, that is a sense of the tentative, which eschews preclusion and false certainty.[26] Restoration aims to complete a building, and it has other purposes. Alteration is progressive and is not an attempted recuperation, such as a pure restoration sets out to achieve. It is in part like a rehearsal for a completed building.

10.6   The elusion of the ideal: Viollet-le-Duc's engraving of the 'perfect' Gothic cathedral (from *Dictionnaire raisonné*)

Restoration is an important component of alteration, but alteration is the agent of re-occupation rather than emptying buildings.

The approach to alteration requires that the designer strives to know everything, and then to improvise,[27] ever alert to the appearance of coincidence, the exquisite affirmation between the existing and the imposed. As ever, improvisation and repetition are twinned.[28]

That an old building should show its age would seem to have the ring of truth about it, which would in addition seem to support the far-flung crusades for authenticity. However, here is another seeming certainty that after a while begins to lose its firm footing in the mind. Modernist buildings seem to need to be restored as if brand new; look at the restoration of the Villa Savoye, or Duiker's Zonnestraal Sanatorium buildings near Hilversum, or any other examples of restored Modernist monuments. This would appear to be accepted wisdom, or at least convention, or the code of practice. One might be led to think that here is an odd confirmation of Le Corbusier's edict that the house is a machine, and so needs the same treatment as, for instance, a classic car. But in all these matters, time is still the architect to a certain extent. I remember, on my first visit to America, stopping in a high car park somewhere in the Sierra Nevada in California to watch the sunset. Similarly occupied, if occupation it was, were an elegant elderly couple with an equally elegant and elderly Chrysler Imperial. Both car and owners were venerable. The Chrysler was undeniably old, as were the owners, but because of the inevitable deterioration of the fittings – the worn leather seats, despite repeated treatment with saddle-soap or the like, the pitted chrome on the fenders – the original inspiration of the designers seemed all the more evident, because the temporal context was legible: one could see, without the distraction of illusion that restoration imparts, that this was an old car, better at transmitting the energy and elegance of the times when it was conceived and then mass produced.[29]

What are the consequences of making a three-hundred-year-old building appear new? Should a building not show its age? One might answer that a building may indicate its age in two distinct modes: it may be maintained, as is the Villa Savoye, as eternally new in order to give clear expression of a style; or it may, as Ruskin believed, gain its architectural status through the wear of time.[30] To maintain a building as seemingly new is a particular form of illusion. Equally, the condition in which the Parthenon is maintained is the result of judgement, as much as of its age. Savoye and the Parthenon are the same in being monuments preserved in a particular chosen condition, in a version that stands to represent authenticity.[31]

The differences between the aims of preservation and those of alteration are made more evident through cases such as these,[32] in contrast to alteration. Formally, for instance, restoration may reinstate symmetry, but alteration causes asymmetry. What is true of both Viollet-le-Duc and the restoration of the Villa Savoye is that the treatment of the built structure is intended as a completion and therefore also a curtailment. But this work is addressed to something other, to a building altered in order to remain in use, occupied and not removed from the transactions of the everyday, a building that has been altered to this end, to accommodate a new use or uses.

What is transient? What is considered ephemeral is a result of judgement. Is dust sacrosanct? One thinks of Man Ray's photograph of dust on Duchamp's *Great Glass*[33] and may be persuaded to consider it.[34] The fading painted advertisements on buildings, particularly those in France, a surviving spectacular neon sign,[35] a building might show its experience as well as its age. Are these contributions to authenticity or digressions? (Figure 10.7).

A surviving piece of the original[36] should, I suppose, be treated generally as sacrosanct, but there is ever the danger of *fetishism*. Does the authentic reside in the surface?[37] How then can it ever survive? The worn element, or surface, is a given (Figure 10.8). How a chosen material ages has a validity, even if it is not as comprehensive and exclusive as suggested by Ruskin.[38] If one accepts that the qualities imparted by time, through scuffing, wearing and the like, have an authenticity, this contrasts with the authentic upon which copying relies, the exercise that aims to ascertain original aspects of the host building.

10.7   What is transient?

10.8   Interior, Primrose Hill, 2006

The quest for the authentic is in part an attempt to curtail speculation or any other form of questioning, but even after admitting this, the itch remains. One might conclude that only the original impulse of the builders, to which they themselves may have been partly blind, is authentic. The physical remains are merely material evidence of that thought, realized in different cases with various degrees of success. The idea of the model, archetype or paradigm is one that is accompanied by the copy, or by work *in the manner of*, derived from an ideal that can only be known with precision in part. But one needs to remember that the worn is a given.

Authenticity, patina and the copy can be seen to constitute a triplet of ordinates, which allows the host building to be treated as the scientific object, as Damisch says of Viollet-le-Duc's method.[39] Stripping back then may proceed by the accepted sequence of hypotheses that must be supported by evidence found within the subject in order to stand. Within this too is the understanding that, as with all scientific truths, it is always interim, awaiting contradiction in its turn. This is the reason for the combination of restoration, the original and an uncertainty, all three present in any correct alteration.

NOTES

1   This term was first suggested to me by my friend Stephen Donald, who taught with me for many years, and was and continues to be a constant source of information, energy and inspiration.

2   Arnold Schoenberg, who made transcriptions of J. S. Bach, among others, said that it was the duty of the transcriber to set a piece free from weaknesses in the original in carrying out the work.

3   The French of course have been engaged for some time in the reinstatement of the legitimacy of copying. 'Plagiarism is necessary, progress implies it. It tightly squeezes an author's phrase, serves his expression, erases a false idea, replaces it with a just notion.' From Centre de Lautréamont, *Poesies*, vol. II (Paris: Librairie Gabrie Questroy et Cie, 1870), brought to my attention by Calum Storrie.

4   Unlike the rebuildings of Ise, this work is not necessarily ritualized, except in an informal manner through the under-praised processes of craftsmanship. One can imagine, however, work *in the manner of* might over time become a canon, amassed through the recognition of the generally accepted excellence of certain examples, probably from diverse projects.

5   One of the most valuable writings on the subject of imitation and related issues is Gerd Neumann, 'Like Yonder Cloud that is Very Like a Whale, On Eclecticism and the Meaning of Conservation', in *Daidalos* 8 (June 1983), p. 87: '"Electio", in the meaning thus attributed to it, is intimately connected by way of the concepts "imitatio" and "mimesis", with the problems of beauty and ideality, and the problems of establishing rules and standards for them. The existence of exemplars and exemplarity pre-supposes their perception and selection.'

6   Although reference has been made earlier (Chapter 5) to fine art practices regarding transcription and copying, certain contemporary artists, such as the Berliner Thomas Demand, deserve special mention.

   Known for his photographs of meticulously constructed environments of cardboard and paper, Thomas Demand uses source material from historical, political and media images. The resultant work enables an eerie merging of the boundaries between the imagined and real. His meticulous craftsmanship means that the photographs often look at first glance like real places. Critic Neville Wakefield observed Demand 'proposes architecture as silent witness to the pathologies of social disturbance'.

   (Parveen Adams, *AA Events List*, 3 February 2006)

7   This will further confirm the requirement of interventional training to contain the study without prejudice of architectural style. Such work has long been abandoned in schools of architecture everywhere, apart from a few trivial exercises in reactionary private institutions in the UK.

8　The universality of Modernism depends, as Cézanne recognized, upon the idea that everything is infrastructurally made up of combinations of pure forms. The true experimental proof of this in alteration is in the insertion of spaces that are the evacuated presences of pure form, the cube, the sphere, the cylinder, the cone, as with Matta-Clark's work at rue Beaubourg. Such operations may be as enabling work and as a bridge or mediation between existing and the new work.

9　Frans Postma, *26, Rue du Depart Mondrian's Studio Paris 1921–1936* (Berlin: Ernst & Sohn, 1995).

10　The designer's absorption in the power of line, point and arc should match that of the geometer. In addition to the work of Preston Scott Cohen discussed in Chapter 7, Peter Beard teaching at the Architectural Association in London has done exemplary work with respect to the role geometry plays in buildings. In 'San Carlino and the Cultivated Wild', *AA Files* 31 (1996), pp. 31–38, he describes an excellent project set in the school working with Borromini's San Carlino church in Rome. In introducing the work, the Unit Master writes:

> Brutta e deforma. Gotico ignorantissimo et corruttore dell 'Architeturra, infamia del nostro secolo.' Borromini was described by his contemporaries as 'a most ignorant "gotico" and a corruptor of architecture'. Using the work of this 'corrupt' figure and his 'ugly and deformed' church of San Carlino in Rome as a starting point, the project described in the following pages approaches themes of Baroque space principally through geometry. Anamorphic and other geometric projections, cupping, splaying and torsional distortion are used as elements of a complex synthesis. The church is read as a space of controlled savagery.

11　Colin Rowe, *The Mathematics of the Ideal Villa and Other Essays* (Cambridge, Mass.: MIT Press, 1976).

12　See Michael Wesely's book of long-exposure photographs of the rebuilding of MOMA in Manhattan, the Potsdamer and Pariser platzes in Berlin and other sites (Sarah Hermanson Meister, *Michael Wesely Open Shutter*, New York: The Museum of Modern Art, 2004).

13　One might note a similar conflict between the ornamented surface and the pure surface of Modernism. In this regard, the recent experiments by Herzog and de Meuren, in particular, in architectural decoration should be noted. These would suggest that there is now available a wider licence for the treatment of surfaces.

14　Probably at the outset I intended to write more extensively on the difficulties of fitting new uses into existing buildings. I now think this is best done by case studies, of some depth and intensity, and that has not fallen within the scope of this present enquiry. I have tried to deal more generally with the issue. It is obviously another two-part problem, the first dealing with dimensional fit, how and how much the existing might be changed to accommodate the new set of uses, or simply is the building big enough? I'm sure there are examples also where the programme of the new occupation has been brilliantly altered to allow accommodation between building and use. The second part is the more elusive correspondence between the new and the previous uses, the new occupation and the original purpose of the building. This touches on what might be called appropriateness or its opposite, of questions of propriety. A building, unlike a ship, will not die of shame. However if such judgements are applied, I have tried to show how much of the poetic might be lost or obscured by such preconceptions. The contrasts and coincidences between the new and the usurped occupation are the cause of much wonder, and a source for the designer in their work. It may be possible and possibly useful to devise a taxonomy of occupancy, an anthropometrics of occupancy as a tool for the designer, that is morally neutral, being concerned with spatial compatibility, and so avoiding or ignoring charges of impropriety. This would be less inhibiting. The old chestnut of 'fit' bobs to the surface here, a cause of much debate in an earlier age. Stemming from functionalism, there was the belief, which was almost a Modernist credo, that there was a tight fit between built form and occupation. This was first challenged in the 1960s with the motto 'Long life, loose fit', which was generally considered at the time to be a reactionary assertion.

15　Regarding recent works, if the great Hawksmoor church, Christchurch at Spitalfields in London, had been deconsecrated, and had consequently undergone a change of use, it may have been more immune to the Ruskian destruction it has recently suffered.

16　See the essay 'Details' in his *Style and Configuration* (London: Academy Editions; Berlin: Ernst & Sohn, 1994, pp. 40–42). This piece may be the best demonstration in print of an elegant architectural intelligence:

> The bridge is a first year project on timber construction in the late 50s . . . At the time I did it in a rush, made the model one week-end and photographed it. I thought the bridge was

elementary in every respect. Just timber scantlings – four-by-twos and six-by-twos – and based on triangulation – underneath and at the first posts. Some twenty years later one looks more closely at Palladio and sees, if not the inverted ties, rather nice unmannered bridges in the same theme, the point being that the gap of 400 years has no meaning at all if one is building in a basic manner. Fashion is absolutely irrelevant and it does not matter whether you are classical, modern or extremely with-it. At root, when one gets down to detailing, the language becomes shared.

17 As mentioned in a previous note on the use of colour, Ben Kelly Design has always adopted an 'art school' approach to intervention in its bold use of new materials and finishes, as well as colour. See *Plans and Elevations: Ben Kelly Design*, ed. Catherine McDermott (London: ADT Design File, 1990).

18 The adoption in the latter part of the twentieth century in certain quarters of computer-generated forms for buildings has perhaps moved the condition from one of belief to one of immersion, from which a total and suffocating aesthetic has emerged, a product of technique outside of any didactic framework, immune therefore to criticism, and freed of the sense of morality which attached to the earlier crusades of Modernism.

19 Picasso's famous 'Still Life with Chair Caning' united oil paint with pasted-on oil cloth, while the first *papiers collés* were undoubtedly done by Braque. As a technique of picture-making, the term 'collage' comes from the French verb *coller*, to paste, stick, glue; and *papier collé* is the more restricted expression referring only to paper. Collage itself is now an accepted art form, making a direct contribution towards creative expression . . . As many artists have admitted in their commentaries, it was the only way out of an impasse that they had reached at some difficult stage of artistic expression, and it has brought to them a new liberation of vision and form.
    (Helen Hutton, *The Technique of Collage*, New York: Watson-Guptill Publications, 1968, p. 9).

20 Roni Feinstein, *Robert Rauschenberg: The Silkscreen Paintings 1962–64* (Boston, Toronto, London: Whitney Museum/Bullfinch Press, Little, Brown), p. 92.

21 'There are two causes of beauty – natural and customary. Natural is from geometry consisting in uniformity, that is equality and proportion. Customary beauty is begotten by the use, as familiarity breeds a love to things not in themselves lovely.' Sir Christopher Wren, quoted by Colin Rowe at the beginning of his essay on 'The Mathematics of the Ideal Villa' – see note 11, above.

22 At the risk of being obvious, the study of architectural style and its history, as well as the study of projective geometry, are to be twinned cardinal interests in any teaching concerned with the art and practice of alteration.

23 Alfred C. Kinsey, author with others of the two *Kinsey Reports on Sexual Behavior: in the Male* (1948) and *in the Female* (1953).

24 This comment may be addressed to the work on Christchurch, Spitalfields, also referred to elsewhere.

25 Lionel Trilling, *Sincerity and Authenticity* (Cambridge, Mass.: Harvard University Press, 1971).

26 One may consider all total restorations, such as the recent work at Christchurch, Spitalfields, as acts of this type. I was, however, first struck by the debilitating and stifling quality of preclusion by the video work recently acquired by MOMA in New York (Eve Sussman, *89 Seconds at Alcazar*, 2004), which purports to show like a scene from a larger film the goings-on in the room as *Las Meninas* was being painted. It is difficult to think of a more potent means of diminishing the original.

27 Improvisation: the art of improvising, to fabricate with what is to hand, combining disparate parts to create a whole; working with the accidental and the coincidental. In jazz, a soloist playing a classic American song, something by Cole Porter perhaps, is an exercise in extending the given musical bases so as to test recognition of the source, a game of explanation and obscuration, dependent always on a spirit of love and reverence for the original tune. In truth, Charlie Parker, the greatest of the be-bop improvisers, would sometimes play a tune quite straight, as with 'How Deep is the Ocean' or 'The Gypsy', almost devoid of improvisation. However, at other times, as with three versions of 'Embraceable You', he would from the first note play such an abstracted line that only slowly does one come to suspect what the song is. (All Dial recordings.)

28 As with, for instance in music, John Coltrane repeatedly playing 'These Are a Few of My Favourite Things' by Rodgers and Hammerstein. This may stand as a metaphor for the richness that can be

drawn from imitative and interpretative work. It may be considered one day that the Modernist expedition into originality was a strange anomaly; however, it indicates more than anything else Modernity's utopian programme, to leave everything else behind. One should note the increasing number of fine artists working in the realm of copying and imitation, so much so that one thinks that they might begin to constitute an important general project for our time, for designers and architects as well as artists. It will be obvious by these references and others elsewhere that the author thinks of these activities as central to the education of the interventional designer. As I completed these notes, an exhibition of Thomas Demand's cardboard facsimiles had opened at the Serpentine Gallery in London. The *Tavern* series in particular seems to give substance to a connection between event and place.

29   Original pieces, prototypes of Modernist furniture, especially those emanating from the Bauhaus, have such a touching quality of aspiration, which the consequent mass-produced item always lacks. It is embodied in creative attempts to avoid certain inabilities and inadequacies at the outset, which will be later solved in production. Such precious pieces are like items from a cargo cult, harbingers of an intensely desired future.

30   John Ruskin, 'The Lamp of Memory' in *The Seven Lamps of Architecture* (London, 1849), p.202:

> But so far as it can be rendered consistent with the inherent character, the picturesque or extraneous sublimity of architecture has just this of nobler function in it than that of any other object whatsoever, that it is an exponent of age, of that in which, it has been said, the greatest glory of the building consists; and therefore, the external signs of this glory, having power and purpose greater than any belonging to their mere sensible beauty, may be considered as taking rank among pure and essential characters; so essential to my mind, that I think a building cannot be considered as in its prime until four or five centuries have passed over it; and the entire choice and arrangement of its details should have reference to their appearance after that period, so that none should be admitted which would suffer material injury either by the weather staining, or the mechanical degradation which the lapse of such a period would necessitate.

31   In this respect, one might understand the contrary positions of Ruskin and Viollet-le-Duc as being between two different notions of authenticity.

32   The Villa Savoye may be compared with the Acropolis and its buildings, with regard to the decisions taken to ascertain the condition in which each monument was to be maintained. One might consider that one emphasizes a view of dimensional authenticity, a quality of a newly completed building which can be re-captured, and the other a conviction in the physical remains alone as authentic. It will be seen that the first will emphasize spatiality, and the other will focus upon surface.

33   Man Ray and Marcel Duchamp, *Dust Breeding* (1920).

34   In many museums, the ephemeral production of certain times, of the 1960s for instance, is a cause of many conservational quandaries. The conservation of the inflatable plastic furniture from that era is a case in point, to which the Victoria and Albert Museum in London has given much effort. See *The V&A Conservation Journal*, October 1996.

35   Much of this is the territory of architectural salvage, but where the borderline is between retention and salvage seems very difficult to delineate exactly. Of course in practice the designer comes upon the building with much that was considered of value having been removed.

36   In the confusion between actual and authentic, isn't the authentic also always a result of judgement, by an authenticating authority, an individual or a group? The actual is quite different. In the arguments that derive from Ruskin, those which perhaps come closer to forming a convention than any other set of arguments, a convention of assumed conservation and pretended non-alteration is clearly based upon the physical remains of the original building. The remains are revered as much for their being worn down by age as for their being authentic. There is nowhere suggested that the wear of time dilutes the piece's authenticity. In fact, for Ruskin in *The Seven Lamps of Architecture*, the opposite would seem to apply. Because of this lack of a clear central idea, these arguments are prone to deteriorate quickly into picturesque and sentimental considerations.

37   Ruskin, 'The Lamp of Memory'.

38   *Ibid*.

39   Hubert Damisch, 'The Space between: A Structuralist Approach to the Dictionary', *Architectural Design* 3/4 (1980), p. 88.

CHAPTER 11
THE WIDER CONTEXT

a novelty today, tomorrow a ruin from the
past, buried and resurrected every day, lived
together in streets, plazas, buses, taxis,
movie houses, theatres, bars, hotels, pigeon
coops and catacombs,
   the enormous city that fits in a room three
yards square, and endless as a galaxy,
   the city that dreams us all, that all of us
build and unbuild and rebuild as we dream,
   The city we all dream, that restlessly
changes as we dream it.

I speak of the city, shepherd of the centuries,
mother that gives birth to us and devours us,
that creates us and forgets.[1]

THE CITY IS IN OUR head; any language would be exhausted if one tried to
describe its actuality. Many hands make the city: the builders, the legislators,
the developers, both public and private, the traffic and railway engineers, the
services engineer, the architect, the designer, the anonymous dead. It is the
greatest manifestation of the collective spirit. The citizens' allegiance to their
city contains its definition; to their respective denizens, all cities are eternal
(Figure 11.1).

   No-one understood this better than Aldo Rossi. By referring to the paintings of Giorgio de Chirico,[2] he provides evidence that the city resides in the

11.1   Berlin in the 1930s

collective unconscious (Figure 11.2). Although Rossi's influence has faltered in
recent years, and his ideas no longer have such dominance in architectural thinking, their coherence contains important implications for the matter of change and
the city. One might say that his thesis of the city is similar to that here proposed
for the individual building: that in changing, the essential nature must survive.
The only destruction that is threatened by alteration is the corruption of this
immutability. Of course his address is to those planning new buildings in an
urban context, but unlike Rowe and Koetter,[3] his interests are wider:

> The architecture of the city offers numerous examples for these theoretical
> theses through its continuous transformation; these examples [the transfor-
> mations evident in Spalato referred to earlier] are the reality of architecture.
> They show us that the routes for reunion between past and present are much
> more complicated than is usually believed and that operating in historic cen-
> tres can offer contemporary architecture a field for even the most unexpected
> experiment. As an architect I have never had a clearer understanding of
> Roman architecture than when I saw the Roman theatre and aqueduct in
> Budapest; where these ancient elements are set deep within a busy archi-

11.2   The city resides in the collective unconscious: the paintings of Giorgio de Chirico

tectural zone, where the Roman theatre is a football field for local boys and where a crowded tramway crosses the remains of the aqueduct. Obviously these images, this use of the monument, is [sic] not generally to be advised; but it invites a compositional vision of the ancient elements within the city which is certainly not that of the city as museum. A field, therefore, not of sterile conservation but where architecture can open up new lines of research and give new answers to the question of the progressive city.[4]

The question of context therefore lies central to Rossi's thought. The familiar becomes for him the Holy Grail of architecture, inverting the campaign of Modernism to make the world anew. Although one might think of Venturi et al.'s study of Las Vegas[5] as being contextual in intent, this and Rossi's most influential book, *The Architecture of the City*,[6] represent opposite political points of view.[7]

Dan Graham explained it thus:

> In the early 1960s, certain influential younger architects, such as the American Robert Venturi and the Italian Aldo Rossi, emerged, publishing polemics against functionalism, but each from a different ideological perspective. Venturi proposed a semiotic and essentially non-judgmental approach. Aldo Rossi rejected what he took to be Venturi's linguistic acceptance of socially conventional present codes, arguing that they merely reflect capitalist development at the current moment. He wished to recover the dimension of history concealed behind the modern ideology of 'progress'.[8] (Figure 11.3)

Rossi's idea of the *progressive* therefore is in opposition to Modernist functionalist *progress*, where obsolescence and demolition are cohorts. Peter Buchanan comments:

> And the deep fascination of Rossi's writings and architecture is that both project a profound disenchantment with this fractured world, acknowledge the impossibility and futility of resurrecting the pre-modern world complete,

11.3   Two Lights, Cape Elizabeth, Maine

yet nevertheless attempt to salvage some of its essentials . . . Through typology the functional, mechanistic city of Modernism is to be replaced with the urban artefact and city pregnant with psychological resonances. And so the inhabitants will be rescued from being mere users and re-instated to the dignity of citizens.[9]

The arguments that Rossi develops contain concepts which link alteration and new build, and puts them within the same universe of thought, so to speak.[10] In talking of continuity, and deriving his ideas from this, Rossi must speak of the existing; and, brilliant man that he is, he regularly recognizes this in his writings. According to Buchanan, Rossi has a deft delineation between city buildings which will alter over time (propelling primary elements) and those which remain unaltered (pathological primary elements):

> Those that are pathological . . . do not adapt to changing conditions and so freeze time, retarding the life of an area. As an example he cites the Alhambra. Rossi is not interested in the cosmetic conservation of these sorts of elements. His interest is in propelling elements whose original forms persist through changing functions and whose role is catalyst and anchor to city life, as well as consolidating the unique identity of an area. An example he gives is the amphitheatre at Nîmes, which after the fall of Rome became a fortress sheltering a small town inside and around which grew the city as it is today. Rossi hopes his own buildings will display some of the same longevity and flexibility.[11] (Figure 11.4)

Of course the eternal city was not always eternal; it seems to me that cities acquire this status, and need to acquire it to become true cities, through particular acts or phases. Or at least some cities are realized in this way: they are founded, so to speak, sometimes long after their inception. They are 'completed'. Sometimes this might be a question of circumference, of marking an edge, but it is never only that. Thus, for London, with its sprawling two-storey suburbs stretched indiscriminately over hill and valley, as one flies over it, the old town seems now to have been finished, if only temporarily, by the Millennium Dome and the London Eye, two impermanent circular structures, so that now you could imagine the whole assemblage sitting in the palm of one's hand.

Other cities are formed more succinctly, as for instance from the building of the Empire State Building and the Chrysler Tower in Midtown Manhattan in

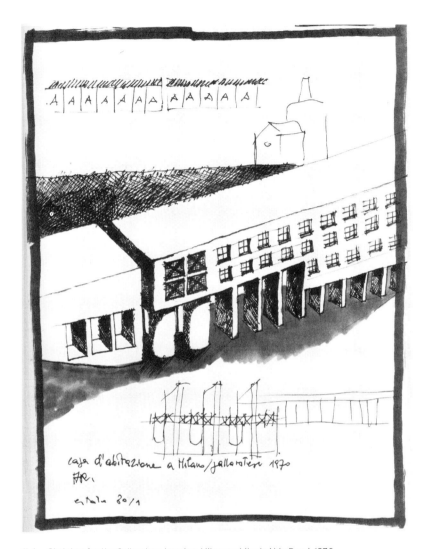

11.4   Sketches for the Gallaratese housing, Milan; architect: Aldo Rossi, 1970

the 1930s, New York had the template for its unchanging condition, viewed from the Staten Island ferry night and day, the enchanting silhouette, the slow rising up of the profile from the Battery to the Midtown group of towers, and beyond that the slow descent to Central Park. Both river edges, the East River and the Hudson, were then devoid of any tall buildings, so a similar, more pronounced profile east–west was established as well. Although it seems strange to recall it now, in the current atmosphere, many people were unhappy with the siting of the World Trade Center because of the disruption it caused to this once seemingly sacred skyline,[12] now by terrible events restored to us, for a short time at least.[13]

Kyoto was formed much earlier.[14] When preservation orders were introduced in the 1930s, the first such order passed by the city council was bestowed upon the protective horseshoe of mountains surrounding the east, north and west of the city. Paris, too, despite Le Corbusier's self-serving analysis in *Vers une Architecture*, was made by Hausemann and others in the nineteenth century, and completed with the positioning of the Eiffel Tower in correspondence with his plan.[15]

> The essential style of Paris has remained unchanged for 125 years. True, but with one or two exceptions, such as the Centre Pompidou and the Institute Arabe, the handful of modern developments in Paris have been poor or disastrous. The reconstruction of les Halles, the former wholesale food market, was so badly bungled in the 1980s that the town hall now wants to rip it up and start again.[16]

In the late nineteenth and twentieth centuries, the city's decided nature has been necessary to the sharp focus of countless art and political works, from *Les Fleurs du Mal* and the laboratories of Surrealism, to Jean Luc Godard's *A Bout de Souffle* and *Two or Three Things I Know about Her*, to the writings of Georges Perec and the urban investigations of Guy Debord and the Situationists.

It is a matter of identity rather than dimension. The city complete is more likely to offer opportunities for intervention than for new building. With the demise of Modernism, major building schemes in Europe, such as at Lille, or Potsdamerplatz in Berlin, or la Defense in Paris, must now be made in unusual sterilized contexts, and no longer within the fabric of the ancient town that Modernist theory once dreamed of sweeping away. It may be different in China.

In some places, the city lies upon previous cities, sometimes seven deep. Old cities often contain the ghosts of lost hierarchies. There is a certain quarter of Beziers, where in shop after shop there are exposed arches and other remains I suppose from the twelfth to the fifteenth century, strange persistent intrusions, apparently appropriated for the purposes of boutique interiors; in several the ancient is employed in the service of selling the most transient of female underwear. One can imagine a future time, the shops withered away for whatever reason, and through some revival or other the lost city, the seemingly contiguous building that was once this quarter, emerging again coherent, although necessarily incomplete (Figures 11.5 and 11.6).

Kafka, talking of Prague, said, 'Today we walk through the broad streets of the rebuilt city, but our feet and eyes are unsure. Still we tremble inwardly as if we were in the wretched old streets. Our hearts have not yet registered any of the improvements. The old unhealthy Jewish district within us is more real than the new hygienic city around us.'[17] One might say such problems of perception will pass away with the generations. The dangers of the cosmetic, however, are eternally present in urban renewal. Rossi himself is more ambivalent towards a similar zone of Venice:

> Furthermore, if we get out of practice, we shall forget how to justify this old environment because often it is merely a reminder of old poverty and it is

11.5   The monumental and the boutique: Beziers

11.6   The monumental and the boutique: Beziers

dear to us as evidence of a people's pain . . . I believe that when the image of the wretched old streets has disappeared completely from within us, we shall also lose the sense of the beauty of those places. Don't we already see the Venice ghetto only in this way, as a desolate place, an embarrassing place to direct tourists to? . . . The process of urban dynamics destroys the old buildings. Habits, customs, social groups, functions and interests inexorably change the use and form of the old city. The dwelling place, which is renewed according to new cultural standards and altered in accordance with new technologies, has a relatively faster cycle of consumption; under the present conditions, the renewal of old houses has no sense and can only be viewed as an elite operation. But in fact houses largely form what we call the environment and so we must inevitably abandon this environment to its fate, knowing that whatever sentimental reasons bind us to it is just a fragment of personal or group experience and not the collective memory of the town, its events and its history. On the contrary, we know that the characteristic elements which have a primary function in the structure of the cities remain immobile and persist in the urban dynamic.

These are, for the most part, monuments.[18]

This is contradictory on so many levels, it is difficult to know where to begin. Rossi himself built housing projects as monuments; in the Gallaratese district of Milan, for example. This proposal largely confounds much of what he has written elsewhere, for instance about the amphitheatre at Nîmes. It also confounds those changes that Rodrigo Perez de Arce so wonderfully charts in his investigations,[19] which are the largely anonymous workings of the citizens within their own cities, the most tangible manifestation of the collective, accredited by both Rossi and himself. There is suddenly within this piece of writing an alien exclusivity, a selectivity as to what constitutes a model. Who is to make such a decision? There appears here a potential for arrogance which one knows to be at odds with Rossi's political beliefs. Is it expediency or irritation at gentrification of certain quarters that is behind his conclusion?

For any architect to renounce the house and therefore also housing must cause a raised eyebrow at least in anyone who knows the damage done, and the supposed damage done, to old cities worldwide by Modernist housing schemes. This is an issue which surely cannot now be excluded from archi-tectural dialogues; reassessment, and, with it, intelligent alteration, hangs gravid, in particular over the extensive housing projects of the Greater London Council and many London boroughs, which are often the work of the most talented architects of the time in which they were built.

The bigger issue is the one that Rossi shares with Kafka: remembrance.

If the city is a receptacle of the collective memory, then it will contain the memory of the events that occurred there. Without this, there is only amnesia, and with that the loss paradoxically of the city's claim to the unchanging, to being timeless, of being superior to the everyday which is its bloodstream, whose authentic purpose is to nourish the collective uncon-scious. The conscious loss or suppression of events is an assault on the identity of the citizenry. This is true for all cities. It has particular poignancy with regard to the capital of Germany.

Berlin was largely destroyed by the bombing of the US and British air forces. Following that, the Eastern sector in particular suffered colossal damage during the invasion of the Red Army, and from the bitter resistance that it met.

Writing on the rebuilding of the Pariser Platz, inside the Brandenburg Gate, since the collapse of the Berlin Wall in 1989, Bernhard Schneider comments on the style of the new buildings.[20] It is a complaint against a false historicity imposed on all those involved in the rebuilding by the city authorities, and the resultant new historicity of the platz itself. Schneider's article concentrates on the diminished status of the gate as a result of the redevelopment, compared with its gaunt detachment during the time of the partition of the city.

At the end of the war, only the remains of the French Embassy on the north side of the platz were left standing, and these were demolished by the Soviets in the 1960s. From then until 1989, the gate stood in magnificent isolation, the Quadriga on the apex, eternally poised to travel eastward,[21] the wall bulging and skirting to the west of it, the Platz marked only by the footings of the disappeared buildings back to the opening of Unter der Linden.[22]

> Developers and landowners were eagerly waiting for the opportunity to erect new buildings. The first project to be put forward was the reconstruction of one of Berlin's best-known hotels, the Adlon. Others were the American and French embassies, and the Academy of Arts . . . However, given the intensity of the debates on the 'critical reconstruction' of the centre of Berlin, it was all too obvious that some kind of consensus among architects, their clients and the public would have been impossible, and it was this that had to be prevented by any means.[23]

Schneider makes a pointed description of the gate's strangeness within its context from the time it was built in 1791:

> The Gate was a novel departure, ruthlessly contradicting the existing order. It was meant to herald a new era, but later developments in the area were not of the kind envisaged. It consisted instead of a series of attempts to tame the Gate's novelty, to integrate it into a symmetrical network of neo-baroque axes (which are again so popular today) and thereby subdue its disquieting otherness . . . in other respects too the history of the Pariser Platz throughout the nineteenth century could be read as a process of reaction to the Brandenburg Gate.[24] (Figure 11.7)

Certainly, visiting it today, it is difficult to imagine how the original tension between gate and square could be more thoroughly tamed and dispelled than it has been by the new buildings of the past dozen years or so. Its potency

11.7   The Brandenburg Gate in the 1960s

when it stood isolated before the collapse of the wall is now impossible to envisage when visiting the site. Schneider describes well the primitive and ignorant historicism that underlies the planning rules developed and enforced by the city. His analysis of the authorities' inability to distinguish between mistakes and achievements in the history of the platz is essential to the understanding of the mediocrity of the overall result of the new development. But there is a deeper issue.

The reconstruction of Berlin has been uncritical. Schneider's article contains this pronouncement:

> After Reunification, the politicians and authorities who established the reconstruction policy for Pariser Platz naturally wanted to overcome as quickly and as radically as possible the horror of the city's destruction and the shame of the Gate's isolation behind the Wall. They wanted to shape the image of the new born-again Pariser Platz through an act of incantation recalling better times somewhere between 1871 and 1933, as if the destruction and eradication had never occurred. Ignoring the apocalyptic history of the sixty-five years since 1933 may be a necessary act, a way of destroying the destruction.[25]

I should not have to say this: mainly in Berlin in living memory, the worst events in history were planned and commissioned. These events were orchestrated from an almost consecutive sequence of buildings running along Wihelm-Strasse (Figure 11.8), 'the centre of the terror apparatus',[26] from Dorotheen-Strasse in the north to Prinz Albrecht-Strasse in the south, where the Gestapo headquarters were located. Pariser Platz was the major space included within this conglomeration.

Surely the purposes of humanity would have been best served if the relics of this quarter which had survived the Second World War,[27] that once stretched unbroken along the west side of Wilhelm-Strasse, had been cauterized and removed from the everyday life of the city, and maintained empty in perpetuity as a reminder to everyone of the peculiar fragility of civilization under certain conditions. One street in the whole of Europe, one urban intervention, given over as an unavoidable memorial in the heart of Berlin to the terror of fascism, so that its scope and power might never again at its inception be overlooked. The events are too monumental for the city or for anyone else to argue that it was in some way a matter of mischance that they happened in Berlin, and consequently that the locaton is somehow incidental.[28] The commemoration should have been a project at an urban scale, and commissioned by Europe, rather than of single isolated entities, chosen at the city's discretion. I realize this verges on fantasy, that the Soviets had already destroyed all the remains above ground by the 1960s. But the footings

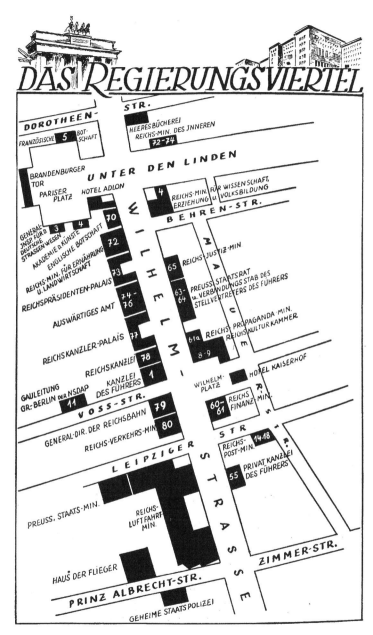

DAS REGIERUNGSVIERTEL

DOROTHEEN-STR.

FRANZÖSISCHE 5 BOT-SCHAFT

HEERESBÜCHEREI
REICHS-MIN. DES JNNEREN
72-74

BRANDENBURGER TOR
UNTER DEN LINDEN
PARISER PLATZ   HOTEL ADLON
4   REICHS-MIN. FÜR WISSENSCHAFT, ERZIEHUNG u. VOLKSBILDUNG

BEHREN-STR.

GENERAL-JNSP. FÜR D. DEUTSCHE STRASSENWESEN 3 4 70
AKADEMIE D. KÜNSTE
ENGLISCHE BOTSCHAFT 72
REICHS-MIN. FÜR ERNÄHRUNG u. LANDWIRTSCHAFT 73
REICHSPRÄSIDENTEN-PALAIS 74-76
AUSWÄRTIGES AMT
REICHSKANZLER-PALAIS 77
REICHSKANZLEI 78
GAULEITUNG GR. BERLIN DER NSDAP 11
KANZLEI DES FÜHRERS 1

65 REICHS-JUSTIZ-MIN
63-64 PREUSS. STAATSRAT u. VERBINDUNGS STAB DES STELLVERTRETERS DES FÜHRERS
61a REICHS PROPAGANDA-MIN.
REICHSKULTURKAMMER
8-9
WILHELM-PLATZ   HOTEL KAISERHOF

VOSS-STR.

GENERAL-DIR. DER REICHSBAHN 79
REICHS-VERKEHRS-MIN 80

60-61 REICHS FINANZ-MIN.

LEIPZIGER

REICHS-POST-MIN. 14-48
55 PRIVATKANZLEI DES FÜHRERS

STRASSE

PREUSS. STAATS-MIN.
REICHS-LUFTFAHRT MIN.

HAUS DER FLIEGER

ZIMMER-STR.

PRINZ ALBRECHT-STR.

GEHEIME STAATSPOLIZEI

11.8   Map showing the offices of the Third Reich in and around Wilhelm-Strasse. That the Gestapo resided here was never concealed; it was listed in travel guides and on city maps as a matter of course.

remained at reunification, and in many cases the basements, and these would have proved sufficient support for the proper impulse to make a record at the correct scale of the terrible events.[29] It remains in my mind as a potential project, a necessary project for the future Europe.

In the Pariser Platz in Berlin, what ground is the acclaimed DG Bank by Frank Gehry to be built upon, or wherein is the intended United States Embassy to be built? This is a question not of superstition but of remembrance.[30] As the two lovers discover in *Hiroshima, Mon Amour*[31] there is a horror in forgetfulness.

With regard to remembering and forgetting,[32] the role of pure architecture, of new building, is more likely without conscious effort and direction to serve the latter, and the role of alteration of the existing more likely to serve the former.

Two restorative projects in Germany may be used to contrast different approaches to remembrance.

In rebuilding the Reichstag in Berlin, Foster Associates[33] achieved what was considered by many to be the practice's greatest accomplishment. The resultant built scheme, although very unlike the winning competition entry from the practice, is sufficiently widely published to be familiar, or easily made familiar to everyone. A fully illustrated book on the history and the rebuilding of the Reichstag arrived in 2000. Its Introduction, 'Reichstag as World Stage', contains a résumé of the practice's other works: 'As with the Reichstag, openness, transparency and lightness are all fundamental to the Sainsbury Centre's design.'[34]

The project for the new assembly for the German Parliament is a major, perhaps primary exercise in the marrying of the aesthetics of literal transparency and the architectonics of a nineteenth-century building. The building itself did not occupy a central place during Nazi rule from 1933 to 1945, despite its prominence in the final fall of Berlin to the Red Army, somewhat standing aside. It was a building, as Martin Pawley records, for which Hitler had little respect: 'Contrary to popular belief, Hitler never spoke in the Reichstag. He visited the building only once, deriding it as an "old shack".'[35] A month after Hitler became Chancellor, the building was severely damaged by a fire whose cause remains unknown. It was converted for use as a maternity hospital and a military archive during the Second World War, and was not involved in tthe governance of the Nazi empire.

The recently rebuilt Reichstag has won widespread praise: it sets new standards for energy conservation, with the claim being made that the building creates more energy than it uses, and there are examples of unusual ingenuity throughout, most famously perhaps where, with one mirrored device, daylight is dragged down into the chamber and the interior is ventilated. The standard of building throughout is exemplary.

The architect of the Reichstag restoration explains the entrance thus:

> For example, upon entering the Reichstag, members of the public are offered a clear view into, and through, the chamber via the glazed screen that closes the tall lobby, and another that forms the back of the chamber. This view introduces the theme of transparency and so of the accountability of politicians. Yet this same device could just as easily be read as a tantalising glimpse that emphasises physical inaccessibility. Such are the quandaries faced both during and after design. The architect did in good faith what was possible, within the constraints set by the demands of security and the limitations of the existing building to achieve transparency: perhaps it is now up to critics and the public to interpret the results in similar good faith.[36]

Of course making a debating chamber transparent in order to raise the level of accountability within it is naïveté of a sort. This is a misinterpretation of openness, and of scrutiny, wrongly assuming a literal equivalence with transparency. A debate has to be scrutinized by the ear, not the eye; debate is not spectacle. The degree of surveillance surrounding the chamber from all sides, one would imagine, is more likely to correct the dress sense of the delegates rather than their oratory. The literalism of the transparency is also probably to blame for the positioning of the cantilevered public and press galleries, the tribunes in the chamber, from which only the President of the Bundestag, the Chancellor, 'other national leaders' and the Eagle can be easily seen. For many also in Germany and elsewhere, a giant eagle to hang above the President's chair is an unfortunate choice. It hangs like a suave, rapacious exhibitionist looming over the assembly, as if throwing open its Armani coat; it is perhaps more surreal than its authors intended. The Eagle and the huge internal window through which it confronts visitors at the head of the entrance stair from the front provide a parody of the social consequences of transparency discussed elsewhere.[37]

The omnipresence of tourism now may be thought of as the global victory of transparency: everything can be seen, but in return there must be no involvement.

If I were to record my own unease while visiting the rebuilt Reichstag, it would centre on the overall affect of slick late twentieth-century Modernism. For instance, the east corridor, which 'rises through three levels, [is] a legacy of the Baumgarten reconstruction of the 1960s which entirely disregarded Wallot's vaulted nineteenth century spaces'.[38] Well, this new rebuilding also disregards Wallot's original building, repeating the mistake that attention is drawn to here; no typological restoration is attempted anywhere; the space rises up to the second level, and apart from the preserved graffiti and other fragments at the lower level, the Modernist aesthetic is total, as it is throughout. The major pieces are autonomous; the old building is revealed only at the convenience of the new.

The architect writes: 'The scarred and graffiti-marked fabric of the Reichstag bears the imprint of time and events in a palpable way. It is more evocative than any exhibition. Preserving these scars allows it to stand as a living museum of German history for future generations.'[39] This claim is inflated. The retention of much of the surviving graffiti from the invading Red Army soldiers can be seen easily only from within the east corridor, spaces reserved for the deputies. In no sense do the writings, mostly in the Cyrillic alphabet, dominate; they are treated as interior decoration, incidental to the renewed building. The rebuilding is in fact a new building fitted into an old shell, one which was 'as limp as a sack'. A few picturesque elements are retained, but kept strictly in subservience to the new.

There are hints of what a different distribution of emphasis might have achieved, as when in the east corridor the old stonework, together with the graffiti, is broken through with a new door, and handled with great assurance. 'Where the new meets the old the junction is clearly articulated.'[40] The incident looks like a drawing by Jean-Jacques Lequeu.

The building as actuality formed too much of the basis for alteration from the outset. I am aware that most of the war damage was repaired earlier in the 1960s, but it would appear that no determined attempt to describe the building in terms of ideal or the original condition, of stripping back the host building, was attempted at the outset. Without a structured understanding of the given that such an exercise would yield, the intervention would always tend away from assimilation, towards autonomy and incident.

Also without this, the programme of demolition was always liable to be excessive, without precise direction: 'We have gouged through the building from top to bottom, opening it up – especially the chamber – to natural light and views. Members of Parliament on the floor of the chamber can now look directly up and see people on ramps in the cupola . . . above their heads.'[41]

The initial diagram for the work, if one ever existed as such, seems to have been too comfortable, the disposition of the main spaces plonked down in an obvious manner, excluding any prospect of struggle in the plan between the existing and the intended, no twist or tricky fit, which could have led to the old fabric revealing itself more candidly. There is no indication of an attempted asymmetry at any stage, for instance, to set against the determined axiality of the old building. Because of the cosy accommodation of the new plan by the old, no compositional tension is able to develop.

While the graceful earlier Foster intervention at the Royal Academy in London[42] is a well-composed poetic assemblage of new and existing, this is never matched in the rebuilding of the Reichstag. The economy of means evident in the London intervention in Berlin seems more like a limited vocabulary. The intervention at the Reichstag is at once too literal and too autonomous, characteristics that are quite absent from the Academy project.

> Following the opening ceremony, the Reichstag's doors were thrown open to the public from 21 to 25 April 1999. On the first day 24,000 people stood patiently in line. An astonishing total of 150,000 visitors was recorded in the five-day period. Most climbed the ramps up to the viewing platform on foot, but some very young ones made the trip in buggies and others in wheelchairs. The atmosphere on the roof terrace was celebratory, like the Christo event but more so. Within the cupola, hushed voices carried across the space as they might in the whispering gallery of a cathedral dome.[43]

The photographs of the event printed in the book, apart from that of a young couple kissing,[44] largely record the familiar blank gaze of the tourist, neither interested nor disinterested, undertaking the task which is now a global responsibility for all: to travel, to visit places and to look. It would be surprising if it were otherwise. The terrace, with its elegant ramp, its extensive views across Berlin and beyond, its smart restaurant and cheaper coffee bar, is a tourist destination *par excellence*. The circulation confirms this: tourists enter through the great portico at the front of the building, and immediately within elevators await to rise unencumbered to the terrace. The hierarchy could not be more clearly expressed (Figure 11.9).

In architectural terms the prime purpose of the building is explicit. The glory of the building, in architectonic terms, is the cupola and its brilliantly planned ramp, with the hanging mirrored cone venting the parliamentary chamber far below. It is the primary destination within the Reichstag; in the architect's own words, 'the result is an aesthetic and technical tour de force'.[45] As with tourist attractions everywhere, a certain suspension of personal credo is expected of the visitor. This is the endemic propriety of such places and the reason for the sightseer's quietism; a tourist is above all an apolitical being.

The inclusion of an assembly chamber consequently seems a secondary consideration.[46] The relationship of the ramp and cupola, with the rather remote views down into the chamber below, verges on the contemptuous; one is reminded of an *oubliette*.

In Munich the city art gallery, the Alte Pinakothek, was heavily damaged by Allied bombing in 1944. The central bays on the south façade were destroyed, as were the internal spaces back to the north wall. The architect of the original building was Leo von Klenze. It had been built between 1826 and 1836.[47] The building lay close to the most sacred places of the National Socialist Party, the fascist acropolis,[48] a short distance south of the gallery on the Konigsplatz.

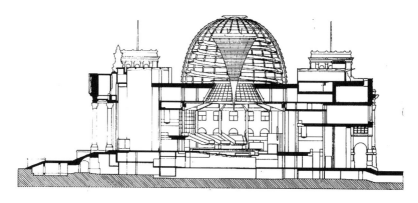

11.9   Section through the Reichstag

11.10   Women reclaiming bricks, Germany, 1945

After the Second World War, despite much opposition and the final frustration of his overall scheme for the rebuilding of the gallery, the architect Hans Dollgast made good the south façade using reclaimed bricks from other bomb sites in the city, emulating the form of the neo-Classical stone façade that had stood there before.[49] In bombed cities all over Germany after 1945, bricks were reclaimed from the ruins by women, the only available labour force. The mortar was broken off and the bricks then used in rebuilding. The women worked in lines with one picking out the brick then handing it back along the queue. They were called the rubble women or the brick widows (Figure 11.10).

When Dollgast finally came to mend the façade in 1952 with such reclaimed bricks he made a frank commemoration of the aerial destruction of Munich and of the austerity that followed, and provided a memorial to the women who with their hands had begun the reconstruction of their homeland after the disasters that had befallen it (Figures 11.11 and 11.12).

11.11 The Alte Pinakothek, Munich, ruined

11.12 The Alte Pinakothek, Munich, restored

NOTES

1 Octavio Paz, 'I Speak of the City' (from *Arbol Adentro / A Tree Within*, New York: New Directions, 1988) for Eliot Weinberger. This poem was first brought to my attention by my friend Stephen Donald, to whom I refer elsewhere.

2 'The absolute knowledge of the space which can put the objects in the picture, and the space separating the objects, establishes a new astronomy of those things which are bound to this planet by the fateful law of gravity.' Giorgio de Chirico, *Metaphysical Aesthetic* (1917), n.p. 'There is no real contradiction between a girl with a hoop and a simplified Renaissance building, between shadows and an even sky. The contradiction resides between the implicit meaning of such a scene and its apparent disconnection from what stands before our eyes.' Albert Cook, *Figural Choice in Poetry and Art* (Hanover and London: University Press of New England, 1985, p. 98).

3 See Colin Rowe and Fred Koetter, *Collage City* (Cambridge, Mass.: MIT Press, 1984).

4 Aldo Rossi, 'Architetturra e citta: passato e presente', *Werk*, September 1972.

5 Robert Venturi, Denise Scott Brown and Steven Izenour, *Learning from Las Vegas* (Cambridge, Mass.: MIT Press, 1972).

6 Aldo Rossi, *Architecture of the City* (Cambridge, Mass.: Opposition Books, MIT, 1982).

7 One might comment that the most marked conflict occurs between Venturi's classification of all buildings as either 'ducks' or 'decorated sheds', and Rossi's theory of *types*. Peter Buchanan writes:

> buildings in cities (or urban artefacts as he calls them) are intended to be so terse as to reveal rather than smother the uniqueness of location and to weather vagaries of time and use by being unspecific enough to accommodate almost any response and elaboration in function. Rossi is attempting more than the sensible but prosaic notion of 'long-life and loose-fit'. To encapsulate (and perhaps escape) history he boils his buildings down to typological essentials so fundamental as to evoke classical and vernacular forms of any period, and so authentic as to resemble such unselfconscious structures as those found at the seashore – fisherman's shacks, bathing cabins and lighthouses . . . An urban artefact can trap and monumentalise the uniqueness of its setting – what Rossi calls *locus solus*. So the urban artefact as primary element is essentially a monument whose material form and presence both generates identitiy and sense of place, and is a record of memory, a repository of memory . . . Type resides in that mythical domain of the late-twentieth century, the collective unconscious.
>
> (Peter Buchanan, 'Aldo Rossi: Silent Monuments',
> *Architectural Design* 172 (October 1982), pp. 48–54).

8 Dan Graham, 'The City as Museum', *Artforum* 20, no. 4 (December 1981), n.p. The author continues: 'Rossi saw Venturi as proposing a semiotic or communicational model of architecture. Rossi argued that if architecture includes, as its content, all other signs present in the surrounding environment, then it is subsumed into this system. He saw Venturi's extension of present-day codes as passively reflecting the environment. If architecture accepts present day ideologically coded "reality" as given, Rossi contended, it forgets its autonomy and loses perspective.'

9 Buchanan, 'Aldo Rossi: Silent Monuments', pp. 48–55. This is the best short account of Rossi's theories that I know. It was very important to us in the development of the idea of alteration at a crucial early stage. His theories contain connections between alteration and the making of new buildings, and consequently allow for a relationship between the idea of alteration and mainstream architectural thought.

10 In my opinion the theory of *types* is of limited use to the intervention designer but I may be wrong, so I have tried to contain in this note and in note 8 above, an explanation of their centrality to Rossi's thinking. It seems to me, as with other architectural theories quoted elsewhere, to be concerned primarily with the production of new buildings. Rossi's theories hinge on the notion of type as the mediator between the citizen and the city, between their personal memories and the collective unconscious. The reference to type stems of course from C. J. Jung:

> One of the many contributions of Carl Jung was to forward such concepts as the collective unconscious, the archetype, and the symbol. Jung contrasted the notions of personal uncon-scious, which had been postulated by Sigmund Freud, with the collective unconscious, a deeper

layer that does not derive from personal experience. He notes that this phenomenon is therefore universal in character '. . . in contrast to the personal psyche, it has contents and modes of behaviour that are more or less the same everywhere and in all individuals. It is, in other words, identical in all men and thus constitutes a common psychic substrate of a suprapersonal nature which is present in every one of us.'

(Joy Monice Malnar and Frank Vodvarka, *The Interior Dimension: A Theoretical Approach to Enclosed Space*, New York: Van Nostrand Reinhold, 1992, pp. 275–76).

11 Buchanan, 'Aldo Rossi: Silent Monuments', p. 49.

12 There is one proposal for not building on the Lower Manhattan site that I know of, submitted in the form of a collage by Ellsworth Kelly to the offices of the *New York Times* (see front page of Arts and Leisure section, 11 September 2003). Looking at the site from the Visitors' Gallery on the west side, one is struck by the unusual beauty of the space. Exposed by the calamity on the east side is an array which seems to include every type and age of the city's tall building, a hetero-geneous company standing seemingly as dumbstruck witnesses to the disaster. They are peculiarly reminiscent of the chorus of towers outside the hotel room, where the Empire State and the Chrysler buildings lie together in Madelon Vriesendorp's painting (in Rem Koolhaas, *Delirious New York: A Retroactive Manifesto for Manhattan*, New York: Oxford University Press, 1978, pp. 134–35).

13 It may be interesting to note in passing that the conflict between Daniel Liebeskind and the man-aging architects SOM over the redevelopment of the World Trade Center site is largely an argument about response to context, which is the essence of the winning project, and the brilliant non-contextual tower developed by SOM. Models of the tower were repeatedly presented as models of a free-standing object during the early stages of the fraught collaboration. The tower's structural brilliance depended upon it being autonomous, and so free-standing.

14 There is a very attractive project for bridges over the river in Kyoto, a competition-winning entry by Gunther Nitschke, a long-time resident of the city. The bridges are intended to be built slowly over a period of 100 years, as opportunities arise. They are to be commissioned from a variety of designers, as time goes by. The anecdote about the preserved mountains is also from him, included in a lecture at Brown University, Providence, 16 September 2003.

15 Balzac complained that he, a native Parisian, had been made a stranger in his own city, such was the degree of change in the mid-nineteenth century.

16 From John Lichfield, 'Paris Mourns Passing of a Cathedral of Industry', *Independent* newspaper, 16 July 2004:

They are knocking down the old factory at last, ending 90 years of French industrial and social history. The original Renault plant occupies all of a long, curving oval island in the Seine, only three miles downstream from the Eiffel Tower. Central Paris once contained both Renault and Citroën factories. In the 70s Renault emigrated to a new factory in the suburbs at Flins to alter rigid work practices at Billancourt, or, seen from another viewpoint, the trade union solidarity which had won so many social advances . . . For years, Jean Nouvel, one of the most distinguished French architects . . . said that the factory was an important architectural and social site and should be preserved. 'The completeness of the wall of the outer buildings to the water's edge gives the factory a nobility, which ordinarily one only finds in a chateau or military fortifications,' Nouvel wrote in *Le Monde* in 1999. 'It is as beautiful as the Krak des Chevaliers . . . It is the Krak of the proletariat.'

17 As quoted by Aldo Rossi, 'What is to be Done with the Old Cities', foreword to a special issue of *Architectural Design* on the School of Venice, No. 55, p.19 5/6 (1985).

18 *Ibid.*, p.3. One might add that this habit of dissolving away the urban fabric so as to leave only the important buildings standing is echoed by both Le Corbusier and Leon Krier at different times.

19 Rodrigo Perez de Arce, 'Urban Transformations and the Architecture of Additions', *Architectural Design*, 4 April 1978.

20 Bernhard Schneider, 'Invented History: Pariser Platz and the Brandenburg Gate', *AA Files*, 37 (1998), pp. 12–16. This is the report of his contribution to the conference at the Architectural Association in May 1998, 'In the Name of Modernity: The Politics of Conservation and Restoration', organized by Dr Eleftherios Ikonomou.

21 'The Brandenburg gate was built in 1791, and its post-war years standing in isolation therefore span almost a quarter of its existence.' *Ibid.*, p. 12.

22 I visited East Berlin in the spring of 1982, and it left a very strong impression. Very little had been repaired then, and there was effectively no traffic on the streets. It was the city of Schinkel, in partial ruin. The buildings and their settings were all, the Guard House, the Opera House, the Alte Museum. The marks of the final battles for Berlin in May 1945 were inescapable; the elegance and the savagery were enmeshed. Regardless of rank, the people behaved towards each other with a directness, which was for me exemplary. My disappointment at revisiting East Berlin in 2004 stays with me. It now looks like everywhere else: that is, it is now looked at the same as everywhere else. Transparency holds the visitor in a semi-trance the length of Unter der Linden and along Friedrichstrasse; one looks into shop windows and, not without conscious effort, at the buildings. They have become a backdrop and peripheral. For those who did not see the old city before its commercialization, it is perhaps impossible fully to convey the grandeur and beauty that have since been dispelled.

23 Schneider, 'Invented History', p. 14.

24 *Ibid.*, p. 15.

25 *Ibid.*, p. 12.

26 *Topography of Terror: Gestapo, SS and Reichssicherheitshauptamt on the Prinz-Albert-Terrain*, ed. Reinhard Rurup, trans. Werner T. Angress, chapter 1 on 'Administrative Center of the SS-State: Addresses and Institutions'. *Topography of Terror* is the catalogue of an exhibition from 1987, which was a prompt to the building of a permanent archive of SS documents. A building by Peter Zumthor was commissioned, but has recently been abandoned. See 'DW-World', *De Deutsche Welle*, 9 June 2004.

> Here stood the desks of Himmler, Heydrich, Kaltenbrunner and Heinrich Muller . . . Here was the 'Hausegefangnis' of the Gestapo, but also the hub of the network of Gestapo Regional and Local Commands and the administrative offices of the Higher SS and Police Commanders . . . that was strung out across Germany and large parts of Europe. From here the genocide of the Jews was prepared, and deportations and exterminations were co-ordinated by the state authorities. The Special Units operating in Poland and the Soviet Union sent their reports here concerning their murderous exploits. From here the persecution of the opponents of the regime in Germany, and subsequently in all occupied territories as well, was organized.
>
> (Topography of Terror, p. 11)

27 Wilhelm-Strasse was in the Soviet sector, near the wall. Photographic evidence shows that many of the National Socialist buildings survived at least in part into the 1950s. The basements survived, which commonly were the sites of cells, many of which were later uncovered. All the standing remains, some of them considerable, such as the Gestapo headquarters and the Prinz-Albert-Palais, seat of the Security Service (SD) of the SS, were demolished by the early 1960s, and the ground levelled.

28 The Jewish Museum by Daniel Liebeskind and the *Holocaust Memorial* by Peter Eisenman might be thought to be adequate. However, the Memorial is on a site of no particular historical significance or prominence, beside the Tiergarten, at the back of the proposed site of the new US Embassy in Pariser Platz. In addition, by only commemorating the Holocaust, that is the planned genocide of the Jews, the full scope of the terror is diminished and to a certain extent contained. The Work to Death programmes, largely applied to Slavs and other 'inferiors' of the 'Master Race', were of equal horror. Any recent history of the Third Reich will give a fuller account of the acts of the National Socialist government emanating from the buildings along Wilhem-Strasse. Michael Burleigh's *The Third Reich: A New History* (London: Macmillan, 2000) is one of the most notable recent publications, and one of the first to use new sources made available by the collapse of the communist regimes in Russia and in Eastern Europe. Of course this period has in other forms been well documented, and of course environmental design is not best suited to documentation. The Work concern of this chapter is for memorials, to which such design is well suited, as is often demonstrated, as with the *Memorial to the Martyrs of the Deportation* on the Ile de la Cité in Paris (architect: Georges Henri Pingusson, 1962). In the spirit of memorial, the work of the artist Christian Boltanski should not be overlooked.

29 One is reminded of Melvin Charney's project in Montreal, noted in Chapter 4, as a means of evoking lost buildings (*Les Maisone de la Rue Sherbrooke*), albeit in an almost opposite context.

30 Perhaps one might say that what distinguishes the two world wars of the twentieth century is the extensive and concerted construction of memorials, both in home towns and on battlefields throughout France, Belgium and the United Kingdom after 1918 (for instance, the still wonderfully maintained war graves in north-eastern France), and the relative paucity of such acts following the Second World War, particularly in Britain. (I should largely exclude France from this observation; it is scrupulous in marking the assassinations and deportations of civilians during this time.) One is tempted to think depressingly that the vast civilian casualties of the Second World War somehow have had less significance to the state than the mainly military casualties of the First World War, and seemingly that dead soldiers have a greater status than dead civilians in the minds of the authorities. In London itself, for instance, a Pavilion of Remembrance to civilians killed in the Blitz has been completed only recently, sited in a new park, the Thames Barrier Park (architects: Patel & Taylor; landscape architects: Groupe Signes of Paris. The latter are responsible for the acclaimed Parc Citroën on the island in the Seine in Paris). This pavilion is dedicated to the anonymous civilian dead from the Blitz of one London borough only, namely Newham. There are no names, as would be required on a military memorial, or even as are movingly recorded in the Merchant Navy memorial opposite the Tower of London.

Acts of remembrance are rare enough, but in the process of researching this section, I came upon a moving student project from the Architectural Association by Steven Ware, a Diploma Honours student in 1996, titled 'Innocence for Hiroshima: A Ring of White Noise, Following that Now Invisible Circle at the Centre of the Catastrophe . . . In this Zone . . . a Constructed Silence', *AA Files* 32 (Autumn 1996), pp. 90–91.

For reasons beyond my comprehension, the aerial bombing of cities is not considered a war crime. The often unhindered slaughter of masses of civilians from above continues to be allowed as a generally justifiable act of war. Sven Lindquist's *A History of Bombing* (London: Granta, 2001) is a heartfelt account of this strange savage activity.

31 Alan Resnais, *Hiroshima, Mon Amour* (1959).

32 The fate of Beirut after Lebanon's terrible civil war, the invasion of the Israeli Army and the massacres of the Palestinian refugees in 1982 provide further evidence of the tendencies of redevelopment to eradicate the past. The consequences of the plans for the reconstruction of the ancient Islamic city were described in a contribution to a conference at the Architectural Association in London in June 1993 by Assem Salaam (reported in 'The Reconstruction of Beirut: A Lost Opportunity', *AA Files* 27 (1994), p. 11). The Prime Minister, Rafic Hariri, was the major shareholder in the company formed by the state to carry out the work:

What this entails is in fact the total and uncontrolled privatization of the reconstruction operations . . . First, the compulsory participation of owners and occupiers in the REC [real estate company] and the conversion of their deeds and leases into shares will automatically deprive them of their right to return to their premises, and those who still legally reside in the centre will be obliged to vacate their dwellings. Second, this compulsory association dissolves the physical boundaries between property lots and merges them into a single unit to be parcelled and sold off to developers . . . The plan proposes to demolish eighty per cent of the town centre and to increase the density fourfold. With these two policies it has dealt a fatal blow to the memory of this very ancient city, to be replaced by a mirage of a new city, rich in new buildings but impoverished in architectural traditions.

The developers published a fully illustrated book of the results of their work: Robert Saliba (in association with Solidere, the developers), *Beirut City Center Recovery: The Foch-Allenby Conservation Area* (Göttingen: Steidl; London: Thames & Hudson, 2004).

33 Norman Foster, *Rebuilding the Reichstag* (Woodstock, NY: The Overlook Press, 2000). The book contains forty-nine photographs of the architect. Another book derived from this project has also been produced: Norman Foster *et al.*, *The Reichstag Graffiti: Die Reichstag Graffiti* (Berlin: Jovis, 2003).

34 Foster, *Rebuilding the Reichstag*, p. 16.

35 Martin Pawley, 'The Rise and Fall of the Reichstag', in *ibid.*, p. 46.

36 Foster, *Rebuilding the Reichstag*, p. 170. The architect continues:

For those who can penetrate further, the sense of transparency and openness as well as light and lightness that has been achieved within the massive walls of the old building is amazing. The Chamber is flooded with natural light: the space itself seems drawn into the corridors in front of it and behind it and into the courtyards on either side. Here is the horizontal sweep, the views in and out, that in Bonn have been equated with democracy. Yet the space soars upwards, and the eye is drawn with it, to the lantern and the inverted cone of the reflector that protudes downwards from it. This, with the light it reflects down and its energy saving functions, gives an exalted sense of connection to sky, sun and even to the cosmos . . . In this hall, you feel, thought should take wings, and the debate be imaginative and responsible . . . The Reichstag cupola draws the eye upwards to the light and evokes historical associations with Le Corbusier's lantern at Chandigarh and Baroque domes (such as Francesco Borromini's S. Carlo alle Quattro Fontane).

37 See Chapter 9, notes 8 and 19. On further consideration, at the victory of Modernism over the Classic in the twentieth century, transparency might be thought to have replaced symmetry as the trance-inducing mechanism of architecture. By 'trance' I mean the subservience or capitulation of all the other senses to the visual sense, rendering the subject chronically incapable of judgement.

38 Foster, *Rebuilding the Reichstag*, p. 66.

39 Preface to chapter 1, 'Architecture and History' in *ibid.*, p. 60.

40 *Ibid.*, p. 79.

41 *Ibid.*, p. 78.

42 The insertion of a lift and staircase and the construction of an access floor at roof level, upon which were placed the new Sackler Galleries. The insertion is in the gap between Burlington House and the building to the rear. It is one of the most satisfactory assimilations of old and new in recent years.

43 Foster, *Rebuilding the Reichstag*, p. 243.

44 *Ibid.*, pp. 242–243.

45 *Ibid.*, p. 170.

46 *Ibid.* This is to a certain extent confirmed by how little space is given over in the book to the chamber itself, and much of that is concerned with the design and hanging of the Eagle. In fact the planning of the chamber is a mixture of axiality and transparency.

47 The restoration work on the Alte Pinakothek is scrupulously recorded by Erich Altenhofer in 'Hans Dollgast and the Alte Pinakothek: Designs, Projects and reconstructions 1946–73', in a special issue of *9H* magazine: *On Continuity, in Memory of Robin Evans*, ed. Rosamund Diamond and Wilfred Wang (1995).

48 Each November, a nazified Passion Play was enacted on the streets of central Munich, commemorating the sacrifice of those who in 1923 [the failed Munich *putsch* that led to Hitler's imprisonment and thus to the writing of *Mein Kampf*] had anticipated the victory of 1933 . . . Hitler laid a wreath at the Feldherrnhalle, before a procession which had marched from the Burgerbraukeller escorted the coffins to Ludwig Troost's newly built temples on the Konigplatz. If Munich was to be the Rome or Mecca of National Socialism, then this was the inner sanctum.
(Burleigh, *The Third Reich*, p. 264)

49 Altenhofer, 'Hans Dollgast'. The major reconstruction was completed in the mid-1950s. In a letter at the time, Dollgast wrote to Munich State Building Department, 'The Pinakothek will always be the most rewarding task of my architectural career.' Following this, the authorities seem to have tried hard to alter the opinion that the architect had of his own involvement by resisting and finally frustrating later proposals, particularly regarding the roof. Altenhofer reports at the end of his admirable article: 'Hans Dollgast received little gratitude for his greatest project, and his own statements from the time of the Alte Pinakothek's reconstruction are tinged with bitterness. Franz Hart twice remarked, in vain, that Dollgast's name is missing from the brass memorial plaque mounted at the Alte Pinakothek's entrance.'
    As I prepared this text for publication, two excellent related books appeared: Robert Bevan, *The Destruction of Memory; Architecture at War* (London: Reaktion Books, 2006); and A. C. Grayling, *Among the Dead Cities: The History and Moral Legacy of WWII Bombing of Civilians in Germany and Japan* (London: Bloomsbury, 2006).

CHAPTER 12
UNFINISHED

THE ONE GREAT WORK OF interventional design, universally recognized, is the work by Carlo Scarpa[1] at Castelvecchio,[2] the Municipal Museum in Verona. Much has been written of him following his posthumous recognition by the architectural community. His worldwide reputation was

> as belated as it is effusive . . . because of his exceptional personality and style. One of its salient characteristics is the sense of understanding history, not just on a scholarly or bookish level, but through a profound and penetrating 'insight' that is both a gift of providence and the result of continuous study and grand passion. Although it was never recorded in writing, all Scarpa's work displays a consistent, existential interest in visual form and the genetic processes – executive, technical and formative – by which it is determined.[3]

Richard MacCormac said of Castelvecchio: 'The work is literally and metaphorically an instrument of interpretation.'[4]

There is no doubt that at times during his long involvement with the museum that Scarpa had little or no idea how to proceed. He was rescued by archaeological and historical discoveries. Firstly, a lost canal was discovered and excavated which ran to the river, leaving the courtyard at the corner. Consequently the courtyard must have been completed later than the building's beginning. Secondly, a monumental exterior staircase that rose up to the first floor was found through historical research to have been built when Castelvecchio had housed Napoleonic troops at the beginning of the nineteenth century. This allowed Scarpa two decisive demolitions: of the bays completing the north-western corner of the courtyard, where once the canal had passed, thus exposing the full length of the castle wall onto the approach to the bridge; and the removal of the staircase in the opposite north-eastern corner. The former gave Scarpa the site for his placing of the great equestrian statue of Cangrande, on a cantilevered concrete plinth some seven or eight metres above the ground. The latter allowed him to enter the building at ground level in this opposite corner, and there to begin the route which at its mid-point emerges and dances around the statue in the broken open bays, allowing visitors a changing intimacy as they climb or descend around the Cangrande.

Castelvecchio shows the importance of archaeology, and the value of slowness (Figure 12.1). So Scarpa's slow discovery can act now as a common resource, an indication of method, which he had time to discover slowly and haphazardly, but which later generations may now adopt as a result of his quest stretching over some seventeen years.[5] This is the most important common legacy for all present and future interventionists: the luxury of time that Scarpa was allowed by a sympathetic client,[6] to find his way, to recognize relevancies, and to assemble a comprehensive working pattern for alteration, for general application by others to other buildings at the beginning of conversion.

12.1   Excavations at the Archbishop of Canterbury's Palace, Southwark, London

Installing new uses into existing buildings traditionally is carried forward at a faster pace than new buildings, so time is an unlikely luxury for the designer. Therefore, he must use such discoveries as those which Scarpa slowly uncovered as immediate references and resources. Of course I don't mean that everything Scarpa did should be considered sacrosanct. To many, the rather pretty fiddling about with materials and finishes in some of his projects will forever prove tiresome. But the revelation of the role of archaeology in the work of alteration to historic buildings, for instance, is fundamental.

Above all, the lesson of Castelvecchio is one of the significance and potential of incompleteness, of the complete made incomplete. When Scarpa started work on the buildings, the museum was complete; the photographs reproduced in Richard Murphy's book are evidence of this. There are pictures of absolutely entire interiors; all these Scarpa ruined. When he is finished, he leaves clear indications that the building has been rendered into a state of suspended completion, shown primarily around the broken open section that now contains the statue, in the detailing of the walls, especially the brickwork, and the structure of the complex roof, its layers progressively slid back from the edge of the void.[7] The museum is rendered by the great Venetian into a condition of beautiful incompletion. The art of unfinishing, the incompleting of the Castelvecchio, has achieved here the floating suspension of the building between its past and its future (Figure 12.2).

Incompletion is the clear aim of alteration because of two prime purposes: it is only by such means that the allusion to the ideal, or paradigm, can be made; and it allows the building to become an element of continuity. Christopher Wren said that buildings should aim for eternity, and perhaps the strategies included herein are just a way in which they may continue to do this for the length of their existence. The work of alteration should aim for an incomplete perfection, or a perfect incompleteness.[8] Do I hear an objection to such purposes?[9] The incomplete is hardly unique. One could begin a list, but that itself would be endless: it could start with Schubert or Mozart, Janáček's violin concerto or Hopi sand paintings, the *Mona Lisa*, the temple at Luxor, the Parthenon, Alberti's Tempio Malatestiano in Rimini, itself an alteration, Geoffrey Chaucer's *Canterbury Tales*, the 'Ballad of Kublai Khan' by Samuel Taylor Coleridge, *The Mystery of Edwin Drood* by Charles Dickens, *Amerika* by Franz Kafka, *The Man without Qualities* by Robert Musil, the *Arcades Project* by Walter Benjamin, *The Last Tycoon* by F. Scott Fitzgerald,

12.2   Castelvecchio, the Municipal Museum of Verona

Pandemonium by Humphrey Jennings, Michel Foucault's *History of Sexuality*, Westminster Abbey, Beauvais, Narbonne Cathedral and nearby, by the same team, the great Gothic church at Capestang, Chartres, the Duomo in Siena, the North Yorkshire abbeys and ruins everywhere, uncompleted motorway links in London, Glasgow and elsewhere, some 100 uncompleted tower blocks, including cranes, in Bangkok abandoned in 1997, the unfinished hospitals and other Soviet state buildings in Russia,[10] the mud mosques of Mali, partially dissolved each year by the rains, and, according to Marcel Duchamp, *The Great Glass*, also the Elgin Marbles, Josef von Sternberg's film of *I, Claudius*, Sergei Eisenstein's Mexican documentary, and *Ivan the Terrible*, which was intended to be a trilogy, the operas *Turandot* by Puccini, *Prince Igor* and other works by Borodin, and *Moses and Aaron* by Schoenberg, Michelangelo's captive slaves, the *Tondo* in the Royal Academy, many of Vermeer's paintings, in the London National Gallery alone *The Adoration of the Shepherds* by Goltzius with the missing infant, *Whistlejacket* by George Stubbs, and two unfinished Michelangelo paintings, the *Entombment* and the *Manchester Madonna*, Manet's third butchered version of the *Execution of Maximillian* and some twenty other paintings, Monet's *Dejeuner sur l'Herbe*, Le Pont St Beneset in Avignon, the Saltworks at Chaux by Ledoux, Les Heures claires with its missing top floor, les Quartiers Fruges at Pessac . . .

NOTES

1   I have an under-researched idea that those who are good at intervention and alteration are not as brilliant at pure architecture. I know many will argue that they consider that Brion Cemetery to be Scarpa's masterwork, but I would disagree. Is the plan, the layout of the site, in particular the positioning of the two tombs and their relationship to the other landscape elements, and they to each other, well resolved? Isn't the chapel, for all its beautiful light, a little frenzied with the incessant application of the serried steps motif? One might also add the Banco Populare in Verona, even though this is a posthumous work, could never have rivalled the nearby Museo Municipale. His houses in the Veneto and Piedmonte would have gained him little more than a footnote in the history of post-war Italian architecture, whereas Castelvecchio is a masterwork.

In another age, the exteriors of Robert Adam's buildings are all a disappointment compared with his work on the interiors.

Perhaps similar observations can be made concerning Viollet-le-Duc: Pierresfronds, Notre Dame or some other work of restoration is his best work. His independent proposals, the drawings for instance done for les Entretiens are never more than interesting. Summerson comments:

In the second volume of his lectures, he illustrates and describes several designs he has prepared in order to test and elucidate his theory. One is a concert hall for 3000 people; another is for a town house, another for a country house. He is very modest about these products of his own pencil and repeats many times that he makes no claim to having evolved anything new and that the designs are only given in order to indicate the kind of approach which the 19th century architect should adopt. The designs are at once unattractive and fascinating. As one follows their author's description one sees that they are disciplined, daring, economical, ingenious. There is a reason for everything; geometry is paramount and ornament is admitted with nice discretion. But there is one thing missing. It is difficult to find the right word for it, but I think the word is style.

(John Summerson, *Heavenly Mansions*, New York: Norton, 1998, p. 154)

Neither Scarpa nor Viollet-le-Duc received an architectural education; both were self-taught in many respects. In fact, the architects of Venice once organized to try to prevent Scarpa from becoming registered as an architect. So this is a half-formed theory, but nevertheless persistent, that the sensibility of an interventionist is different from that of a pure architect.

2 Any discussion of this building must at the beginning acknowledge the work of Richard Murphy, his students and his associates, who first set out to prepare a set of record drawings of the Castelvecchio, following a visit to Verona in 1983. From this exercise sprang an exhibition, *Carlo Scarpa at Castelvecchio. Survey of a Journey*, shown at Edinburgh University in 1987, and the Building Centre, London, in 1988. From that followed the book which is the standard work on the building, a wonderful achievement: Richard Murphy, *Carlo Scarpa and the Castelvecchio* (London: Butterworth Architecture, 1990). He more than anyone has been responsible for the subsequent universal recognition of Scarpa's genius. Any description of the museum and Scarpa's involvement with it will tend to end up as a précis of part or all of Murphy's book.

3 This is extracted from Pier Carlo Santini, 'Architecture as a Continuous Dialogue with Pre-Existence', in *Carlo Scarpa: il progretto per San Caterina a Treviso*, ed. Vianello Libri (Ponzano: n.p.), p. 28. Santini suggests: 'Scarpa was obsessed by the unrenouncable need to investigate and understand a work's linguistic identity, from the general to the specific and vice versa, in order to understand its liabilities, excesses, motivations and original streaks.' This is a more succinct and elegant description of the purposes of stripping back than I was able to summon up. The article continues:

His custom was to subject everything coming into his field of vision to immediate judgement or problematic and dialectical examination, whether it was of a really expressional nature or not. His pupils, collaborators, and friends were the beneficiaries of a multitude of expressions, revelations and reactions in which paradox often figured as the impromptu, provocative intro-duction to a more considered argument. Walking or travelling with Scarpa was an adventure within the very adventure of knowledge. Personally as one of his frequent companions, I always regret that what remains of his talk, gestures and habit of illustrating them in pencil is but a fleeting memory.

4 Richard MacCormac, writing in the *RIBA Journal*, September 1991.

5 This is Scarpa's own explanation of his approach:

I have a great passion for works of art, as you know. I have always taken the trouble to learn, to know, to understand, and, it seems to me, to have a real critical awareness. I would not be able to write, to produce a critical article; but I have a lively sense of critical values, and they move me. Indeed, I would rather, on the whole, build museums rather than skyscrapers – though logic may say otherwise, since the latter may perhaps be creative, while the former requires one to adapt and subordinate oneself to things as they are. One might also say that there is a certain mimicry involved, not of a formal kind, not of equivalence, but rather as an attempt at interpretation.

(From *Incontri a cura di Gastone Favero: Unora con Carlo Scarpa*, RAI documentary, c. 1970)

6 Lisisco Magnanato, the museum director, was the man responsible for Scarpa's appointment by the municipality, and it was he who supported and protected Scarpa during the work. The remod-elling took place in two phases between 1957 and 1964, with the final phases completed in 1967 and 1973. The museum has recently undergone a new phase of post-Scarpa changes.

7 The roof's complex make-up is perhaps the most blatant signal of the incomplete nature of the treatment of the courtyard, but also the broken wall onto the garden.

8 I first came upon this description as the title of a special issue of *Daidalos* 31 (1989).

9 Fans of completion should go to see the grinding efforts to complete the Sagrada Familia in Barcelona.

10 Recorded by the photographer Uryevich, and available on his website, www.abandoned.ru/about. php.

INDEX